Finding Light

'With patience, thoroughness and good humour, Chris Smaje is charting a vitally needed path beyond the dead end of industrial modernity, into the kind of world in which we're likely to find ourselves. I can't think of a better companion for that journey, and I look forward to seeing this book illuminate our conversations along the way.'

DOUGALD HINE, author of *At Work in the Ruins*

'This is how we make it through. Amid all the greenwash and business as usual, facing denial, deflection and despair, Chris Smaje brings his trademark integrity, generosity of spirit and clarity of thought to the world as it is – and as it could be. It feels grittily real, this mosaic of ideas. Of communities of place, purpose and passion welding themselves together with a plan B when the lights have gone out and we're past the point of fighting over toilet roll because the supermarkets are empty and dark and – horror! – the internet has gone down. Who are we then? What values do we share that really matter to us? How can we build something from the emergent rubble that makes our hearts sing? This is a blueprint, and Every Single Individual who can read should have a copy and refer to it. Our world would be quite different if we did.'

MANDA SCOTT, author of *Any Human Power*; host, *Accidental Gods* podcast

'As Gaia lays waste to the hubris of capitalist modernity, it's becoming clear that we humans need to unlearn many lifeways and invent new ones. A big thanks to Chris Smaje, then, for expanding our imaginations and giving us courage. He explains how, in the coming epoch of the Ecocene, we can create institutions and cultures that honour care, social reciprocity, bottom-up empowerment and respect for Earth as alive. All will be essential.'

DAVID BOLLIER, activist-scholar of the commons; author of *Think Like a Commoner*

'With a blend of deep academic wisdom and of-the-land pragmatism, Chris Smaje looks to a fascinating medieval history to show us how humankind can not only persist but thrive – reclaiming autonomy, community, even joy – in the face of civilizational collapse. *Finding Lights in a Dark Age* is indeed the antidote to our fear about the current looming global catastrophe. But it is also the push so many of us (myself included!) need to start working in our own small ways, now, for what might be needed in the precarious years ahead.'

JENNIFER GRAYSON, author of *Unlatched* and *A Call to Farms*

'At once pragmatic and visionary, *Finding Lights in a Dark Age* is a meditation on how we might make the best of the difficult times ahead. Smaje brings every bit of himself to this book, daring us to upend conventional wisdom about progress in service of a richer and more natural kind of human thriving. Count me in.'

PHILIP LORING, author of *Finding Our Niche*

'Farmer and social scientist Chris Smaje offers a credible, and delightful, glimpse of a small-scale agrarian future. He combines personal experience, cross-disciplinary scholarship and pragmatic analysis with that rarest of grails in future-focused writing: plausible optimism.'

SAMUEL MILLER MCDONALD, author of *Progress*

'Incisive and irenic, this is Chris Smaje at his wide-ranging best, exploring the territories of liveable-but-realistic human futures. Chris sweeps away the cobwebs of late-modern thinking to sketch what a sober pathway through the coming morass might look like. A guiding light!'

CARWYN GRAVES, author of *Tir: The Story of the Welsh Landscape*

'The source of our collective insecurity has its roots in the land – and has erected fences to keep us out. Chris Smaje's erudite and compassionate investigation shows that our own wellbeing cannot be secured without Earth's. He offers a vision for how we, the people, can secure our future by giving the labour of our bodies to the land and to each other. In a time of warring narratives, Smaje's call for sovereignty invites us to tear down the fences that exile us from our own histories.'

RACHEL DONALD, creator and host, *Planet: Critical* podcast

'In this literally vital work, Smaje gazes into the near-inevitable harrowing collapse that is the "future" of this civilisation, with a doughty realism – and a quotidian eye for the likely – that is rarely matched. He refuses to be daunted: he sketches, and quite beautifully so, "thrutopian" possibilities for what deep and transformative adaptations can yield for us, through what is coming. These begin with his wry setting out of how, quite often, as empires decline and fall, plenty of ordinary folk (not to mention other beings) can actually end up better off. This is probably Smaje's most important book yet – and that is really saying something.'

RUPERT READ, emeritus professor;
co-director, Climate Majority Project;
author of *Why Climate Breakdown Matters*

'The strength of a set of ideas is not in whether the reader is moved to agree with them immediately. It's that they are compelled to ask themselves why they shouldn't. That's what Chris Smaje has achieved here, in a significant and most welcome development of ideas latent in his two earlier books.'

ADAM GREENFIELD, author of *Lifehouse*

'This is a beautiful book – full of insight, wit and earthy humility. Whether or not you agree with Smaje's view that we're inevitably headed toward an energy-descent future, there is a lot to learn from him on how to navigate our escalating polycrisis and build new futures and ways of life beyond capitalist modernity. If you agree, as Smaje says, that "the main point of being a person isn't to get maximum cheapness and convenience", then read this book!'

DR MICHAEL J. ALBERT,
lecturer in global environmental politics;
author of *Navigating the Polycrisis*

FINDING LIGHTS IN A DARK AGE

Also by Chris Smaje

A Small Farm Future
Saying NO to a Farm-Free Future

FINDING LIGHTS IN A DARK AGE

SHARING LAND, WORK AND CRAFT

CHRIS SMAJE

Chelsea Green Publishing
White River Junction, Vermont
London, UK

First published in 2025 by Chelsea Green Publishing | PO Box 4529 | White River Junction, VT 05001 | West Wing, Somerset House, Strand | London, WC2R 1LA, UK | www.chelseagreen.com
A Division of Rizzoli International Publications, Inc. | 49 West 27th Street | New York, NY 10001 | www.rizzoliusa.com

Copyright © 2025 by Chris Smaje.
All rights reserved.

No part of this book may be transmitted or reproduced in any form by any means without permission in writing from the publisher.

Publisher: Charles Miers
Deputy Publisher: Matthew Derr
Commissioning Editor: Muna Reyal
Project Manager: Susan Pegg
Copy Editor: Susan Pegg
Proofreader: Sarah Greaney
Indexer: Charmian Parkin
Designer: Abrah Griggs

ISBN 978-1-915294-73-9 (paperback) | ISBN 978-1-915294-74-6 (ebook) | ISBN 978-1-915294-75-3 (audiobook)
Library of Congress Control Number: 2025029969 (print)
A CIP catalogue record for this book is available from the British Library.

Our Commitment to Green Publishing
Chelsea Green sees publishing as a tool for cultural change and ecological stewardship. We strive to align our book manufacturing practices with our editorial mission and to reduce the impact of our business enterprise in the environment. We print our books using vegetable-based inks whenever possible. This book may cost slightly more because it was printed on paper from responsibly managed forests, and we hope you'll agree that it's worth it. *Finding Lights in a Dark Age* was printed on paper supplied by TJ Books that is certified by the Forest Stewardship Council.

Authorized EU representative for product safety and compliance
Mondadori Libri S.p.A. | www.mondadori.it
via Gian Battista Vico 42 | Milan, Italy 20123

Printed and bound in Great Britain by
TJ Books, Padstow, Cornwall.
10 9 8 7 6 5 4 3 2 1   25 26 27 28 29

CONTENTS

Preface: Ragnarök Revisited?   xi
Introduction: An Arc of Future Earth   1
  1: Dark Age Ahead   17
  2: Building New Structures   31
  3: Open Country   45
  4: Home Economics: Producing   59
  5: Home Economics: Caring   71
  6: Land   91
  7: A Dark-Age Distributism   107
  8: Making a Living   121
  9: Working for Others   143
10: Politics of the People   155
11: Divine Comedy: Or, the Stranger King   173
12: Walking West   187
Afterword: The Distributist Moment   203

Acknowledgements   207
Notes   209
Bibliography   219
Index   227

PREFACE

Ragnarök Revisited?

Fenrir will feast
On the fallen,
Summer sun blackens,
The Great Winter comes.

Hel's hound Garm howls,
His bonds will snap.
Death comes for the Gods
At Ragnarok.

Brother kills brother,
Sons betray their kin:
Axe-age, sword-age,
Wind-age, wolf-age.

The world-ash groans
As Fenrir breaks loose.
All-father heeds Mimir,
But the wolf will slay both.

Another green Earth
Will rise from the sea.
I see eagles over fells,
Sporting for fish.

The black dragon flies,
Over dark-of-moon hills,
Bearing corpses to Hel.
Where I must go too.

'VÖLUSPÁ: THE SEERESS'S PROPHECY'[1]

Around the middle of the sixth century, devastating volcanic eruptions shrouded the world in veils of dust. Written sources from East Asia to the Mediterranean attest to failed harvests and civil unrest. In Europe's far north, temperatures may have dropped by more than 3°C and a dust-veiled winter gripped the land continuously for at least three years. The margins for livelihood in this region were already thin. By some estimates, the resulting famines killed as much as half the population in parts of Scandinavia. Forest replaced field.

Scholars continue to debate the historical accuracy of the Norse sagas that were written down much later. But some argue that lines like those above from 'The Seeress's Prophecy' represent in mythic memory what once happened in real life when they tell the story of Ragnarök – the mythological end-time when both gods and humans perish, foretold by the groaning and shivering of the 'world-ash' tree, Yggdrasil, that unites the cosmic realms, and by the Great Winter that lasts three years with no summer in between.[2]

Before this sixth-century catastrophe, many parts of the Scandinavian peninsula comprised petty kingdoms where ordinary people were small-scale farmers exercising rights of landownership over family plots handed down over generations. In this deeply local, agrarian world, 'the property owned the owners', as one scholar puts it.[3] But the Great Winter stoked a process, already underway, where land was concentrating in fewer hands and was then let out as tenant plots by absentee owners. These owners were self-made warrior aristocrats with retinues of men-at-arms – a heroic-styled culture of fragile allegiances and codes of honour, underlain with the constant threat of violence, of the kind celebrated in epic literature like *Beowulf*.

Shorn of such self-representations, in many ways this social world resembled the gangster or pirate cultures of more recent times. It involved sophisticated and relatively egalitarian codes of conduct within its own community, but a ruthless and predatory expansionism outside it, oriented to enrichment from captured booty and enslaved people.

Such were the origins of the Viking period in the so-called Dark Ages of Europe. Conventional histories date its emergence into wider European consciousness with the Viking raid on the island monastery of Lindisfarne in northeast England in 793. It was a small affair compared with what was to come, involving a handful of men in a couple of boats, but it shocked Christian opinion in England and beyond with the turn to violence among erstwhile trading partners from the pagan north.[4]

Before long, the self-reinforcing cycle of interlinked trading, raiding, slaving and adventuring built a vast economic and military Viking diaspora stretching from the Arctic to the Mediterranean and from the edge of

PREFACE

North America to the western Eurasian Steppe. The access of some more than others in Viking society to the fruits of this extractivism-fuelled social stratification within it. The gap between lord and peasant widened.

Eventually, the Vikings embraced Christianity and their story merged with the development of a relatively unified medieval culture in northwest Europe, woven out of more disparate earlier strands.

But it retained a combative edge. William, Duke of Normandy – a Norse settler culture in northern France, Norman meaning Norse or Northman – famously invaded England in 1066 and installed himself on its throne. The *Domesday Book* he commissioned was a colonial document prefiguring many later ones. It asked, in enormous quantitative detail, exactly what the country could yield, and in what quantity, with a view to appropriating as much as possible to the Anglo-Norman exchequer. The Norman conquerors bequeathed to England a centralized and extractive state apparatus that arguably prepared the ground for England's own expansion much later as a global power, helping to spread this predatory mindset across the Earth.

TODAY, WORLDWIDE, our societies and governments are still asking exactly what our countries can yield, and in what quantity. It's too easy to see this as benevolence – lifting the poor, feeding the world and so forth. It's as much because they're still conquest societies – Viking societies. The trading-raiding-slaving nexus of Viking-era globalization is *our* world, directly paralleling the globalization of modern centuries.

The modern style of globalization has sometimes been tamer and more rationally framed than its medieval precursors. Nowadays, it's typically expressed through an implausible universalism: everybody can aspire to being a Viking, organizing a flow of trade goods and labour services to their personal advantage, while nobody has to be disadvantaged and reap the consequences of this plunder. Or else it manifests in an embrace of a 'Viking' warrior or winner-takes-all attitude, typically among social-media-saturated young men who are not very plausible candidates for effecting it.

Either way, these implausible positions reveal the beating dark-age heart of our modern age of enlightenment: a world built on slavery, colonialism, labour exploitation and the levelling of nature in pursuit of a relentless material throughput.

※※※

A MILLENNIUM AND A HALF after these possible origins of Ragnarök, I'm doing the rounds of my own small farm in the county of Somerset in South West England. I live on the edge of the Mendip Hills, whose western scarps sweep down to the sea north of the flatlands in the Somerset Levels – 'the land of the summer grazing' that gives the county its name. Beyond the Levels and the anvil head of Exmoor, the southern reaches of the Bristol Channel empty into the Atlantic, three thousand miles of open ocean toward Newfoundland and the western limit of Viking activities. Not far to the east of the Mendips, King Alfred fought Viking armies to a stalemate in the 880s and stabilized the Anglo-Saxon kingdom of Wessex, until the Duke of Normandy came calling two centuries later.

Many of the young ash trees we planted here are sickening with fungal dieback disease. Leafless twigs bronzed with lesions point skyward, too vertical and crabbed. I'm not going to draw some cloth-eared parallel between the fate of these stripling Somerset ash trees and the groaning of the world-ash Yggdrasil. All the same, it's hard not to take these small signs in nature – ash dieback, the decline of familiar birds and insects, the blighting of plants by new insect arrivals such as leek moth and alder beetle, and strange patterns in the weather – likewise as portents of something badly wrong in the world.

We know all too well what that something is. Wildlife loss, chemical pollution, water stress, soil stress. Also, climate change and global heating that threaten disturbances easily as challenging as the dust-veil years of Norse prehistory. The warnings grow louder but we continue down a path that's now deeply threaded into our own version of Ragnarök. Fenrir, the wolf of economic increase, has slayed old gods like 'All-father' Odin and old knowledges (Mimir) that grounded people locally. The doom of the old gods ushered in an age of global violence that we still inhabit. And now we face the doom of our new modernist gods, which will also undoubtedly spell violence – the more so the longer we cling to them.

Our politics, too, seems to have imbibed the apocalyptic spirit. Electoral choices are increasingly framed on all sides as titanic battles between good

PREFACE

and evil rather than the dilemmas between lame options of old. Perhaps they *are* titanic, since it's political choices that are ultimately responsible for all the other dysfunctions. But a belief that any present political leader has the answers requires equally epic levels of faith.

Some thinkers talk of a multipronged contemporary 'poly-crisis' or 'meta-crisis'. Whether the doom of our modern gods comes about in any given place through climate change, energy squeeze, water scarcity, soil loss, nature deficit, political or economic disaster, or some combination of them is unknowable. It's as well to prepare for worst-case scenarios as best we can, without assuming they're necessarily escapable or that we're the masters of our destiny. Without assuming, too, that whoever that 'we' is, somebody will come to save us if those worst-case scenarios manifest.

Still, if Ragnarök indeed came at the dawn of the Viking era, it was not in the end the doom of gods and people, or at least of all gods and all people. People endured and, afterward, the Seeress said, 'Another green Earth will rise from the sea.'

Hope springs eternal, then. We may not always be able to stave off the worst outcomes, but we can work toward better ones. There are any number of visions of how another green Earth might rise from this sea of our present chaos. They span the gamut from tech-happy ecomodernism to 'coming home to the Pleistocene'.[5] What I offer in this book is neither the former, with its perfected progress story of our Viking modernism, nor the latter, with its dreams of a return to past purity. Instead, I sketch something grittier, less perfect, more grounded in existing technologies and knowledges painstakingly built up around the world and too easily tossed aside – an orientation to land, craft, work and community, which I believe can more plausibly ground another green Earth rising out of the profound crisis of the present than anything else.

INTRODUCTION

An Arc of Future Earth

To begin, let's fly over an arc of the present Earth, starting at the other end of the North American continent that the Vikings visited a millennium ago – in Los Angeles, let's say. It's easy to do with Google Earth. Zoom to a camera altitude of 100 kilometres and look down from your majestic perch onto the second-largest city in the US.

From the Port of Los Angeles on Terminal Island, the coastline arcs gently southeast along Long Beach. We follow the curve of the beach but then course correct northeast over the city, noting the regularity of its patterning – a grid of square blocks in city grey, each tessellating neatly with the next. Zooming in, we see their fractal pattern, smaller blocks within the larger, and individual houses within the small blocks replicating this world of quadrilaterals, but with more randomness and colour. Here and there, a sports field or a park.

Back at our 100-kilometre vantage point and heading east, we soon leave the city and enter a less geometric world of nature, albeit one that from this height we can see has its own kind of order. Brown and yellow, a landscape of desert, rock and hill. Before long, we reach Lake Havasu on the California–Arizona border, an artificial lake created by the Parker Dam, from where the Colorado River Aqueduct that provides Los Angeles with much of its water makes its way to the city we've just left.

From Havasu, we follow the twists and turns of the Colorado River north, observing the ribbon of human development the river creates – irrigated fields and more urban grids. Further out from the river, solar electricity facilities, with their own rigorously geometric architectures.

Entering Nevada with the river, the city of Las Vegas is just to our west. Smaller than Los Angeles, but with a similar grey grid – though more dotted with green, which seems surprising given the greater aridity of the area. Zooming in, we see that many of these green areas are golf courses.

To the east is Lake Mead, another artificial lake created in the 1930s by the Hoover Dam. Its sinuous arms scribe the brown desert with a signature in water dark as ink. The dam was a New Deal project of President Roosevelt's that now helps slake the thirst of croplands and cities across the Southwest.

We continue northeast, across Utah and into Colorado – a sparsely populated landscape of desert and mountain that greens a little as we go. East of Denver, another gridded cityscape, the country changes completely.

We're now in the High Plains: farm country. This land is gridded too, but instead of the grey circuit board of the cities, the squares are larger – the browns and greens of fields. They have less fractal complexity when we zoom in, although often we can see the lines of field crops and a tracery of tracks and water movements in the landscape. Many of them have the telltale circle-in-a-square geometry of centre-pivot irrigation systems, pulling water from the Ogallala Aquifer to quench the thirsty crops.

As we head east and north, this farm country stretches a long way over the central United States – eastern Colorado, Kansas, Iowa, Illinois and onward. Its enormous production of arable crops far outstrips the needs of the people living in these areas – a breadbasket region exporting grains not only to other parts of the US, but across the world.

As night falls, we notice the lights below form another linear grid pattern. Lines and nodes, roads and towns. We thunder past Chicago, the city that invented modern agribusiness by connecting beef and grain from the west with wood from the north, consumers from the east and money from … somewhere. Then the postindustrial city of Detroit.

To the east of Detroit, Lake Erie and Lake Ontario are fingers pointing us toward our ultimate destination, but first we take a detour south over Washington, DC, capital of this great superpower nation-state. The spirits of presidents Washington and Lincoln stand watch from their memorials at either end of the National Mall near the left bank of the Potomac River. Just to the north, the forty-seventh president, Donald Trump, has recently moved into the White House for his second term as I write these words.

INTRODUCTION

Departing northward, we fly over New England where, unlike further south and west, the fields play second fiddle to the woods. Leaving the US behind, we island hop over the Viking sea – Newfoundland, the ice giant of Greenland, Iceland, the Faroes. Then we take a dogleg through my homeland of the British Isles – the brown moors and mountains of the Scottish Highlands, striped green here and there by crofting communities.[1] The more extensive field systems of Ireland and Wales, interleaved with mountains and boggy rough grazing, all greener and smaller than the field systems left far behind in the central United States.

We pass over Bristol, once a major slaving port in the grim trade linking Africa, Europe and the Americas in the first era of globalization. Today, the harbourfront is incomparably more genteel – a world of museums, pubs and coffee houses.

Zooming east far above the M4 motorway, we cross the fields of southern England until we reach the capital, London. Another grey tracery of streets, but less orderly than its American counterparts.

Northeastward out of London, field systems resume in the flatlands of East Anglia, the arable heartland of England. And then we're flying over the shallow waters of the North Sea. Only a few millennia ago there was a land bridge here, Doggerland, linking the British Isles to the mainland peninsula of Europe. Once we've crossed this sea, we'll end our journey in Amsterdam, which some centuries ago vied with London to be the colonial and trading capital of the world. In the late seventeenth century, the Dutch Republic, of which the city formed a part, even donated Britain a king. Depending on whose history you read, William III (1650–1702) arrived either by invitation or, like his earlier Norman namesake, by invasion. In any case, from the sea defences of the Dutch coast we follow the Noordzeekanaal a few miles into the heart of this watery city, and touch down.

LET'S RERUN THAT FLIGHT, unspecified decades into the future from still-watching satellites. I offer the following in a spirit that's less than prediction, but more than mere provocation.[2]

We start at the same point in Los Angeles, but Terminal Island has gone, and the coastline now runs north of what was once Long Beach. There's still a tessellation of city blocks as we head northeast, but the city is smaller now, with long fingers of nature's greens and browns probing from the edges of the old city into its present interior. Some of the city blocks look less orderly. Some of them look black. What were once sports fields or parks, smoothly green from this height, seem to have been repurposed – still green, mostly, but now with shrubs and a more complex ordering of lines and curves suggesting cultivation. Smaller patches of green dot the city here and there.

Heading east, Lake Havasu is mostly gone, and the Colorado's thread is narrower. The irrigated fields alongside it have gone, while the ranks of solar panels have grown – though it's hard to tell from here whether they're still in working order. We follow the Colorado again into Nevada. Las Vegas has shrunk to almost nothing, and its golf courses to nothing at all. Lake Mead has also mostly gone.

There are many changes in the High Plains, too, as we head east. The irrigated fields have all but disappeared, along with most of the aquifer that supplied them. Some of the old field systems are intact, but with greater variation. Some, particularly as we get further east, are green, more complex in form, and smaller, with woodland threading around them. Others look brown and dusty, marked by the signature curves of wind and water rather than straighter lines of field crops. It no longer looks like a global breadbasket region.

As night falls, we see no checkerboard of light across this farm country, or indeed much light at all, but there are a few clusters here and there. They seem to correspond to no linear human geography yet speak of small settlements unseen in this darkness. Maybe they hint at a collapse of postcolonial urbanism in the region, parallelling on a grander scale the fourteenth-century collapse of the precolonial city at Cahokia in present-day Illinois.

As we pass the Great Lakes region, Chicago and Detroit are depleted like Los Angeles, though not quite as badly, and dotted with green in the same way – impressively so in the case of Detroit.

INTRODUCTION

The forests to the north are receding poleward, while some of the plains to the south are sporting their own sparse garb of woodland. Chicago has long since stopped brokering the connection.

It's hard not to wonder about how the relationship between cities – these huge, tight aggregations of people – and the continental-scale field and engineering systems they rely on, is faring in the new world we're seeing below. T.S. Eliot's great, post-World War I poem of disenchanted urbanism, 'The Waste Land', springs to mind as we pass over these Midwestern conurbations:[3]

> *Unreal city*
> *Under the brown fog of a winter noon*

Washington, DC, seems to have experienced similar degradations to other cities we've seen – if anything, worse. But the National Mall is still there, its presidential statuary now guarded by river flood defences almost as monumental.

Repeating the flight over rural New England, the dance between field-light and wood-shade that we saw in the eastern side of the plains has tipped toward sun-drenched field systems. Small fields snake its valleys and spread further up their sides.

The coastline of eastern North America has changed, just like its western counterpart. We see one reason as we fly over Greenland. It still has its icecap, but it's shockingly depleted – as if someone had scored fiercely around its coasts with a dark pen. The Scottish Highlands have turned darker too in many places – deer country becoming venison country becoming crofts, with their distinctive pattern of small cropland areas, small pastures and small woodlands. In some ways, they now look more like Ireland and Wales.

Like other cities, Bristol has grown smaller, and its coastline is altered. It has the same interdigitation of grey and green like other cities, too. The harbourside museums and bars have gone, and it seems to be a working port again, with barges and small boats nuzzling its edges.

> London has experienced much the same fate as the other cities we've passed over. Depleted, greened in some places, blackened in others, newly scalloped by the ingress of water from the River Thames. London, T.S. Eliot's original unreal city, isn't quite submerged under the lagoon depicted in J.G. Ballard's classic climate-change sci-fi novel, *The Drowned World*, but things have certainly changed. In parts of its hollows, there are what look more like encampments than bricks-and-mortar housing.
>
> Flying north, some of the field systems of East Anglia are still intact, though obviously not the ones now reclaimed by the sea. Finally, we fly over the undersea realm of Doggerland – now a bit more undersea than before. We end our flight again in Amsterdam. It's truly now an unreal city, in that half of it has gone.

※※※

I'M NOT, FOR NOW, going to abandon the lofty vantage point of the flight we've just taken and come down to Earth to explain in detail exactly what happened to generate the world we saw in our second pass over the territory. I'll colour in some of that story as the book proceeds. But our simulated flight was intended to suggest that some of the things we currently take for granted in rich Western countries may come to a dramatic, unscripted and chaotic end.

The apocalyptic imaginings of the twentieth century focused mostly on nuclear war and pandemic disease, with sides of totalitarianism and techno-dystopia. All those possibilities remain alive, although I won't say much more about them. Recently, climate breakdown has emerged as a new threat that no longer inhabits the outer realms of science fiction, as it did when Ballard wrote *The Drowned World* in 1962.

Contained within a growing body of obscure technical communiques, policy analyses and mainstream writings too, this sense of an ending is becoming science fact. Even a report for the resolutely business-as-usual investment bank J.P. Morgan stated, 'It is clear that the earth is on an unsustainable trajectory. Something will have to change at some point if the human race is going to survive.'[4] On another front, the Asian financial crisis of 1997 and the global financial crisis of 2007–9 look like warning tremors of bigger economic earthquakes to come.[5]

Misery upon misery, then, and fear upon fear. Yet my future flight was also intended to suggest that this sense of an ending may be a beginning as well. The end of the world as we know it isn't the same as the end of the world.[6] Some communities endure. New ones form. For all we can tell from 100 kilometres up, some of them may be thriving.

The focus of this book is on helping us find ways to survive and thrive. Therefore, it's not so much about why the human world as we know it may be coming to an end. I and many others have written more about this elsewhere.[7] Still, it's probably helpful to lay out the main reasons briefly first. Some of them we'll have occasion to fill out later in the book.

Changing Times

The modern world economic system has found ways to generate extraordinary amounts of money. Not only does this system usually grow the amount year-on-year, it actively depends on growing it. Money is just an idea, a promise, but it has real-world consequences.

Those consequences are partly material – the use of nonrenewable resources, or the use of renewable resources at nonrenewable rates. They're also political. Increasingly, the growth of the global economy creates geopolitical tensions between countries or groups of countries. It also creates tensions between political factions within countries. One dynamic of world system collapse is the probably irresolvable nature of these resource, economic and political tensions in their own terms, regardless of other drivers. A global trading system once underwritten by US military power in the context of Cold War rivalry with the Soviet Union is disintegrating. The world emerging out of it is vulnerable to supply-chain shortages, trade conflicts, turbulent politics and further towering economic crises similar to or worse than the global financial crisis of 2007–9.[8]

A second dynamic of collapse, as I've already mentioned, is climate change – a grave threat in its own right and a multiplier of other ones. This loomed large in my opening dramatization, for example in the issue of sea-level rises and city inundations – estimates for US sea-level rises by 2100 above 2000 levels are in the range of 0.6–2.2 metres.[9] And that's not all. Other effects include supply-chain disruptions, food crises, extreme weather events, wildfires, droughts, chronic heat stress, ecological collapse, new diseases and political-economic meltdowns – at worst, a beyond-Biblical litany of plagues.

In my years of writing about human-caused climate change, I've often encountered the notion that it's a hoax geared to entrenching government power. Former US president Barack Obama's recent house purchase right by the rising seas around Martha's Vineyard, an island in Massachusetts, has set these tongues wagging. But Obama is a multimillionaire with lifelong secret service protection. Whereas I, and probably you, aren't. If things go south, Obama will be fine even if he loses his beach house. The rest of us may have to be more inventive. For those of us who don't have big bucks or hired guns to get us out of trouble, the next best thing is building community. That's largely what this book is about.

Still, it's true that climate change and other crises might be used by governments as excuses to further their own agendas rather than genuinely helping ordinary people. So let me be clear: my argument in this book is that while people need government, they don't so much need The Government. In other words, centralized modern states won't deliver solutions to climate change and other problems top down, whatever their political flavour – left, right or in between. People mostly need to figure out their own approaches themselves, bottom up. Hopefully, that's what those near-invisible communities we glimpsed through the darkness in the US Midwest were up to, as the erstwhile residents of Cahokia apparently had to do in an earlier era.[10]

Building on that, I'll introduce a distinction between *publics* and *communities* that I'll draw on later in the book.

A public is a group of people organized around rights they claim from a state. We're very familiar with this in modern times. Most of our politics are built around it.

A community, on the other hand, is a group of people organized around livelihoods they claim from the place where they live and not from the state. They may need to make claims upon the state to define or defend their occupancy of place, strategically becoming publics. But ultimately, they're playing a different game. They're not publics or citizenries, and their way of life isn't held in the container of the state.

We're less familiar with this idea in modern times, but I believe we need to get familiar with it, fast. The arc of future Earth that we took suggested that, in the future, states may be less able to organize territorial space politically than they now do. That will require a new politics grounded in livelihood communities.

Energy is another key issue pointing toward a radically different future world. The world that we saw in our arc of present Earth, with its dense cities, huge dams, long-distance supply chains, golf courses, intensive irrigation systems and global breadbasket regions is a world of cheap, abundant energy. In 1750, at the dawn of that modern world, global average primary energy consumption was less than 20 gigajoules (GJ) per capita. In 2000, the corresponding figure was 65 GJ per capita, and in 2023 it was 77 GJ per capita.[11] Currently, over 80 per cent of global energy consumption is provided by nonrenewable and climate-change-promoting fossil fuels. Globally, despite all our decarbonization efforts, total consumption of fossil fuels has increased every year since 1982, with the exception of 2009 (due to the financial crisis) and 2020 (due to the Covid pandemic).[12]

To avoid dangerous climate change, we need to stop using fossil fuels. That's not happening at the moment, despite much talk about an 'energy transition' into low-carbon forms of energy, such as solar or nuclear electricity. It's true that the richer countries have made strides in decarbonizing their electricity sectors. This falls far, far short of adequate decarbonization, which has to occur rapidly worldwide. Nevertheless, the key lies with the four largest energy-using countries: China, the US, India and Russia. The geopolitics of rapid decarbonization do not look promising there.

Smooth energy transition to low-carbon sources remains the great hope of many for avoiding climate and other breakdowns (solar electricity is now heading the race, over the nuclear boosterism of the past). The fact that it's not happening yet doesn't mean it won't, although the time window is now wafer thin. The technical obstacles are prodigious, but it's not only a matter of technology – if anything, the politics, the economics and the interactions between all these factors are even more daunting.

Indeed, science historian Jean-Baptiste Fressoz shows in his aptly titled book *More and More and More* that there have never been any past energy transitions – merely the addition of new energy sources to old ones, involving what he calls 'the entanglement and symbiotic expansion of all energies' as part of the ever-growing material flows of modern life. For example, we tend to think of wood as an old-fashioned source of energy that was replaced by coal, and that coal in turn is being superseded by newer, cleaner energy sources. The truth is that we have never consumed more wood or coal globally than we do today; these and all other energy sources lie entwined behind the vast material flows that structure the world of cities, bright lights, highways, concrete, plastic and fertilized, irrigated commodity farmland we saw in our flight over the present Earth.[13]

The belief that there can be a transition to clean energy that will not only preserve this world but extend its (mixed) blessings beyond the charmed circle of wealthy people and wealthy countries isn't securely grounded in past historical fact. Inasmuch as it's based on an evidential grounding at all, these are usually paper exercises involving, at best, optimistic assumptions about the replacement of fossil energy and feedstocks with renewable energy – an optimism increasingly verging on the heroic, with each passing year of non-transition – and a certain political and material naivety about how, in the words of one of the more sceptical experts in this area, 'the world really works'.[14]

My assumption in this book is that these transition hopes won't be realized. This potentially catches us in something of a scissor movement – either lower energy use or climate breakdown, or elements of both. My arc of future Earth dramatization involved the working out of that dynamic, with degradations of existing urban and rural-agrarian spaces dependent on high-energy infrastructure and their replacement with lower energy lifeways in the context of climate change and other drivers. A world of lower energy use needn't be something to fear. A world of unexpected energy squeezes and global competition over energy resources might be.

Although financial, climate and energy dynamics are important, they're not the only factors impelling us toward such futures. Other physical drivers of our challenged future include water, critical minerals and ecological collapse. There are also a range of political and economic factors pushing in the same direction. But I'm going to leave it there for now. In a sense, these physical and social drivers are immediate causes that reflect a deeper cultural and spiritual problem represented in what I'll call the hero's journey.

INTRODUCTION

The Hero Is You

The hero's journey is a common storytelling motif in Western culture. The way it goes roughly is that in a world full of disorder and trouble, a special person sets out on a quest to put things right. He (it's usually a he) encounters many problems, false dawns, narrow escapes and imposters along the way but eventually finds some key or secret knowledge that enables him to sort things out back home among much acclaim from his grateful people, who live happily ever after.

Many of our stories along these lines involve technological mastery, going back at least as far as Greek myth and the story of Prometheus, who stole fire from the gods and gave it to humanity. The idea of the techno-fix that redeems modern humanity still dominates much of our contemporary myth-making, with the scientist, the engineer and the entrepreneur cast in the hero role. This is sometimes called 'Promethean environmentalism'.[15]

There's always been a vein of ambiguity in the hero story concerning hubris, overreach and unintended consequences. Mary Shelley's Gothic Romantic novel *Frankenstein*, published in 1818 at the dawn of the modern industrial era, was subtitled 'The Modern Prometheus'. The novel was Romantic in the sense that it dramatized the ideas of the Romantic movement, not in the sense that it was a love story. In modern terms, those ideas are that purported mass technological solutions to problems usually create new problems and risks, and draw down on more energy and resources.[16]

This tends to be forgotten nowadays in the hero tradition of the 'technological sublime' described by historian Eugene McCarraher in the context of US history as 'the mesmerizing veneration of technology and its creators – and the conviction that the nation had a "manifest destiny" both to possess the continent and to superintend the redemption of the world'.[17]

The technological sublime crops up all over the place – especially in mainstream political discussions and academic futurology, where to break out of the story that things will be like now but better is to court ridicule. Tellers of fictional tales give themselves more licence but the technological sublime crops up here too.

Stephen Markley's blockbusting novel *The Deluge* is a case in point. In the near future that Markley depicts (spoiler alert!), climate change wreaks havoc across the world and specifically in the US, where most of the action occurs. Unprecedentedly ferocious storms lash the eastern seaboard, floods plague the Midwest, Los Angeles burns in wildfires (some of these things are already happening). Food prices go through the roof while the economy crashes. At one point, an economic expert proclaims, 'This depression will not be great, greater or greatest, it will be the fucking dark ages.'[18] Bad actors take control of both main political parties, while 'patriot' militias and rogue politicians cause mayhem. Shops are looted, casual violence mushrooms. Inhumane militarized borders spring up worldwide. There seems to be no solution. Scientists issue grim warnings. Doesn't work. People try the usual technocratic political interventions and policy wonkery. Doesn't work. NGO lobbying of government. Doesn't work. Civil disobedience and political direct action. Doesn't work. Increasingly violent ecoterrorism. Doesn't work.

But then eventually, eventually, after all the mayhem, just when it seems like there's no hope, things turn around. A radically reforming Democrat president pushes through a huge economic package, implicitly based on the ideas of post-Keynesian economics that governments with monetary sovereignty can support socially beneficial projects without fear of running out of cash. The bad guys inside and outside government are rounded up and brought to justice. Arctic areas now in the hands once again of Indigenous people welcome global migrants to work in new critical mineral mines. Nuclear-powered geoengineering in Antarctica stems the melting of the ice. High-tech methods like aquaponics start stabilizing the food supply. China turns to democracy, with help from the US. Humanity isn't out of the woods yet, but things are looking up.

Much as I enjoyed reading the novel and found many of its future projections plausible, this happy ending is basically Prometheus and manifest destiny once more. In Markley's hands, it's a progressive liberal vision of the government sorting things out and making America great again. There are, of course, conservative and illiberal visions with the same goal.

Notions of manifest destiny, even implicit ones of the kind Markley mobilizes in his novel, repress other stories that might serve us better today. In his fine book *Finding Our Niche*, anthropologist Philip Loring references an Indigenous American myth about a girl who drowned in a river, became a salmon, spent a lifetime living among other salmon learning of how they wanted humans to treat them, and was then reincarnated among her people, telling them of what she'd learned and thereby enabling them to thrive locally for generations as fisherfolk by following these rules.[19]

The girl in this story wasn't a heroine with a magic solution. She was an ordinary person who brought knowledge to share, enabling others to work more successfully at generating a sustainable livelihood from a local ecological base – and, importantly, knowledge that isn't just a story about greater human control over nature but one about negotiation with non-human agents (salmon) as active participants.

Métis scholar Zoe Todd has elaborated this point in relation to Indigenous legal philosophies and human–fish interactions in Canada, explaining its importance for Indigenous people in surviving colonial violence.[20] As I see it, such thinking is much less well developed within European and European-settler cultures, but it does still manifest in these cultures among those relatively few people who generate livelihoods directly by working with land and water in low-input ways – if not as a legal philosophy, then at least as a way of being.

My argument is that we inheritors of this modernist European culture need to make these ways of being more central to our practices, perhaps by (ironically) learning from Indigenous people about dealing with forms of violence that we're increasingly inflicting on ourselves. Or by looking to disinter the knowledges of other livelihood communities buried under modern disdain. In other words, by listening – really listening – to the salmon and to other beings and learning from them.

In any case, the livelihood model of the salmon-girl story is not a technological fix like nuclear fusion that you don't understand and have no agency over, but that the government uses to keep the lights on so that you can carry on getting to work, paying the mortgage and taking your mind off things with Netflix in the evening while your wider culture trumpets its manifest destiny. The model is that you yourself can learn the skills to live well in the place you call home by working to generate your livelihood, and that this work, this way of being, *is* your culture, of which you are an important bearer. If there's a hero in this story, it's you. And it's everyone else at the same time.

I've spent a lot of time in recent years arguing against heroic modern techno-fix stories, and in favour of shared local livelihood stories. I've written detailed, quantitatively grounded critiques of new 'saviour' technologies like manufactured microbial food, demonstrating their technical and energetic implausibility.[21] One kind of response that's come my way is a belief that a future renewable-energy cornucopia makes my calculations irrelevant. As I've already argued, I think the belief in this cornucopia is ill-founded. It's certainly not based on any sound evidence. But it does inadvertently shift the debate onto the right terrain – namely, our spiritual orientations toward the future and to our true aims, which I discuss in later chapters.

I've also found that critiques of saviour technologies and the alternative case for local livelihoods tend to get dismissed by the new Prometheans as mere backward-looking romanticism. This is to misunderstand Romanticism, which – to quote Eugene McCarraher again – stems:

> *not from a facile and nostalgic desire to return to the past, but from a view that much of what passed for "progress" was in fact inimical to human flourishing: a specious productivity that required the acceptance of venality, injustice, and despoliation; a technological and organizational efficiency that entailed the industrialization of human beings…*[22]

… and so on. You get the picture. In my experience, a lot of ordinary people do get the picture, whereas acceptable public narratives remain fixated on Promethean and manifest destiny myths to be delivered technologically by centralized states. Even radical critics of the status quo find it hard to let go of the state-technology-high-energy nexus and are apt to dismiss views of lower-energy futures beyond the circle of the modern state as mere 'anarcho-primitivism'.[23]

In this book, I show that non-state forms of organization needn't imply anarchism, and reduction of energy use needn't imply primitivism. But I'm not going to spend much more time explaining why our existing social world is coming to an end or justifying the case for building culture and livelihoods bottom up on a local ecological base. The hour is getting late, and I focus instead on trying to help with that building process. I don't claim to have easy answers or solutions. And, while I cite a lot of evidence, I try to avoid the trap of claiming that the evidence lends unambiguous support to my favoured positions. The interpretation of evidence is usually contextual, making sense within the framing of the particular story it illuminates. But many of our current stories ill serve us. Instead, I look in these pages for the light of some different stories to guide us.

INTRODUCTION

On that note, I should mention that I use the words 'we' or 'us' quite often in these pages. The we in question could just be my wife and me in our work on our farm. Or it could be humanity as a whole, or any number of subgroups in between. Hopefully, it'll be clear from the context. Often the 'we' in question is we people from the rich countries of the West or Global North. I believe that that we, of which I'm a part, can be the heroes of our own stories, but we've already written a lot of hero stories about ourselves. We now need some different ones, in which we dial down our sense of ourselves as world-transforming history-makers and instead tell tales of ourselves as heroic local livelihood-makers.

※※※

BUT THERE'S ONE MORE version of the hero story I want to mention, arising out of a modern antihero with a largely deserved reputation as something of a bogeyman. The Reverend Thomas Robert Malthus (1766–1834) first published *An Essay on the Principle of Population* in 1798 with its famous argument that the growth of human populations tends to outstrip the growth of the resources – especially food – needed to meet their needs.

To say that people need to live within limits, as I do in this book, is not a Malthusian argument. To say that the poor will always be with us, and that it's counterproductive to try doing anything to help – as Malthus did to the delight of industrialists and the upwardly mobile in the rising economies of the nineteenth century – *is* a Malthusian argument.

Not many influential people publicly espouse that kind of Malthusianism today. More common nowadays is a flipped version of the Malthusian narrative – what some call neo-Malthusianism.[24] The argument here is that the Malthusian perils of mass poverty and starvation forever lurk, but for the heroic intervention of science and technologies that keep humanity one step ahead of these miseries. This, of course, is the Promethean hero narrative that I mentioned above. 'Threatening dystopias' like impending climate breakdown further fuel the narrative that solutions lie with technical development and expertise.[25]

There's a left-wing version of this Promethean narrative that argues the scarcity and suffering experienced by so many people today results from capitalism. This artificial scarcity, the argument runs, would disappear with its abolition, ushering in a world of abundance.

It's true that capitalist economies create artificial scarcities, but it strikes me that these arguments about easy abundance come from people who aren't well versed in actually producing a material livelihood for themselves, a practice that focuses the mind on the obstacles involved. Equally flawed, though, is the notion that without the benefits of modern technological civilization, life is one long, grinding struggle merely to survive. The truth is that with the help of the salmon and other such intermediaries, people can live well enough if they work hard enough, with enough skill, and no more. A world of judgement and sufficiency, of knowing when enough is enough, where limits are enabling as well as constraining, and where 'more' is not necessarily 'better'.

I'm certainly not arguing there's no role for modern science and technology in local futures grounded in making livelihoods from the ecological base. It's just that science and technology are at best helpmates rather than 'the solution' or the hero. The hero, as I've said, is you. And everyone else. This contrasts with what I call the 'world environmental problems framework' that claims big global problems require big global solutions that only clever and powerful people can command. I believe this framework itself is a big global problem, to which there is no big global solution. Only a lot of small local workarounds from local heroes.

But neo-Malthusian narratives are everywhere. The word 'moonshot' is a giveaway. The narrative often involves a request for government money to be put into the hands of corporations to supposedly solve people's problems, which they're regarded as incapable of solving for themselves. As Mary Shelley among others recognized, the new Prometheus usually fails in unanticipated ways to solve the problem, while creating further and often bigger problems, requiring more government money to be put into the hands of more corporations to solve more problems.

And so it goes on. I believe there's a tiny chance this kind of government-driven solutionism, the kind that redeems humanity at the eleventh hour in Stephen Markley's novel, may somehow find a way through the treacherous seas of climate change, technological limitation and political and economic impasse, allowing us to forget about the salmon girl for another generation or two. But the chance is vanishingly small and getting smaller by the day. That leaves us contemplating what one of Markley's characters called 'the fucking dark ages'.

CHAPTER 1

Dark Age Ahead

'There is, henceforth, no path to a liveable planet that does not pass through the complete destruction of business as usual.'[1]

So say two climate-change scholars in their book, *Overshoot*. But we can draw more or less the same conclusion if we're talking about other biophysical drivers. Or economic meltdowns of the kind projected in Stephen Markley's novel. Or the kind of political, moral and cultural terminus of present times diagnosed by such celebrated thinkers as Jane Jacobs in her book *Dark Age Ahead* or by Alasdair MacIntyre in his argument for local forms of community to sustain us through what he called the new dark ages.[2]

Not all these endpoints necessarily culminate in a planet that's unliveable, but they do all suggest at minimum the collapse of the kind of modern lifeways taken for granted by most people in the world, and certainly by those of us in regions of the Global North like Europe and North America. For my part, I see no way of getting to the kind of livelihood communities I discussed in the introduction, to worlds where we're prepared to live the lessons of the salmon girl, without passing through disorder and uncoordinated breakdown.

Partly, then, this book addresses the idea of a dark age ahead in this everyday sense of inevitably troubled times – times that demand us to keep looking for the light. But as I outlined in the preface, there's a more specific history of past 'Dark Ages' that's also relevant.

※※※

THE TERM 'DARK AGES' is disreputable among contemporary historians because of its moral loading – for example, in the way that modern

European thinkers of the Renaissance and the Enlightenment vaunted their own rebirth, their belief they could now see things in the clear light of a reality they thought had been obscured in the 'dark ages' of medieval thought after the collapse of the Roman Empire.

People still unthinkingly use terms like 'medieval' and 'dark ages' as pejoratives, to the extent that two historians titled their popular history of medieval times *The Bright Ages* in a worthwhile but probably fruitless attempt to redress the balance.[3] In this sense, I invoke the idea of a dark age ahead ironically. There are things we can learn today from the ruralism and political innovation of the post-Roman or postimperial Dark Ages, and there are things we can learn from the medieval moral and political thinking that preceded our modern age of self-proclaimed Enlightenment.

In times of trouble, grassroots intellectuals have been articulating localism and agrarianism at least since the fourth century BCE with the School of the Tillers during the Warring States period in ancient China.[4] The case for going back to the land is not some uniquely modern affectation of nostalgia for a lost past we've definitively left behind, but a permanent counter-civilizational possibility, which is constantly being refreshed. Maybe it's time to get over ourselves a bit, slow down, and listen to some voices from the dark circle beyond the fire of our self-absorbed 'enlightenment'.

In that sense, as well as looking for some light in a dark age, in this book I'll be looking for some dark in an age of light – figuratively, but also literally. Lower energy use, the dimming of the light we saw as we flew over the nighttime US in our arc of future Earth, the reduction of all the ecocidal practices associated with high-energy civilization, will bring some relief to a beleaguered nature but might also bring relief to beleaguered people. It's hard to see from a hundred kilometres up what people are doing in the darkness of the modernist state's decline, but I'm not going to assume they're always either miserable or up to no good.

Indeed, historians of earlier dark ages have made the point that life for many of those living through them could be pleasant enough. What struck the literate elites of the time as a catastrophic decline in politics and culture was experienced by ordinary people as a lessening of taxes and of military conscription – a lessening, generally, of the depredations from state centres and organized political power. Historian Susan

Oosthuizen shows, for example, how living conditions improved for ordinary peasant households in 'Dark-Age' Britain after the withdrawal of the occupying Roman powers from the end of the fourth century CE.[5] The anthropologist and archaeologist duo of David Graeber and David Wengrow go further, arguing that:

> *The same portrayers of world history who profess themselves believers in freedom, democracy and women's rights continue to treat historical epochs of relative freedom, democracy and women's rights as so many 'dark ages'. Similarly ... the concept of 'civilization' is still largely reserved for societies whose defining characteristics include high-handed autocrats, imperial conquests and the use of slave labour.*[6]

To press the point, 'dark-age' situations where people build local land-based autonomies in the shadows of state power – deliberate autonomies, geared to keeping that power at bay – have been a near-permanent historical possibility that people have often jumped at when they get the chance.

It would be wrong to overdo the idea of merry dark ages actively chosen by ordinary people only too delighted to get the exactions of elites and state bureaucrats off their backs, but there's a grain of truth to it all the same. Ideally, I'd like to emphasize it more wholeheartedly than I do in this book; creating bottom-up livelihood communities of the new dark ages that stand largely outside the modern nation-state and that build rich, local human-to-human and human-to-nature interactions could be a powerful and beautiful thing. But it's a challenging task for our present high-energy world, making it harder to take a sunny view of the present meta-crisis and its possible descent into a new dark age. In the past, the means for a tolerable day-to-day life in the absence of state power were close at hand for most people. Consider by contrast what would happen now if the remit of the state and the supply chains it underwrites were to crumble.

On the upside, your landlord's or your mortgage lender's calls upon your resources might wane. On the other hand, the water supply to your house, its sewer connection, energy to heat or cool it and to drive your car, food and clothes in the shops, cash from the ATM, and – horror of horrors – your internet connection may no longer be reliable. Public workers may go unpaid. The lengthy cast list of doctors, teachers, care workers, waste collectors and so on serving your daily life would dwindle. Things would not, in sum, look good.

So, it's understandable that almost every shade of acceptable political opinion nowadays cleaves to the notion that these decencies of everyday life must be protected, and that the only politics up to the job emanates from the powerful reach of the modern state and the resource caravans it enables via high-energy high-technology and via agencies like transnational corporations.

Yet, as I've already argued, the modern state probably *isn't* up to the job, whoever's in charge of it. I'm not suggesting we should wantonly abandon the existing one, but it might be wise not to hold too tight to the idea that it will ultimately come through for us, as it finally did in Stephen Markley's novel. Indeed, there's every sign that, increasingly, nation-states are wantonly abandoning *us*, their citizens, in terms of the services and security they can provide.[7] New political structures for which nobody possesses a blueprint are usually built out of moments of deep crisis. And we're in a moment of deep crisis.

One way that crisis can go is the axe-age and wolf-age of 'The Seeress's Prophecy'. Even if that happens, trying to build local livelihood communities still seems like a wise bet. But another possibility is her green Earth rising from the sea … not to mention rivers full of salmon. I'd argue that this green Earth, if it rises, is likely to be farmed earth, tended earth – tended mostly by and for the people local to it. How we might best amplify that possibility out of the dark-age ruins of the present global economy is the subject of this book.

Hopefully I've now made the contours of those dark-age ruins clear. If we avoid the axe-age and the wolf-age, we face a dark age ahead in the loose sense of hard times to come arising from climate change and other biophysical drivers, along with political, economic and cultural conflict and decline. We also face a dark age ahead in the almost literal sense of a lower-energy world, with all that that implies for the material conditions of life. And we face a dark age ahead in the more specific sense of declining state power, a growing inability of political centres to organize and control local day-to-day life as powerfully as they've done in recent history – which, I've argued, may not be altogether a bad thing.

From Liberalism to Distributism

It's worth examining the political ruination of the present global economy I just mentioned in a little more detail.

There's a large literature from the political left on why private markets are generally a bad way to secure people's wellbeing and to address global environmental problems. There's a large literature from the political right on why government bureaucracies are a bad way to do those things too. I agree with both these literatures, and – skating over much detail – I broadly align with writers like Patrick Deneen who label both these wings, left and right, as different facets of a modern liberalism (progressive liberalism versus classical liberalism or, now, neoliberalism) that relies on the excessive power of the centralized state.[8] For that reason, I use the term 'liberal-modernism' in this book as a catch-all for this broad gamut of mainstream modern politics.

Another way to look at this is that both the left and the right have an essentially individualistic view of modern mass society as composed of autonomous and sovereign individual people in their multitudes who need to be organized by the state to realize their ends. This happens either directly, in the case of the left, via political parties and bureaucracies or indirectly, in the case of the right, by state-corporate management of money and markets.[9]

State power also looms large in the post-Keynesian economic approaches that were implicit in the salvation narrative at the end of Stephen Markley's novel *The Deluge*, as I mentioned earlier. One such approach is modern monetary theory (MMT). A key idea behind it is that governments with control over their own money (like the US and the UK) don't need to raise taxes or borrow on international markets before they can spend money.[10] They effectively spend money into existence, with taxes being the way they create demand for their currency. They cannot go bankrupt like a business or a household because they are currency issuers, not currency users like these other entities.

This means that such governments have a lot of choice over what they do. They can happily run large long-term deficits and fund programmes like healthcare and social services regardless of the money supply.

But it doesn't mean they can do whatever they like. Their choices cannot be overly inflationary if the economy is running at full capacity, and the choices have to be based on the real underlying resources available to deliver whatever they choose to do.

Unfortunately, that last sentence is quite a rub, especially when put alongside another reality of government. This is the gigantic global private business and financial sector geared to maximizing and accumulating profits however it can, including through virtualized financial instruments like derivatives, which are untethered from any real-world resource constraints.

This sector is now the proverbial tail wagging the dog of global governance – what political analyst Wolfgang Streeck calls a 'consolidation' phase of the state, where commercial market obligations take precedence over political citizenship obligations, and where the wellbeing of citizens is secured, if at all, essentially as a side effect of profit accumulation.[11] Others have more evocative names for this. Energy analyst Nate Hagens calls it 'the Mordor economy'. Writer Paul Kingsnorth calls it 'the machine'. A sense of something deathly, inhuman and implacable, over which humans have lost control.[12]

Whatever we choose to call it, this inhuman economics is occurring in multiple ways and at multiple levels – for example in net transfers of resources from poorer (Global South) to richer (Global North) nations, and from poorer to richer people within those nations.[13] It mobilizes a kind of poor-to-rich or periphery-to-centre pipeline variously of things, people, money and energy that will not be sustainable in the long run and is likely to prompt system breakdown. I focus in this book mainly, though not entirely, on the privileged European and North American parts of the picture, largely to keep my task manageable and because it's what I know best. But, as I try to make plain, this is a whole-world problem.

Without going through all the arguments in detail, I think this whole-world problem involves irresolvable tensions in global governance, grounded in the fact that the present level of monetization in the global economy is completely out of whack with the real underlying resources available. Far from learning from the salmon how to live sustainably with them, present levels of loose capital globally are probably enough to buy the salmon in all the rivers of the world – which obviously wouldn't be sustainable.

Another example is the disparity between land values and income from farmland in the UK (although not only in the UK), which is in the news as I write due to recent changes in inheritance tax on farmland. According to some calculations, a modest family farm of about 200 acres typically has a paper land value of about £3 million, and an annual income of only about £30,000, which seems about right from my reading of agricultural economics in my locality.[14] Farmers would be better off selling the farm and investing the proceeds – but then there would be no food.

I'll explain some of the apparently baffling economics behind this later in the book. To oversimplify, the basic point for now is that such examples of excess capital in search of limited land or resources illustrate the disparity between the real underlying material base upon which we can build enduring societies and the much greater theoretical resources our present economy lays claim to. This is a signature of complex systems operating far from equilibrium, and therefore in danger of collapse.[15]

Almost everything about orthodox contemporary politics and economics is built on the assumption that these systems will not collapse – that persisting worldwide economic growth and centralized sovereignty will keep delivering improved, or at least not worsening, welfare to citizenries in the long term. Almost everything we think we know about 'development' – moving people away from making their livelihood directly from a local ecological base, and toward making it indirectly and supposedly more prosperously via the medium of money from many unknown ecologies worldwide – is built on these same assumptions. Promethean hero stories claim we can keep this ball in the air via new technologies. But, as I argued earlier, these generally turn out to create new problems – often the problem of requiring more energy, which is another limited real-world resource.

As these assumptions reach their expiry, it's hard to overstate the scale and the urgency of the back-to-first-principles approaches that are needed. Back to the salmon, back to productive farmland. It's inevitable that this dangerous moment will involve conflict and violence in some places. These are not, after all, qualities the modern state ever vanquished – indeed it's augmented them often enough. But it's worth staying open-minded toward other, more elevated possibilities.

ONE OF THE BENEFITS of modern monetary theory is that it draws attention to the fact that the centralized state has a lot of freedom of manoeuvre in principle – due, among other reasons, to its monetary monopoly. It doesn't always have this freedom in practice because of its subordination to profit accumulation – to Wolfgang Streeck's 'consolidation state'. But its freedom-in-principle through monopoly raises a question. What if it didn't have such a monopoly?

There's been a long history of states asserting their monetary monopolies upon their citizens by force, notably in the US. But that may not be so easy with freefalling monetary systems coming back into balance with underlying real resources. In such moments, the case for more distributed political, economic and monetary systems may assert itself.

An approach that I draw on heavily in this book is called, appropriately enough, 'distributism'. One of its key ideas is *subsidiarity* – decisions are made at the smallest and most local level possible within the hierarchy of political communities, where the local, smaller levels aren't inferior to wider, larger levels or exist only under their sufferance. In practice, this means that there's widespread or distributed private access to land and other means of generating a livelihood for most people, securing a level of autonomy against the aggregated power of private capital or the state and the 'publics' associated with it, as discussed in the introduction. I address the nature of landownership further in chapter 6. Distributism also has important ideas about justice, work and human relationships that I'll consider in later chapters.

Distributism emerged originally out of Catholic Social Teaching. I'm not myself Catholic, but I became an accidental distributist after distributist thinker Sean Domencic rightly pointed out to me that my book *A Small Farm Future* was effectively an articulation of distributist principles.[16] Those principles don't necessarily have to be tied to Catholicism as such, and I'm not an uncritical adherent of distributism – or of any other specific doctrine. But religious-political history in general, and Catholic history in particular, brings some important dimensions to bear on the wider issues considered here. I come back to this later in the book.

Another influence I draw on in exploring the heretical idea of breaking state monopolies of money and sovereignty is populism. Populism – a politics of and for the people – gets a bad press in mainstream political analysis, and it's true that 'the people' can be a dangerous idea in the hands of demagogues who claim to control the state in the name of 'the people' as a kind of formless mass untethered to any local commitments or sources of political autonomy – which regrettably is the end of too much contemporary politics. Yet when government is truly vested in ordinary people and not in those claiming to rule on their behalf, a politics of the people can have a remarkably radical, effective and generous edge.

The politics of the people I'll draw from in this book is largely what's known as *agrarian populism* – mobilizations of ordinary people around access to land and other necessities so they can make a direct livelihood. This form of populism is barely known or talked about in everyday political discussion these days, at least in the richer countries, but it's been an enormously important politics worldwide over the last couple of centuries. It's perhaps best known through figures such as Mohandas Gandhi in India and Emiliano Zapata in Mexico. In the contemporary West, its recent influence has been more countercultural – renegade economist and pioneering green thinker Fritz Schumacher springs to mind – but it's worth remembering that around the turn of the twentieth century, the Populist Party in the US was a serious electoral force.

Probably the main reason populism is no longer well known in the richer countries is because it won many of its political battles, but in ways that turned out to be Pyrrhic. Populists wanted to foster prosperous local communities, which to some extent they achieved but only through a kind of devil's bargain with the liberal-modernist state: 'We'll give you your prosperous community, but only in the form of a mass urban-industrial society orchestrated by the centralized state and its corporate allies.'

In many poorer countries of the Global South, agrarian populism has long been and remains an important form of politics, geared around improving rural and agrarian communities and livelihoods, rather than 'developing' them out of existence. This is well known among scholars in rich countries, but unfortunately rarely makes it into public discussions here. I take up this story in chapter 3.

Scrolling forward to the present, this anti-populist history of 'development' in both the richer and poorer countries has culminated in Promethean, growth-oriented techno-salvation narratives of the kind I examined in the introduction. These have brought us to the brink of the new dark ages and traverse the entire mainstream political spectrum from tech-focused communisms to the competitive, fossil-fuelled growth orientations of the populist right.

This is one reason why old left-wing/right-wing political distinctions are breaking down. Just as mainstream left and right politics realigns around a joint commitment to tech-heavy liberal-modernism, so it's possible to imagine, in the words of Stephen Quilley, 'a realignment built on the overlap between libertarians, Burkean localists, and religious communitarians currently (sometimes unwillingly) camped out on the political right on the one hand, and green/anarchist anti-moderns on the left.'[17]

This book represents an attempt by one particular writer inclined to green anti-modernism on the left to find the overlaps with those groups camped out on the right. An easy point of agreement is on the benefits of rich, local associational communities grounded in livelihood-making. Letting go of currently high levels of fossil-fuelled plenty may be a harder journey for both left and right, but if my arguments about our impending dark age are accurate, we don't have much choice about that. Probably most challenging to traditional left or anarchist thinking is the need to let go of a sense of individualist freedom and self-fashioning, and to embrace the idea that self-realization is possible only within the limiting (but also enabling) structures of already given communities and families – and, what's more, communities with spiritual underpinnings.

Yet I believe this step is necessary, for reasons I outline later in the book – particularly chapter 10. Sticking for now with easier challenges, both distributism and populism usefully inform the necessary idea of detaching sovereignty – the final power to command – from the centralized state and returning it to local communities, even if sovereignty ultimately operates at a transcendent realm that such communities can only mobilize and not control. In the language of secular politics, what this means is that there's a need for governance at different levels in society, but there is no 'ultimate' seat of government.

THE RETURN OF sovereignty to community may happen by default. In the impending dark-age moment, state sovereignty depends on delivering welfare – keeping the lights on, if you will, and delivering all those other services to the modern household – that ultimately centralized modern states probably can't keep delivering. One possibility in these circumstances is that they'll double down, in the process becoming techno-authoritarian disaster states. Another is that they'll lose some of their ability to organize geopolitical space.

Probably, both those things will happen. Much of this book is addressed to the latter scenario, in the hope it can contribute to sketching a distributist politics that might be able to claim further space from the declining liberal-modernist state. But it can be hard to imagine plausible alternatives to that state because we're so habituated to its stories. We're not used to real self-government. And we've allowed ourselves to be naively bought off by the liberal-modernist state with consumerist promises and bureaucratized forms of care it's unlikely to be able to sustain.

New thinking in social policy is traversing similar ground. For example, in her book *Radical Help*, Hilary Cottam writes:

> *Our current welfare institutions cannot provide care. Worse, they cannot even speak a language with which we might begin to think warmly and humanly about what is needed. ... The question is not how can we fix these services, but rather, as I stand beside you, how can I support you to create change. ... The emphasis is not on managing need but on creating capability.*[18]

Those ideas writ large strike to the heart of my arguments in this book, not just in terms of a makeover for the welfare state, but for the state in general, for society in general, for people's relationships with each other and for their relationships with the natural world. We need to detach sovereignty from the state and return sovereignty, capability and self-possession to ordinary people, families, households and communities. We need to do this not in the form of a politician's soundbite – 'giving power back to communities' – but for real.

Another challenge is that few of us know much about how to generate a livelihood and secure food, clothes and shelter in low-energy, low-capital situations where the organs of the modern liberal state are no longer generating it for us.

Still, for all that we've lost and for all the challenges ahead, people are by nature skilful learners and weavers of new cultures and new relationships, and it's on this that we must build. Moral philosopher Alasdair MacIntyre wrote some years ago of the parallel between present times and the period when the Roman Empire gave way to Western Europe's post-Roman Dark Ages. In that earlier crisis, he said, people stopped identifying with the Roman imperium:

> *What they set themselves to achieve instead – often not recognizing fully what they were doing – was the construction of new forms of community within which the moral life could be sustained so that both morality and civility might survive the coming ages of barbarism and darkness. ... For some time now we too have reached that turning point. What matters at this stage is the construction of local forms of community within which civility and the intellectual and moral life can be sustained through the new dark ages that are already upon us.*[19]

I'd add that those local forms of community, to be sustained, must be built materially on the skilled practical work of local producers, farmers, builders and craftspeople – people who can deliver a plan B when the grocery shelves lie empty, there's a queue around the block for fuel and the internet falls silent.

But MacIntyre was right to emphasize the importance of constructing new moral and communal frameworks within which those skills can be exercised. And he gives us a richer and more critical sense of tradition to work with, viewing a living tradition not as mere obedience to a dead weight from the past but, in his words, as a 'historically extended, socially embodied argument, and an argument precisely in part about the goods that constitute that tradition'.[20]

All this suggests there's a lot of work to do if we wish our emerging dark age to be as merry as the ones enjoyed by some of our forebears. We need to abandon the dead tradition of the sovereign liberal nation-state, build livelier new local civic cultures in productive argument with themselves about their goals, and learn how to create local livelihoods for ourselves.

Like the women and men of the early post-Roman Dark Ages MacIntyre described, I believe the time is ripe to turn away from our Frankenstein liberal-modernism. We need to 'hospice modernity', and build as best we can the new forms of community that we need, even if inevitably we won't be able to recognize fully what we're doing, we'll only have partial control of the narrative, and we're likely to be frustrated at every turn by the distracting, centre-stage drama of modernity's last hurrah.[21] Hence in this book, I try to take both a short-term perspective on the future – what can we do right now on the basis of what's to hand? – and a longer-term one geared to the dynamics of more glacial institutional change.

What's to hand includes some recurrent patterns in human culture, good answers to learn from with local variants in many times and places. With its scorn for history and traditions, liberal-modernism has done its best to bury many of these answers – with considerable, but happily not total, success. A big part of this book involves trying to uncover some of those good answers that it buried, putting them into a cultural framework to illuminate present questions and help find some light for this dark age.

CHAPTER 2

Building New Structures

I'm standing in a rainforest, haloed by a shaft of low autumn sunlight piercing the shade of the trees above me. The trunk I'm leaning on has a thick coat of moss girding its base. Higher up, its skin is mottled with lichens. The ground encircling it has no such adornments. It's scuffed and torn, unzipped to naked brown earth. Nearby, I hear the undergrowth rustling, and then a series of unearthly squeals. A pig – wild-looking, hairy and ginger – bursts from a hogweed thicket and comes sprinting toward me, closely followed by a second. Here's the cause of the earthworks around the tree. Ears pricked like hunting dogs and saliva flying from toothy mouths, they'd be a frightening sight if I didn't already know these rascals. I've come to give my Tamworths a tubful of crab apples.

Twenty years earlier, I'd stood with my wife on pretty much the same spot. The dry summer grasses scratching at our knees were the tallest vegetation around us. We'd spent six months in a frustrating search for a little farmland and had come here on a tip-off from a friendly auctioneer after another failed bid. We hadn't been there long, but my wife was already wielding her Nokia purposefully in that familiar way: let's do this. Yes, we'd like to buy it.

This rainforest, then, was the work of our own hands, and those of the people who helped us plant it. To call such a small and intensely humanized ecosystem a rainforest might sound exaggerated, but a movement has arisen in the British Isles in recent years laying claim to the country's status as a rainforest nation. Its working definition of a rainforest is a woodland where the trees support epiphytes like mosses and lichens. That's good enough for me – we planted a rainforest!

My delight at being a rainforest-maker took a bit of a knock when I noticed that mosses and lichens were also growing on my tractor. Either it's so rainforesty here that epiphytic life can even grow on rusty steel, or else the working definition is a tad overgenerous.

Actually, I have misgivings about representing wet British woodlands as rainforests.[1] There's something to be said for it in making our landscapes as precious and worthy of protection as the tropical jungles in other countries that we've grown up learning must be saved. But there's a danger that in doing so we assign them to the 'wilderness' slot – places we regard as unpeopled, ungrazed, wild and needing to remain so.

Many tropical jungles and other supposed wildernesses have been endlessly manipulated and managed by conscious and skilled human intervention, while Europe's own woodlands and other habitats were long manipulated too, without such destructive ecological consequences as we've seen in modern times. Much global modern nature damage has arisen not because people were there in the landscape but because they weren't – because they relied instead on proxies like agrochemicals, futures markets, mineral mines, colonial adventurers, loggers, trappers, traders and other middlemen to mediate their relationship with the wild and to draw down on the natural bounty of other places that shouldn't have been theirs to command.

With minimal disturbance and no external nutrients added, the biological life of a given place tends toward what ecologists used to call a 'climax' state – which in parts of the British Isles can be wet, biodiverse, temperate rainforest full of mosses, lichens and other organisms specifically adapted to tapping whatever scarce resources come their way. But it's quite common, quite natural, for places not to reach this climax. Things like herbivore grazing, fire or floods disturb and nutrify the landscape, setting it on a different course. 'Mosaic' is a ubiquitous contemporary term used to describe the world arising from these agents of disruption.

Humans are arch agents of disruption. At our best, we can help build complexity in the habitat mosaic. Britain's apparently wild rainforests are a historic part of this, having often been grazed and harvested for timber over centuries. But it's fair to say that frequently humans are not at our best. Both here in Britain and globally we've too often let things get quite out of hand.

On our farm, my wife and I have experimented – very imperfectly – with restoring some balance to our own local mosaic. Along the continuum of disturbance and nutrification we've created rainforest (arguably), pasture, small fruit and nut orchards, and cropland in the form of a market garden growing vegetables for local sale, along with allotments where local people grow their own produce. The buildings encompass dwellings, composting toilets, a forest school and a campsite. The pigs bearing down on me in the rainforest contribute to this web of organic interaction as waste-recyclers, muck-spreaders, habitat-disturbers, tillers of the soil, providers of food and fat for cooking and preserving, and potentially of skins and fibres for numerous other uses. There are almost endless ways to increase these cycles of beneficial interaction and mitigate their negatives. It's a journey we've barely begun.

Yet to a certain modern mindset, all this seems inefficient and somehow retrograde in comparison to specialist providers. We can get, more cheaply and more easily, timber from the Baltic, fruit from California, nuts from Turkey, vegetables from Spain, pork from Danish feedlots and fertility in a sack derived ultimately from the fossil-fuel industry, the latter perhaps a harbinger of the ultimate industrialization and virtualization of all our material needs in synthetic chemistry and biology. Every country has its own version of this Viking marketplace.

'In wilderness is the preservation of the world.' This phrase is often attributed to pioneering nature-philosopher Henry David Thoreau (1817–1862). What he actually wrote was, 'In wildness is the preservation of the world.'[2] The difference is important. In a sense, it goes to the heart of this book. Wilderness is something separate from people, something pristine and 'out there', whereas the wildness that Thoreau had in mind was an internal property of humans and their societies in relation to the wider world that he wanted to amplify. That's why I'm happy to talk about my rainforest and the wild pigs that live there, even at the risk of overstatement. I'm only a wild man with training wheels, but any step off the tame path of efficiency and progress counts for something. The main point of being a pig-keeper isn't to produce more pork, and the main point of being a person isn't to get maximum cheapness and convenience.

The wildness that might be the preservation of the world today as we hurtle toward our Ragnarök will be the wildness of learning to live and thrive mostly within the local ecology and its limits, as wild organisms do – and as historic agrarian societies have done. The wildness of amplifying organic cycles like pigs, trees, earth and people in reconstructed rainforests. The wildness of growing a vegetable garden that can feed your household year-round. The wildness of figuring out how to interact with other people in these emergent spaces.

❦

THIS WILL INVOLVE rebuilding local mosaics and making ourselves local ecological protagonists as farmers, craftspeople and weavers of human and ecological connection. It's going to mean doing that alone, in families and households, and in neighbourhoods and communities. It's going to mean seeing the consequences of our actions locally and adjusting them accordingly. One thing I've learned about keeping pigs in the rainforest is that the forest will only put up with so many of them. But woodlands, pigs and people operate on different cycles, and it's not always easy to bring them into alignment. This is the kind of wildness we need to learn. This is what we need to rewild.

There's a problem, though. In fact, a set of problems. One problem is that most people can't afford to get access to productive and sustaining local land in the way that my wife and I did. We were generationally lucky beneficiaries of the overproduction of money mentioned in the last chapter that enabled us to parlay a few square feet of London real estate into a few acres of Somerset farmland – even if I like to think we had a certain clarity of vision that enabled us to see how the economy also overproduced university teachers, my previous job, and underproduced food growers. That's likely to change one way or another, and I was ready to jump before I had to.

Another problem is that even those people who do have access to productive land are rarely able to make a decent living from farming it in sensible and renewable ways – or often in any way at all, come to that. A third problem is that most people can't afford to buy sensibly farmed food, and nor can they get a sensibly priced roof over their heads. A fourth is that the material base and craft skills necessary to undergird thriving local sustenance are gone. Until those problems – which are really all the same problem – are overcome, Thoreau's preservation of the world looks unlikely.

I don't particularly offer the case of our farm and community that I describe in this book as an exemplar of how to do this for others to follow.

(Incidentally, I'm never sure what to call our place – none of 'farm', 'market garden', 'homestead', 'smallholding' or 'landholding' quite do it. A municipal officer once told me that I wasn't a 'proper farmer' – since then, my ornery nature has inclined me to call our place a farm, and myself a farmer. This at least helps break down the distinction most of us hold in our minds about what a 'proper' farm or farmer is). So – on our farm, there's been a lot of running to stand still and a degree of burnout that we're perennially trying to address, without complete success. Part of this has arisen from avoidable mistakes, but probably the larger part from the inevitable tension of running a small operation that just doesn't fit with contemporary bureaucratic and economic assumptions. I suspect proper farms in the future may look more like our farm than the proper farms of today, and in this latter respect, at least, they may have an easier time of it.

Still, I think I've learned a few useful lessons from the experience of my farm that I'll share in this book. There remains so much more to learn, but I believe small attempts like ours to bring wildland, woodland, grassland, cropland, craft and human settlement into productive local relationship are on the right course. We need more people embarking on it, experimenting and trying to create beneficial connections at different local scales.

For the reasons I laid out in previous chapters, I think more people *will* be embarking on it in the future, by default if not by design. That could play out in better or worse ways. In this chapter, and in the rest of the book, I try to lay some foundations for the better ones.

I write from the position of being a landholder and having access to productive land, which is unquestionably a position of privilege available to few in contemporary society. However, the problems of creating a just society able to generate renewable livelihoods aren't over if and when present restrictions on widespread access to land are overcome. That, rather, is the moment they get real.

States of Refuge

About ten years ago, my wife set up a small campsite on our farm, despite much grumbling from me. The prospect of meeting and greeting interesting new people and creating a pleasant outdoor experience for them was very much her cup of tea, whereas the comings and goings of endless strangers challenged my well-honed antisocial tendencies. Besides, at that time I still felt more committed to making a go of commercial horticulture, and I wasn't convinced that many people would want to visit our nondescript bit of countryside anyway.

It turned out I was wrong on the latter front. For a few years the campsite did good business, enabling us to earn something approaching the living wage between us, which could hardly be said of the market garden.

The economics of food production isn't my theme here, although it's not entirely irrelevant. If you grow food for sale, you enter a race to the bottom in which you're competing with whoever in the world can assemble the cheapest inputs of land, labour, energy and agrochemicals.[3] Whereas if you run a campsite, you compete only with other campsite proprietors in your region, who are unlikely to be able to innovate significantly lower input costs than you.

However, as more farmers cottoned on to this in our area and opened their own campsites, we found it harder to maintain the cash income. Which is kind of how the economy is supposed to work – endless reinvention to deliver consumer value for money and drive progress. That's one way to look at it, anyway. It's a more plausible economic model for tech-heavy industrial sectors with high-energy inputs driving economies of scale than in labour-heavy service sectors. The logical endpoint is that someday there'll be a single factory somewhere producing everything, while everyone else's home will be an Airbnb. In the meantime, this economic model creates many casualties.

One thing I naively hadn't anticipated about running a campsite is that a small but non-negligible proportion of customers are essentially homeless people, looking for a place of refuge for a while. On several occasions, my wife negotiated low-cost, long-term stays with people who had nowhere else to go.

One of these people was a man doing a low-paid local job who'd recently separated from his partner. The housing department gave him low priority for rehousing, with his ex defined as the main carer for their children. In practice, the children spent several days each week with him, sharing his tent. As winter approached, my wife called the local housing services and pleaded with them to find accommodation for him, which in the end they were able to do.

BUILDING NEW STRUCTURES

It's not hard to imagine a future situation in which even that inadequate state housing backstop isn't there, for the long-term, structural 'dark age' or consolidation state reasons I discussed previously that can't be remedied simply by voting in a more benevolent government. What would happen then? What would happen, to press beyond the immediate issue, if it was no longer possible to secure adequate supplies of food or water locally, and there was no longer adequate state capacity to provide it?

Possibly there would be some radical retrenchment of the centralized state to deal with the crisis – a communist revolution, perhaps, or the emergence of an authoritarian populist regime – in which the state assumes the burden of rationing out the limited available resources carefully to everyone.

Or possibly the state would remain an empty shell, and local political powerbrokers would come to the fore. In our campsite situation, my wife and I might become such powerbrokers, albeit at the small-time end of the spectrum. We might hold the power to gift or refuse the benefit of housing and other needed resources to others. This patron–client situation (some would apply the more slippery word, 'feudal') has been common enough historically and still today, especially in situations where the writ of the state runs weakly.

Or it may be that people create more balanced local alliances cutting across these existing disparities, possibly organized against perceived greater threats from outside.

I don't, of course, know how the answers will play out in our region or in other ones in the future. But I think it's worth asking the questions – where would you go, what would you do, who would you trust, where might such outcomes occur in the arc of future Earth we examined in the previous chapter?

Unfortunately, it still seems to be a bit disreputable to be asking such questions. But more people are beginning to do so. The writer and activist Naomi Klein offers an upbeat take:

The known world is crumbling. That's okay. It was an edifice stitched together with denial and disavowal... It needed to crash. Now, in the rubble, we can make something more reliable, more worthy of our trust, more able to survive the coming shocks.[4]

Political scientist Michael Albert offers a wider range of outcomes in his important book *Navigating the Polycrisis*, bringing some academic rigour and authority to the iffy business of using social science to project future scenarios. Albert's best-case scenarios sit with Klein's in the sunshine, while his worst-case ones are – well, let's not go there. Toward the bad end of the spectrum, he offers a suite of possibilities that he terms 'neofeudalism', described thus:

Some nation-states may retain effective governance capacities, but most would eventually fragment and give way to a complex neofeudal geography composed of political-economic and security assemblages cooperating and competing over territory and resources – including corporate quasi-states, city-states, feudalized rentier capitalists and warlords that offer livelihood protection in exchange for tribute, and numerous communities of surplus populations left to develop their own survival strategies.[5]

In other words, familiar nation-state politics may persist, at least for a while. But if and when it declines, the increasingly empty shell of the old nation-state may get filled with various more or less troubling non-state or would-be state actors trying to stake their claim to its powers. Or the shell may stay empty in places, leaving the surplus populations Albert mentions to figure out bottom up what to do.

Suns, Supernovas and Solar Systems

Albert's various neofeudal scenarios seem to me the most likely options spanning the possible range of dark-age futures. Let's briefly probe the nature of these politics with the help of some celestial metaphors.

It's possible existing nation-states will continue, exerting their smoothly graded sovereignty over their entire territorial space, much as at present in most countries. A rough comparison might be with a sun, a defined body completely suffused with its brightly burning energetic or – in the state's case – political and economic processes.

But retaining that sun-like shape as those political and economic processes run out of juice seems a tall order. The model of the modern nation-state is based on economic growth and increased prosperity, the ability to draw down on more material and human energies and resources.

Nevertheless, there are some informative examples from history to draw from. One is Edo-era Japan. The Edo, or Tokugawa, period began after a time of warfare and instability when Tokugawa Ieyasu (1543–1616) unified the country and became shogun in 1603. Ieyasu sidelined the emperor into a purely ritual role, turned the daimyo warrior aristocrats into state vassals, repressed Christianity, expelled most foreigners in a policy of national isolationism and fixed other social statuses into controlled categories of peasant, craftsman and merchant.[6]

In the face of considerable environmental degradation and pressure on resources, the emphasis in Edo peasant society was on tight, design-intensive resource cycling – a kind of permaculture *avant la lettre*, as described in Azby Brown's interesting book *Just Enough*.[7] Construction practices, farming practices, woodland practices and practices of daily household living were all carefully designed so as to make the most of limited inputs, sustainably managed. It was a heavily taxed society, which, despite state autocracy, involved considerable subsidiarity and relative prosperity, as well as a sophisticated urban-commercial sector built on the back of peasant production.

The Edo period famously ended after Commodore Matthew Perry of the US Navy sailed into Edo Bay in 1853 and forced Japan to open itself to wider trade. Maybe it's worth playing that tape backward as a thought experiment in future history. Supposing the cargo ships and associated naval forces that underwrite global trade and that supply most countries with their world of goods stop coming. Probably the only way the nation-state then survives is through something like a judiciously ecological Edo-style autocracy.

It's possible to imagine more egalitarian versions of that, with a strong ideology of everybody pulling together for the benefit of society. That, in fact, is a model I'll be proposing later in the book. But however we try to slice and dice it, none of these futures look like a bed of roses. At best, they'd probably look like the 'just enough' world of autocratic Edo Japan.

The same goes for more directly communist versions of this vision. The first Soviet leader, Vladimir Lenin, famously defined communism as 'Soviet power plus the electrification of the whole country'. Indeed, the major communist revolutions of the twentieth century – Russia, China, Vietnam – were basically examples of top-down modernization and resource expansion from above built on a base of peasant communalism, whose persisting legacy today is more the modernization and resource expansion than the communism. In future de-modernizing situations of energetic and resource decline, Lenin's definition of communism would become simpler and less appealing: 'Soviet power'. Another version of Edo Japan, at best.

As the nation-states of the global system start running out of political, economic and indeed actual energy, another possibility – my second model – is that the slow collapse of the major state powers prompts them to flare out in a final burst of self-preserving energy. This model (with apologies for the inexactness to any astrophysicists reading) is that of a supernova. Here we get close to some of Albert's worst-case scenarios – world war, totalitarianism, techno-dystopias that burn everything in their path. Once this explosion is primed, it's hard for anyone to stop it or escape it. But at least human systems aren't really like star systems, so there will always be options, and hope. Trying to build local autonomies as well as possible is one of them.

※※※

I'LL BROACH THE THIRD, solar system, model in a more roundabout way with reference to the writing of political scientist James Scott.

Scott authored influential books on the historical emergence and spread of centralized states, arguing essentially that they arose in agricultural areas with a ready surplus of grains (wheat, barley, millet, rice or maize), and with easy terrain facilitating political connection. In Scott's view, the rulers of premodern states – in fact, pretty much of all states – were entrepreneurs of political domination, using a series of carrots and sticks to keep their citizenries in their place. Mostly sticks.[8]

Scott tells the story of 'Zomia', a vast upland region of Asia spanning parts of Cambodia, Vietnam, Laos, Southwest China, Myanmar, Bangladesh and northeast India. Historically, the challenging territory and communications of this area made control from the ruling cities of adjoining lowland states difficult to orchestrate, and prone to collapse. It was therefore attractive to people who preferred not to live under the jurisdiction of such states. Instead of the grand-scale grain agricultures of the plains sustaining the great states, livelihoods in this area were typified more by small-scale mixed farming, horticulture and foraging geared to household and community, along with raiding and volatile local political alliances built on the back of this.

Nowadays, almost the whole world has become a grain state, or at least a series of interconnected ones of coordinated form. In 2023, about 200 million tonnes each of wheat and maize, and 100 million tonnes of rice were traded internationally.[9] At the same time, high-energy modern communications – physical ones like roads, railways and air routes as well as electronic ones – have opened up disorderly terrain like Zomia to state power. One direction the future might take is in the re-emergence or re-disordering of areas like Zomia as buffers against the liberal-modernist state, and as attractive destinations for people fleeing its growing dysfunctions.

My projected arc of future Earth in the introduction hinted at that possibility. Yet it may not be feasible for a great number of people to make a physical escape from the sun-state in that way. A more important question might be what options they'll have within the existing jurisdiction of the state as its dysfunctions begin to multiply.

One possibility is that the legitimacy of the state even in its core areas will weaken as it increasingly fails to provide people with its side of the bargain – health and social services, food in the shops and so forth. Hence, people start figuring out their own local systems as best they can, based on direct livelihood work and mutual aid. This builds autonomies from the state.

There are already temporary occurrences along these lines often enough in emergency situations, such as during the food and financial crises in Cuba and Greece – or occasionally in more enduring situations of ethno-national conflict directed against state power, like the breakaway autonomous administration of Rojava in northern Syria. If such occurrences become more frequent, more enduring and more structural, it's possible that the reach and power of nation-states will become weaker by turn.

Adam Greenfield discusses many such examples in his book *Lifehouse*, making a good case for building out from these bigger and smaller local autonomies to create a wider network of refugia ('lifehouses') from liberal-modernist states in their sun or supernova modes.[10] There's much to be learned from these cases, but they're mostly short-run interventions in contemporary politics arising from local disturbances in the unsustainable longer-term global flow of money, food and materials orchestrated by the existing system of states. Ultimately, they're still part of that flow. My focus instead is on a longer drumbeat as that flow dwindles, bringing a wider range of historical examples into consideration.

※※※

IT'S USEFUL TO CONSIDER different models of state power to the contemporary system of nation-states. Of relevance are traditional (premodern) East and South Asian (Hindu and Buddhist) models of the polity as a mandala or, in fact, as a set of overlapping mandalas – sacred centres whose power diminishes with distance from them, surrounded by lesser satellites. This is what I'm aiming at with my solar system metaphor (a well-known scholarly treatment of the issue uses the term 'galactic polity') – a situation of stars, greater and smaller planets and moons exerting gravitational pulls of varying power on one another but retaining autonomy.[11]

The galactic polity model had its origins in medieval India, but spread widely across Southeast Asia – for example, in various Indic kingdoms across what are now Thailand, Malaysia, Indonesia, Myanmar and Cambodia, such as the Khmer courts of present-day Cambodia from the ninth to fifteenth centuries and the Majapahit empire centred in Java from the thirteenth to sixteenth centuries. In some situations, the model may represent political weakness – the inability of the state to enforce rule or serve its population far from its centre. A state that can't underwrite the wellbeing of its citizens stops being able to claim their full allegiance.

But the galactic polity also represented a particular cultural way of constituting power, and it's interesting in this respect that the mandala models of the Indic kingdoms arose not through invasion from India, but in imitation of it.[12] Here, we're easily misled by modern Western ways of thinking about politics, which tend to be quite reductive and instrumental in emphasizing military violence and economic accumulation as the root of state power.

An example comes from one of the early theorists of this way of thinking, Thomas Hobbes (1588–1679), who wrote 'Covenants, without the Sword, are but Words, and of no strength to secure a man at all'.[13] In this he was quite wrong. I won't revert to university lecturer mode and start discoursing lengthily on the nature of political authority, but the truth is that words, covenants, ideas and cosmologies have enormous strength to secure people. We retain this even in modern Western political thought with ideas like 'soft power' and sayings like 'the pen is mightier than the sword'. It's true that a big part of European colonialism in recent centuries was based on military violence and credit-fuelled economic expansion. But such factors haven't always been central to political power across the world in the past, and they may not be in the future.

A relevant metaphor might be the game of chess (invented, not coincidentally, in India) where the critical centrepiece of the game – the king – has limited power and is in constant danger, while the bigger power dramas of the other pieces roil around him. Global modernization has forced every country into playing the nation-state game and finding ways of building strong centralized governance based on economic power. De-modernization might bring other ways of construing politics into play.

From the point of view of an individual person, town or region within this mandala or solar system model, it may be possible to live happily among overlapping spheres of sovereignty of varying strengths and uncertain boundaries, but which have quite weak claims on their loyalty and day-to-day life. So, we come back to the issue of subsidiarity, with a Southeast Asian twist. Imagine a situation where places like my small-town home of Frome pay symbolic obeisance to larger centres like Bristol or London but otherwise are largely left to get on with organizing their own local political and economic space. (This, incidentally, is what I called the 'supersedure state' in an earlier book, drawing on an analogy with bee behaviour.[14] But in this book I use the solar system or galactic metaphor instead).

Considering my three celestial metaphors at our present point in global history, I'd argue that staying committed to the sun model of the present nation-state system as a way of avoiding troubled future times now looks pretty utopian – rather like the ending of Stephen Markley's *The Deluge*. The supernova model of the rogue, disaster-capitalist nation-state is an obviously dystopian possibility. Something like the solar system or galactic model offers more hope. Neither utopia nor dystopia, it may just offer a feasible route through – what some call a thrutopia. Whatever happens, I think people will increasingly try to build local livelihood autonomies as best they can, but – if we can bring it into being – the galactic model offers the most promise of success.

CHAPTER 3

Open Country

The previous chapter opened with scenes from my farm and some of the people on it seeking a place to live, before jumping into a discussion of political power and the forms that future states might take. This is logical enough in that centralized political power shapes options in our everyday lives. But in this chapter, I want to dial back to the question of seeking a place to live and consider how that in turn may shape future politics.

In her important book *The Long Land War*, historian Jo Guldi describes what she calls the 'global struggle for occupancy rights' – that is, the right for ordinary people to claim a place to live and to produce food and fibre for their households (by fibre I mean animal or plant matter for fabrics, building materials or fuels). Ultimately, this was a populist war against the efforts of modern states to co-opt and displace people from productive land for wider state purposes.

'Occupancy' is a useful term for what these people in the past were fighting for, and it also captures what people will be fighting for in the future. Standard neo-Malthusian narratives tell us that people have always been desperate to get off the land as soon as possible and find a waged, preferably urban, job. It's not that there's never any truth to that in specific contexts but elevating it to a general truth erases an awful lot of real, hard-fought history. As Steven Stoll puts it in his fascinating historical account of Appalachia in the eastern United States, 'Any Scots-Irish, Cherokee, or African-American with a cabin and garden knew that dispossession served someone else's purpose. It was an instrument of control, not a sign of progress.'[1] Studies from many parts of the world confirm the tenacity with which ordinary people fight to retain or reclaim small landholdings to meet their daily needs.²

Guldi's own focus is mostly on rural people in Ireland and India as those countries emerged from the shadow of British colonialism into independent modern nation-states with large populations of small farmers. She then traces the convoluted story of postwar conflicts in international politics over land distribution as a vehicle for economic development, before bringing the land war up to date around twenty-first-century questions of climate change:

> *Distributed landownership has much to recommend it in an era of climate change, both as a way of settling refugees where they can become productive, and as a means to combat carbon emissions through small-scale farming, rather than the more environmentally destructive realities of industrial farming.*³

I think this is exactly right, and I'll draw out some implications in later chapters. Along similar lines to the struggle for occupancy rights Guldi describes, political scientist Michael Albertus discusses what he calls the 'Great Reshuffle' of global land entitlements in recent history, by which modernizing states made more land available to their populations than had been the case in premodern times, often as a result of grassroots pressure. This has certainly brought benefits, at least to some, but has also been part of the wider liberal-modernist package held tightly in the hands of the state that's brought us to the present moment of crisis.⁴

As the quotation from Guldi above suggests, we might well now be poised on the verge of another Great Reshuffle. Yet prevailing neo-Malthusian perspectives make an argument like Guldi's surprising to some in its implication that small-scale farming can 'feed the world'. So, it's probably worth pausing here to justify three points that underlie it.

First, there's a considerable weight of evidence that shows small-scale, low-input farming can be just as (if not more) productive per acre than larger-scale, higher-energy, more mechanized agriculture.⁵ Not per farmworker, but per acre – the latter being a more important measure in the present and future state of the world. So on the face of it, there's no particular problem with the idea that small-scale, low-input farming can feed global populations. Emerging realities like climate change will challenge farming of all types, but there's no reason to suppose large-scale, high-energy, mechanized farming will meet the challenge better. If anything, the opposite, among other reasons because the emphasis in cabin-and-garden farming is to keep the household fed, whereas feeding people is a side effect of profit maximization in the latter case.

Second, Guldi's arguments confront a widespread modern perception that small-scale local farming people live a hand-to-mouth existence forever at risk of hunger. The truth is that the greatest hunger in world history has been a modern phenomenon – in fact, a *modernizing* phenomenon in the hands of leaders like Stalin, Churchill, Mao and Hitler, and earlier in what Mike Davis called 'late Victorian holocausts'.[6] Incorporation into world markets via new technologies like railways has meant that food goes more easily to where it's most demanded, not where it's most needed. As Davis puts it:

> *How do we weigh smug claims about the life-saving benefits of steam transportation and modern grain markets when so many millions, especially in British India, died alongside railroad tracks or on the steps of grain depots? ... Millions died, not outside the "modern world system," but in the very process of being forcibly incorporated into its economic and political structures.*[7]

It's possible that millions will die in the future because of either forcible or de facto disincorporation from the modern world system. But it's important to understand that the problem lies mainly with the processes of incorporation or disincorporation, not with living outside the system as such, which people actively seek often enough.

Indeed, research suggests that equitable local access to productive land is a good predictor of food security.[8] This is why the decline of global breadbasket regions that I hinted at in our flight over the future US in the introduction may be a less fearful result than it seems – maybe even something to be celebrated. Inasmuch as these breadbasket regions and the associated industrial global food system has displaced more local cabin-and-garden forms of food self-provisioning, this can be framed in subsidiarity terms: 'The burden of proof lies always on those who want to deprive a lower level of its function, and thereby of its freedom and responsibility.'[9]

Third, distributed landownership and widespread small-scale farming ultimately implies more ruralism and less urbanism than today. This is part of a larger truth that present levels of urbanism rest on the availability of cheap and abundant fossil fuels to fund the import of food, water and other materials into cities and the export of wastes out of them that won't be sustainable in the long run. (It's muddied by the argument that urban life in high-energy modern societies is more resource efficient per capita than rural life in high-energy modern societies, which is true but beside the point – as is so often the case, it's important not to get the concepts of efficiency and cost mixed up.)

The idea of future ruralization seems to especially challenge mainstream, neo-Malthusian 'world environmental problems' thinking – what David Gilbert calls the 'neocolonial and corporate' narrative that 'urbanizing populations are a marker of progress'.[10] I've often found myself at loggerheads with mainstream thinking on this point. For example, *Guardian* journalist George Monbiot mocks my position on ruralism thus:

> *When the fugitives disperse into the countryside, the inhabitants will doubtless greet them with open arms, saying, "Welcome sister! Welcome brother! Here, have some fertile land. Oh, and some water, knowledge, skills, tools, traction and all the other means to grow your own food and live happy lives as re-peasants in our agrarian wonderland."*
>
> *If history is any guide, this is not quite how it's likely to pan out.*[11]

Much as I'd prefer not to amplify the 'inevitable friction caused by immigration' narrative that already gets plenty of airtime, he does have a point. Indeed, I made it myself in the book Monbiot is discussing in analyzing future rural class conflicts over resources.[12] How to manage population flows and changing future settlement patterns raises huge and intractable problems that are not best dealt with by supposing they won't happen.

But the more I've thought about that passage, the more it strikes me that it tells only one side of the story, and one side of history. Obviously, the truth is never as sentimental as Monbiot portrays it, but since – contra Malthus – people in low-input agrarian societies are in principle and often in practice capable of producing more sustainable benefit (food, fibre, care) than they use, and since there's a lot to be said for being part of a somewhat larger community than a smaller one, the fact is that, yes, newcomers often *are* welcomed into rural societies. And when they are, there's usually an attempt to make the relationship structural rather than just random – the idiom of kinship being an obvious option. Welcome sister. Welcome brother.

James Scott makes this point about the peopling of Zomia: 'It is abundantly clear that all hill groups have incorporated large numbers of "defectors" from civilization by working them into their genealogies' – defectors, often enough, because life as an autonomous mixed farmer and forager in the hills was easier than as a small farmer beholden to urbanized lowland grain states with their onerous tax and labour burdens.[13] This is underappreciated, Scott says, because it's the mainstream voices of state and political centres that get to command the narrative – and to those voices, the idea of actively choosing the backwoods over the bright lights is incomprehensible. Some things don't change.

Yet there's plenty of evidence that poor urban people seek better opportunities in the countryside when they can, and that – particularly for women – this can be advantageous for security, peace and freedom. There's also much evidence that people piece together livelihoods through seasonal labour migration between city and countryside, with city work often being seen as a necessary evil. It's not hard to imagine that future balance tipping toward the rural.[14]

Closer to home, one of the issues we've struggled with on our own farm is navigating both external structural obstacles of wider economy and bureaucracy and internal structural dynamics to create a well-peopled and well 'occupied' landholding that's as productive as it can be in sustainable ways. It's not because we're out of capacity for welcoming people or because there's a lack of people seeking the chance to provide for themselves and others. I discuss these issues later in the book. In view of the profound social changes to come and the likely tensions they'll create, I believe it's wise to embrace and try to amplify whatever possibilities for benevolence may exist in the changing settlement patterns to come.

BUT IT WOULD BE wrong to overemphasize ruralism. What matters above all is that people get occupancy rights that give them the long-term residential security to address their livelihood needs, and it's entirely possible that these will sometimes be obtained in urban or suburban situations.

Crops can be grown in gardens, up walls, on rooftops and in parks and other community spaces. Water can be collected and purified. Pigs and hens can be kept by households or neighbourhood groups in small lots and fed on wastes and byproducts to provide much needed fat and animal fibres. Even ruminants can be grazed rotationally around city lots, like the Street Goat project in Bristol, near to my home – or like the mixed agricultures that go on in a many a Global South city with less fastidious separations of the urban and the agrarian than is typical of wealthy countries.[15] David Holmgren's *Retrosuburbia* provides endless inspiration for making small, built spaces productive of the necessities for life. Ted Trainer's small-town 'simpler way' philosophy is another source of inspiration.[16] Part of my arc of future Earth projection in the introduction suggested such possibilities. To frame it in terms of modern aestheticized lifestyle terminology, solarpunk futures are possible.

Still, the present density of urban residence challenges the notion that urban people at existing population levels will be able to meet their needs feasibly from available resources long-term. Advocates of mass urbanism need to provide brass-tacks answers to how the periphery-to-centre pipeline I mentioned in chapter 1 will be sustained in situations of lower energy and lower political order. Where will the food, water and energy come from? Where will the wastes go? At whose expense? My argument is not an anti-urban one so much as a pro-reality one. As William Rees bluntly puts it, 'What the mainstream refuses to acknowledge is that the dance between energy supply and overshoot (or climate change) poses an unprecedented challenge to the very existence of contemporary urban society, particularly large cities and mega-cities.'[17]

So, greater ruralism beckons. Time for cottagecore to brush up its soft-focus image, toughen up and give solarpunk a run for its money?

It seems inevitable that the future will be more rural than the present, either from people voting with their feet and leaving challenging urban areas or, longer term, from greater population growth in favoured rural areas. Or both. Indeed, this could prove a relatively slow, cross-generational shift – in the US, for example, from increasingly unfavourable places like Los Angeles and the Southwest generally, to more favourable ones like New England and parts of the Midwest.

There will certainly be nodes of concentration and urbanism within those larger geographic shifts. But the balance of relative urbanism and ruralism will depend on a lot of factors around state power, energy, exchange and political economy that are currently uncertain. What people living across the urban-rural spectrum of settlement density consider they owe to one other or expect from one other, and what factors hold them to that settlement pattern, raise important questions, some of which I discuss in later chapters.

Still, more important than the exact patterning across the urban-rural spectrum is the fact that people will favour areas where they can best secure occupancy rights for viable local livelihoods – what I propose to call 'open country'. Open country may be urban or suburban, while many rural areas may *not* be open country – Monbiot is surely right that a warm rural welcome won't be universal. In some cases, newcomers might find ways of *making* rural areas more open (see pages 113–14). In the long run, it seems clear that the urban-rural balance will tip toward the latter from its present extreme and fossil-fuel enabled disequilibrium, but the way to that destination could be crooked.

This brings us back to my story in chapter 2 about our campsite. Will it be open country here, where I live? Will people arriving here from harder situations elsewhere, possibly with few other options, be able to secure occupancy easily or not? Or will we who now live here find ourselves seeking open country elsewhere? Where, generally, will the refugia in the future be, and why will they be in those specific locations?

It's impossible to know what the answers to these questions will be in detail, but it's useful to ponder them in general. This draws us into probing a little deeper into what makes for open and closed country.

Fictitious Commodities

Pick up an economics textbook, and it'll tell you there are three or maybe four 'factors of production' that are needed to make a product and bring it to market. These are land, labour, capital and maybe entrepreneurship. There's a fifth one the textbooks don't mention but presuppose. This is political order.

The economic historian Karl Polanyi called land, labour and money 'fictitious commodities' because, although in modern societies they can be bought and sold like market goods, they are not in fact market goods.[18] Land is limited and not produced by anybody, labour is a property of humans who are not produced for markets – even if they're sometimes treated as if they are – and money is a token of value, ultimately a promise, not a good that's produced.

These fictitious commodities fit into Polanyi's wider argument about how we've built this strange thing we call 'the economy' in modern society, disembedding it from the flow of human relationships as ends in themselves and turning it into a separate and quantifiable thing that obeys its own inhuman logic – hence, Nate Hagens's 'Mordor economy' and Paul Kingsnorth's 'machine'.[19]

This also helps us think about the dark-age realities that might succeed these modern fictions.

Land is, precisely, *land* – the ground around you that, along with air and water, can potentially furnish you with the animals, vegetables and minerals you need to survive.

A lot of present discussion about land and food production assumes that land is a limiting factor in view of humanity's large global agricultural footprint and the negative consequences arising from it. This may be true. It's certainly true in some places, and it will probably become truer as climate and water challenges grow. But a large part of that footprint and its impact has arisen in a profit-driven global agricultural economy with no concern for land-use efficiency or ecological care, reflected in the expansion of agricultural frontiers where land is cheap and relatively unpopulated. Reflected, too, in the overproduction of most agricultural goods – particularly arable grain crops which are wastefully used for biofuels, industrial feedstocks, livestock fodder and processed foods people don't need.[20]

Research consistently shows the enormous food productivity of human labour when applied to land.[21] So on the face of it – albeit with the large caveat of challenging future climate and water dynamics – land in itself may not be a limiting factor for future food production geared to human needs, rather than market wants. Open country beckons.

Labour is your own capacity to work to make your livelihood, not some abstract quantum like the value of labour that you pay for in the checkout price of the goods you buy. In the future, it's quite likely – much more likely than today – that a lot of this work will involve creating your livelihood directly from the land around you, though it's also possible it'll involve providing goods or services to other people doing so. Yet labour isn't just *your* capacity, because people aren't social isolates. You'll be working with others, sometimes at least – but who? I look at this in more detail in chapters 4 and 5.

In a situation where people's labour is mostly devoted to providing their own livelihood from the land, there's never a labour shortage as such because labour is devoted to itself, even if from the perspective of the labourer it might feel like they could do with extra help. Many hands make light work, as the saying goes – although we'll see later that this isn't necessarily always true, with interesting implications. Still, in these situations, labour rather than land can be the scarce limiting factor.

Putting the 'many hands' saying alongside widespread future declines in energy availability sometimes leads people to suppose the future will see the return of widespread enslavement. The persistence of slavery in the modern world certainly suggests that global civilization hasn't evolved to some nobler state where slavery becomes impossible. On the other hand, its absence across large swathes of premodern global history also suggests it's not a given in situations of low energy availability.

The remarks of David Graeber and David Wengrow I quoted in chapter 1 on page 19 are relevant.[22] Slavery is mostly a project of economically and territorially expanding states – in other words, a product of 'civilization' itself. Just as in the past, one impetus toward ruralization and the search for open country in the future could well be the avoidance of labour coercion, slavery at worst, associated with remaining state centres. That doesn't mean there won't be labour coercion in rural areas. But it's less likely to be widespread and systemic. One thing that rings true in Octavia Butler's novel of a dystopian future California, *The Parable of the Sower*, is the way it depicts slavery as an urban-industrial tactic of the decaying centralized state. Her protagonists give cities and factories a wide berth when they can, in a counternarrative to their more familiar place within tales of modernist freedom.

In the present liberal market economy, lack of appropriate labour is a perennial short-term local issue but not really a structural or systemic issue, because the impetus of the system is toward cutting inputs, especially labour. This is easier when cheap fossil energy is available. The result, over time, has been the kind of patterns we saw on our flight over the US, with far more people living across the 500 square miles of city blocks in Los Angeles than over the 70,000 square miles of field blocks in Kansas.

So, a lot of available human labour is currently located far from the land that's best suited for producing food and other material needs, with the existing high-energy, high-capital, high-political-order liberal market economy doing a lot of the work that connects food production with consumers – we could call it the Kansas to Los Angeles conveyor. This is an instance of what I called in chapter 1 the periphery-to-centre pipeline, which works within countries as well as between them. As I've already argued, that pipeline may start to malfunction – which may become a problem for places like Los Angeles.

※※※

LAND AND LABOUR are the two key factors of production, on which producing a livelihood ultimately depends. The other two – money and entrepreneurship – get inordinately more attention in modern economic discussion but are really just ways of putting the other two in motion, ways that can easily go wrong.

On that note, critics of the industrial food system have labelled some of its biotech developments 'Frankenfoods'. I share their misgivings, but – referencing my discussion of Mary Shelley's *Frankenstein* in the introduction – it's tempting to say that the bigger driver of dark-age futures will probably be the overreach in energy and economic complexity involved in animating the agro-industrial flow of food from places like Kansas to places like Los Angeles. A break in the flow along the pipeline. In that sense, the monster that kills you may prove not to be the food provided by the industrial system, but the food that it ultimately fails to provide. It doesn't have to be that way. We could develop more resilient local agroecological food systems. But generally, we don't.

So, money is ... complicated. In the future it might, like today, be a head on a banknote or a digital gate in a computer, symbolizing a promise of benefit that will be kept. But in that future the promise will be less likely to be kept. In which case, that kind of money will become just a piece of paper or electronic junk, symbolizing nothing, and there will be a need to create new ways of making promises. I consider this further in chapter 8.

Entrepreneurship will, like today, be about creatively bringing these factors of production together to create a livelihood. The circle of its operation is likely to be smaller than today – probably for many people not much more than furnishing food and fibre directly for their household. At best, this could involve being part of creating new kinds of society and pro-social arrangements, or finding fulfilment in the skilled work of household self-provisioning. At worst, it might involve being a failing entrepreneur of your own physical survival. That outcome, as I've just argued, is likely anyway if we continue along the present agro-industrial food route.

Both capital and entrepreneurship work as limiting factors in the present liberal market economy. They'll be limiting factors in the dark-age future too, but in opposite ways. In the present world, a globally tiny number of people and institutions can easily raise capital in dizzying quantities. This becomes self-limiting variously by creating debt, inflation, political pushback and the increasingly challenging need to find new frontiers for capital (one of the less Freudian reasons that very rich men are obsessed with big rockets). Meanwhile, and by the same token, most people worldwide can barely raise any capital at all. Generally, this means the vast capital that's available doesn't get spent on useful things, while efforts to turn poor people into micro-entrepreneurs within the existing system bear limited fruit, at best.[23]

In the dark-age situation, instead of this problem of too much capital that's concentrated in too few hands, there can be the opposite problem of too little capital that's too widely distributed. Sometimes *way* too little – major industries, buildings, towns, roads, even farm tools can be a stretch. It's good to aim for a happy medium – a place where promises like money are trustworthy enough that economic action in society doesn't collapse completely, and enough to generate economic exchange and permit some concentration of capital via appropriate levels of entrepreneurship.

In an ideal world, it might be good if the pendulum of capital could swing back from its present overabundant limit without going full dark age. But it's an unfortunate property of pendulums not to stop in the middle of their arc – socioeconomic pendulums as well as physical ones. At least the dark-age part of the swing can create new entrepreneurial opportunities to build capital and social linkages. The challenge is to make them prosocial opportunities that build general wellbeing, and not Viking opportunities.

Political order is at the crux of the issue. It takes a lot of it to be able to turn a sack of seed wheat in Kansas into a pastry in Los Angeles or Amsterdam, let alone to achieve many of the more complex things that residents of those cities require or expect. The story of the liberal-modernist state is the extension of its particular forms of political order worldwide. The story of its dark age to follow is the dismantling and scrambling of that order, its growing inability to smoothly structure political space and keep delivering the endless stream of commodities – and also the peace – that contemporary consumer societies have come to rely on and expect.

Lifehouses

One part of the question as to where open country can be found is biophysical. Is there water to sustain life? Are there food-generating possibilities? Materials for clothes and shelter? Energy to realize these potentials?

Another part is political. Who claims authority over this place? What demands do they place on ordinary people that help or hinder their livelihood-making? Who else, in other places, does their authority affect?

For many people today, the answers to the first set of questions would be things like, 'Yes, from the tap, or the shop, or the wall socket, or from my money income.' The challenge of the new dark age is that those answers may stop being true, and people will have to start finding some different answers for themselves. Who claims authority over the place where they live may change too. And all of it will probably be more uncertain, volatile and hard to second-guess.

Much depends on the biogeography and human relations of a given area. But it seems likely that there will be sun-polities in some places where the state retains considerable organizing power, particularly in major metropolitan areas. Political power, energy availabilities and other means of technological control might be dwindling but could still be used forcefully to secure basic livelihoods for core urban populations.

In certain rural areas – western Kansas, for example – it's possible that a combination of climate, water and global-supply-chain issues will return much of it to something resembling its premodern state. A world of prairies frequented only seasonally by hunters or pastoralists in small numbers, with limited and probably quite dangerous opportunities for newcomers.

Or it may be that farming remains viable, but with a greater emphasis on low-input, labour-rich production for local needs – possibly the way things might go in eastern Kansas and the north-central US.[24] In that situation, the urban push and rural pull could re-attract people with roots in the area and an understanding of its ways when the promise of urban prosperity loses its lustre. This may not amount to many people in the case of Kansas, but city populations in the Global South are often full of temporary or seasonal migrants well connected to their rural roots who wouldn't need much of a push to return.

As I mentioned earlier, despite narratives of land scarcity and overpopulation, land abandonment and rural underpopulation are also a reality.[25] The idea of new agricultural frontiers opening up that are welcoming to incoming would-be farmers may sound a wildly optimistic take on the future. I'm certainly not suggesting it will be the norm. But it's happened often enough in the past, and it's worth considering among the suite of future possibilities. Frontiers open to a wider range of possible kinds of society.

But it's as well to consider old structures as well as new frontiers. Earlier, I mentioned Adam Greenfield's interesting 'lifehouse' idea (see Suns, Supernovas and Solar Systems, page 38). While some of the lifehouses he discusses emerged in short-term, emergency situations and may not be so relevant to a longer-term 'dark-age' future, nevertheless the pro-social politics of occupancy in that future will surely be well-advised to draw on existing associational patterns and groupings.

Greenfield's examples are drawn mostly from left-wing liberatory movements with a somewhat urban twist, such as the Black Panthers and Occupy – and more broadly from grassroots traditions of mutual aid and co-operativism at the more libertarian end of left-wing and anarchist thought, such as the libertarian municipalism of the influential Murray Bookchin. There are parallels in food and ecology movements: food sovereignty, La Via Campesina, Transition Towns, bioregion and watershed inspired movements, and the grassroots politics associated with climate protest movements like Extinction Rebellion.

These are part of a longer radical tradition. For example, here in England, Thomas Spence's 1793 pamphlet 'The Rights of Man' laid out a vision of landownership exclusively vested at the parish level, with land rented to residents who were represented in parish affairs through universal suffrage.[26] Spence's radical plan tiptoed gently around the question of centralized state power, although his views still landed him in jail.

Such land radicalism has parallels in more conservative thinking – for example in groups like the American Solidarity Party and the 'small-town' civic associationism represented by Front Porch Republic, Slow Cities and Strong Towns. And in religious organizations, from the social activism of individual churches or other communities of worship, to more structured ideas or movements like the distributism I draw on in this book and associated groups, such as the Catholic Worker Movement established by Dorothy Day and Peter Maurin in the US, or ideas emerging from Orthodox Christian forest churches.

There are also 'back-to-the-land' movements of various political colours and agendas. In Britain, they remain quite marginal politically and lean countercultural or left-anarchist, but elsewhere in the world they can be Marxist (Latin America, South Asia), right-libertarian (the 'crunchy conservatives' of the US) or nationalist (Eastern Europe).[27] And this is just a small top-of-the-head selection of groups I know about. Their political differences can be sharp, but it sometimes strikes me that the learned political languages of these groups conceal more common ground than you might think, especially in terms of their practical commitments. Perhaps there's scope for the kind of left-wing/right-wing political realignments anticipated by Stephen Quilley (see From Liberalism to Distributism, page 21)?

In many ways such initiatives are limited and frustrated by the container of the centralized 'sun-state', arising in its gaps and incoherences – wherein danger lies. Here in Britain, and more widely in Europe, the environmental scapegoating and economic disciplining of mainstream commercial farmers by state and public is propelling some of them into the arms of anti-environmentalist and right-wing populist mobilization. On the left, improbable dreams of renewable energy transition, 'farm-free' manufactured food and extensive rewilding reflect at best a smugly superior and improbably dematerialized urbanism. Ultimately, there is no better lifehouse than a farm. Both these moves exacerbate rural–urban tensions and ill prepare us for the 'Great Reshuffle' to come.[28]

CHAPTER 4

Home Economics: Producing

If my analysis in previous chapters is even halfway correct, the future will see a lot of people occupying, moving to and otherwise making account of open country (and open towns) in the world to come, largely by making local land-based livelihoods from it. This chapter and the next one look at the face-to-face social relationships involved in that process.

What seems certain is that these relationships won't suddenly be forged afresh out of nothing in the new circumstances. They'll emerge instead out of existing ones, which are already heavily structured and which I'll discuss under four loose terms: households and commons (this chapter), and family and community (chapter 5). Every historical society I know of is woven in some way out of these elements and it seems inconceivable that future ones will be any different.

Partly, I'll be drawing on my own experiences — how the bare land that my wife and I bought twenty years ago gradually acquired a household, a family, then more households of people working the land or passing through in one way or another, and how it fitted into wider frameworks of commons and communities.

This 'acquiring' was a matter of luck, active choices we made, a lot of work and more than a few mistakes. I won't be telling that story in detail, but I'm struck by the way our modern narratives of localism, land-work and community — both in favour and against — are often quite generalized, stereotyped and bereft of lived complexity. So, I hope some personal story-telling will be informative. At the same time, there's a lot to be learned from the global history of the multitudes who have gone before us living these kinds of lives, and this often doesn't get the airing it should. I'll draw on that history, too, and do some generalizing of my own.

So, households, commons, families, communities. There are grounds for thinking that none of these building blocks are in great shape in our modern urban-industrial societies for stepping up to the role of creating local ecological societies of the future. I acknowledge that view, but here I'm going to press a different one – given a chance, people are pretty good at creating effective social relations bottom up to meet present needs, inevitably using the four building blocks I've mentioned. A focus on this, on creating those chances, is critical to a congenial future dark age.

That future will involve a lot more of us spending a lot more of our time in local work geared to provisioning our homes. In the present world, 'home' is the place where we sleep, eat, relax and often socialize, but it's accorded little status as the place where important things happen – history, politics, economic development. The latter is especially ironic given the etymology of 'economics' from the original Greek word for 'household management', *oikonomia* – from *oikos*, meaning 'house', and *nemein*, which has connotations of 'managing' and 'distributing'. Consider the relative status of home economics vis-à-vis economics as academic disciplines – the former barely still in existence, the latter with its own version of the Nobel Prize. Still, home economics will have its day again. In the future, there'll be a lot less economics and a lot more *oikonomia*.

There's obviously a gender dimension here. Part of the modern devaluation of the household and of home economics arises from their association with women and women's work within patriarchal status values. The concept of labour in economics is a fictitious commodity, as discussed in chapter 3, partly because it's abstracted from the household and the unacknowledged work, disproportionately female, that generates it.

The impetus of much modern feminism has understandably therefore been to challenge the overidentification of women with the devalued *oikos* and seek opportunities for liberation and livelihood beyond it. However, if my earlier arguments are correct that those opportunities are going to be increasingly restricted in the future for everybody, there's a need to revalue the house and the work that goes into it.

In this chapter and the next, I try to develop a home economics of care and domestic production compatible with feasible opportunities for local livelihood-making in the future, which stays attentive to the potential for forms of domination like patriarchy involved in them – and tries to mitigate against them. Obviously, that amounts to less than claiming I know how to eliminate patriarchy and other forms of domination. I don't think I'm alone in that, and I doubt it's entirely possible – nor are the economics of the contemporary world of work beyond the home remotely free of them. But I'll try to stay attentive.

Households

By household, I mean the people – one or more of them – who occupy a living space. When there's more than one person in the household, coresidence often implies, though not always, sharing in some of the activities that go on within the household: for example, eating together, caring for children or other residents, sleeping together.

In many societies historically and still today, it also implies working together to produce directly the things the household needs: food, fibre, clothing, tools, housing materials and so forth. So, the household here is the unit of both consumption and a lot of the production for what it consumes.

In modern industrial societies, it's more usual for a household to be a unit of consumption only, with its members earning money to meet its consumption needs by working outside it and buying things produced elsewhere. The declining ability of states to organize and control political space that I've described in earlier chapters is a major reason why this latter kind of household is likely to lose ground in the future to joint production-consumption ones.

The boundaries of the household can be porous and, as ever, hard-and-fast definitions can never capture the complexity of human life perfectly. But they can capture it well enough. On our farm, there are currently ten and a half people (I said it wasn't perfect!) split clearly into six households, albeit sharing some household activities some of the time across the six (ditto). Our average household size is therefore a little smaller than the England and Wales average of 2.4 (the US average is 2.6), although it's set to grow soon.[1] That's another thing about households – they fluctuate in size over time.

But they don't necessarily fluctuate greatly in average size over long historical time. Contrary to popular misconceptions that small households are uniquely modern, relatively small households are historically common worldwide – if anything, the norm – with evidence from times and places as diverse as Stone-Age Ukraine, ancient Mexico and preindustrial England, albeit that household size does tend to decline somewhat with modernization.[2] English data from 1574–1821, for example, suggests more than half of households had four or fewer members.[3]

So, at this crude level, it seems that people may not have to radically reinvent the basic structure of the modern household to make it a suitable vehicle for low-energy, local livelihood-making. Many other societies have shown the way. There's plenty else that needs reinventing, so at least this is one less thing to worry about.

One thing that does need reinventing, or at least rethinking, is the orientation of the household to producing the things that it or other households need. On this point, the research literature has generated two apparently contradictory findings about the productivity of the joint production–consumption household.

On the one hand, production organized at the household level can generate enormous abundance. For example, the economic take-off in China in recent decades after the breakup of the collective farms of the later Mao era was driven in large part by semi-autonomous rural household production in what post-Mao governments called the 'household responsibility system' – telling phrase – a move which in many ways was driven from below by householders themselves. Postwar land reform programmes that de-concentrated landownership in favour of small-scale farmers in South Korea, Taiwan and Japan were likewise the spark for those countries' push to modern economic growth – part of the 'Great Reshuffle' I mentioned in the previous chapter.[4]

There's a deeper story in those latter countries concerning US policies geared to pro-peasant 'capitalist' land reform as a means of preventing them going down the communist route taken by China, a direction abandoned with the debacle of the Vietnam War. But my point for present purposes is simply that evidence from every inhabited continent points to the ability of small household production to create abundant livelihoods.[5]

On the other hand, famous studies suggest there is a 'structure of underproduction' to the household economy – the household orients to its own perceived needs, not to the maximum amount of production it could in principle attain.[6] It lacks the impetus to keep ratcheting up its productivity, growing its output relative to input and seeking new outlets for its products to drive wealth increase in the way that modern capitalist firms and societies do.

I won't plumb the many depths of this issue here. But essentially both positions are correct and might be a happy result as we contemplate future challenges.

Enormous productivity over and above the needs of the joint production–consumption household *can* be willingly given, persuaded or forced from it, as many a local chief, feudal lord, priestly caste, capitalist planner and communist autocrat have proved historically. It's good to know this capacity exists, although the consequences aren't always good for household producers themselves when subjected to demands from one or other among that gallery of economic chancers. This will almost certainly happen in the future under the auspices of the 'corporate quasi-states, city-states, feudalized rentier capitalists and warlords' who are waiting in the wings of the new dark ages, as identified by Michael Albert (see States of Refuge, page 35). That's why people will be seeking open country when they can.

But as the ability of centralized states to organize space politically declines, we're unlikely to see the kind of extrapolation of household productivity that's characterized recent capitalist development in countries like China. On the contrary, this is likely to reverse, creating possibilities for open country. The greater threat in that situation is local overlordship, possibly in cahoots with declining centralized power – in other words, the Viking gambit.

At the same time, the tendency of the household toward underproduction is encouraging in several respects. The spare capacity it implies contributes to the possibilities for the dark-age merriness I mentioned in chapter 1. In my own case, the relative sufficiency of my small farm and its autonomy from external economic pressure enables me to sublimate my dangerous tendencies toward the capitalist work ethic into more harmless activities such as writing books (although this also rests on certain unearned privileges, which I'll consider further in chapter 6). Other writers of books have pressed this point more generally, like Kate Soper's case for the 'alternative hedonism' of slower, less commodity-fixated and more relationship-oriented post-growth lifeways.[7]

I'm not convinced post-growth life in the future dark ages will be quite so leisurely, nor that hedonism is the best lens through which to view it. Still, the tendencies of the household toward underproduction can certainly give its members time for a slower and more associational life, bringing numerous advantages.

Also, those members are well-placed to notice the consequences of their economic activities, not only in terms of their own wellbeing but in the ecological integrity of the local land and water they work. Since the household is both producer and consumer, with a margin of surplus production to play with, this gives options for trimming production or altering productive practices for the benefit of the household or the wider ecology.

All this makes for a different and better scenario to the alienated consuming household that dominates present times. As consumers, we have no idea of the damaging practices associated with the products that we buy, products (cars, mobile phones) that often oppress us even as it's claimed they liberate us. And as producers we often find ourselves trapped in alienating and authoritarian work routines that feed this cycle. When tech-bro libertarians or neo-Malthusian left-wingers scorn as mere romanticism the idea of back-to-the-land autonomy for the joint producer-consumer household, it often sounds to me like the howl of the capitalist beast being unmasked.

Commons

But not everything in the future will be produced at the household level. A past innovation that will persist is regimes of common property, usually known as 'the commons'. Commons will be crucial to people's wellbeing, so they'll need to be constructed carefully. It's therefore important to understand what they can do and what they can't.

In his *A Tour Through the Whole Island of Great Britain* of 1724, Daniel Defoe (1660–1731) described dairying practices in the Somerset town of Cheddar, just a few miles from my home. At that time in Cheddar and other dairying communities, cows were owned, housed overnight and milked by individual households, which also collected their manure. In the morning, they would be gathered together from the individual households and taken as a group by the cowherd, who would watch over them grazing the common pasture. In the evening, they would return and be separated back to their individual owning households to be milked, quartered and given any extra fodder in accordance with household milk requirements. Milk that was surplus to household needs would be taken to a single creamery where it was made into cheese. The cheeses were returned to households, to consume or sell privately.

As agrarian writer Simon Fairlie comments, 'This elegant system paid scant allegiance to ideology – it evolved from the dialogue between private interest and common sense.'[8] The daily oscillation between private property (cows, hay, manure, milk) and common property (pasture, creamery) was a response to the most effective deployment of resources and economies of scale within the given parameters of the system.

The cheddar cheese flying off supermarket shelves across the world today is now produced through much more fully privatized property rights. Cheap energy can support scale-economizing technologies like fencing and milking machines that cut the human work requirement and promote its privatization via money in the form of profits and wages. But the condition of our dark-age future will be less cheap energy and fewer economies of large scale, hence probably more commons.

Technically, a commons refers to a resource that's owned collectively and indivisibly by a defined community of users (commoners), such as hunting grounds, a cow pasture, a river or a creamery (the rights to all of these can be allocated in other ways, of course), along with a set of usage protocols like the ones I discussed in the case of Cheddar.[9] It doesn't necessarily involve people working collectively in a day-to-day sense (the cowherd working on the common pasture in that example may have led a lonelier – or freer – life than householders working together in the cowshed, although the cowherd is probably a householder too). The 'common' aspect of commons refers to property rights, not specifically to work regimes.

Another important point about commons is that they're not free-for-alls in which anybody can take whatever they want. This, notoriously, was ecologist Garrett Hardin's approach to commons, popularized by his influential 1968 article 'The Tragedy of the Commons'.[10] Hardin is regularly and rightly censured for this misunderstanding, and for his problematic wider politics that informed it.

There's a danger, though, that this pile-on distracts from the fact that free-for-alls do exist – for example, using the atmosphere as a dump for greenhouse gases. Or the collapse of various fisheries through over-harvesting. These aren't examples of 'tragic' commons. They're examples of the tragedies that can happen when commons are absent.

But such absences are quite ... well ... common. The distinguished scholar Elinor Ostrom is widely credited for showing via many real-world examples that commons can preserve the integrity of a resource while optimizing its usage in a community. She certainly did show that, but she never claimed that commons are always present or immune to failure (in fact, she meticulously documented commons failures), nor that they're invariably the best way of organizing resource use.

On that last point, Ostrom provides some useful pointers to when commons arrangements might be preferable:

- The value of production per unit of land is low
- The frequency or dependability of use or yield is low
- The possibility of improvement or intensification is low
- A large territory is needed for effective use
- Relatively large groups are required for capital investment activities[11]

On our farm, we use wood from our rainforest trees, planted about twenty years ago, as fuel for warmth and hot water, among other purposes. I won't wade too far into the vexed debate about whether wood fuel is safe or sustainable, although I touch on it again in chapter 8. As with many things, the answer is 'it depends'. But the debate is relevant to my wider theme in that the preferred alternatives to low-tech local wood resources touted by today's wood-maligners are high-tech, high-energy-using, grid-connected mechanisms like heat pumps. The arguments against fuelwood reprise Hardin's in seeing it as an unsustainable tragedy of the commons that should be replaced with privatized, corporate products.

We wood-botherers need a sylvan Elinor Ostrom of the latter day to show how wood commons can work in practice, someone who doesn't assume that they 'tragically' can't by definition. After all, it's unlikely that many of the inhabitants of open country in the future will be powering up off-grid heat pumps. Figuring out efficient and renewable uses of wood will be high on their to-do lists.

So let me offer this cautionary tale. Getting from a standing tree to fuel logs involves quite a few steps: felling, coppicing or pollarding the tree, delimbing it, cutting it into logs, possibly splitting the logs, then moving them to the woodstore and stacking them. When our own household was the only one resident on our farm, I did most of this work as one of my contributions to it. Standing under a hot shower, I was all too aware of the supply chain and resource management behind this luxury, because they were mostly things that were either mine (like my work time) or at least under my control (like the woodland resource).

But once there were other households on our site too, things got more complicated. A woodstore of unpaid-for wood furnished freely for others through my labour with no control on my part over how much they used and over its impact on the standing resource seemed unwise. No doubt some might say this merely illustrates the selfish individualism of a modern Western man like me. Maybe so, but nevertheless almost every society, including non-modern and non-Western ones, mitigates against such free-for-alls by seeking some appropriate blend of private, common and/or public property rights.

So, I arranged to get the bulk of the work done collectively with the wider community of households on the farm. This worked up to a point, but it added an extra mental load for me of negotiating and organizing the work time, and there were sometimes issues with attendance – the 'community workday no-show' problem familiar in intentional communities. We've now moved to a system where each household takes responsibility for furnishing its own firewood from the common resource, the latter managed by me as the woodherd counterpart to the cowherd of old-time Cheddar.

Looking at Ostrom's list on page 66, it's easy to see why the standing trees work as a commons, while turning them into stacked logs doesn't. (Historic firewood commons typically involve rights for commoners to gather fallen wood individually, but not to cut it fresh.) The private and collective aspects of the Cheddar dairying example make equal sense. A distributist would see this in terms of subsidiarity. With due allowance for the pleasures of companionship, the most effective working arrangements are organized at the smallest feasible level: one or a handful of workers when possible, then a whole household, then a group of households, then a wider commons and so on. This also applies in differentiated ways across separate dimensions of work. A building site, for example, is a vast collective enterprise, but individual builders usually own most of their own tools, and there's a reason for that.

Near the public footpath on our farm, we planted hybrid willows, which we pollard in rotation every year. Due to their visibility, we get a lot of requests from people – mostly ones who know us – to cut some for craft purposes. Occasionally, we find some have been cut without asking by passersby, though this doesn't happen often. Most people are remarkably respectful.

However, as the requests have multiplied, we're left to judge case-by-case how much of the resource we can give away at the asking (more mental load). In one sense, this also arguably underscores the low value that people place on land-grown resources like wood (and vegetables). They wouldn't ask us to give them money – but, hey, it's just a bit of wood. In another sense, I'm all too aware of how easy it is to be a dick about this – hey, it *is* just a bit of wood. Small acts of generosity make the world go round, while small acts of selfishness make local gossip spin way faster. Yet nobody ever asks supermarket staff if it's okay for them to take just a few bars of chocolate (though I gather that shoplifting is on the rise). Nor do the vast implicit and explicit public subsidies such big businesses receive usually figure in accounts of their low prices and superior efficiency over small operators.

In any case, it's for such reasons that I embrace distributism. If everyone had the opportunity to plant their own willow coppice, it would be easier to make good judgements about whose requests to prioritize. This winter, I've been establishing a new area of willow coppice for the farm community's use in a less visible part of the holding, with a view to saying yes in the future to every request that comes our way in respect of the original coppice. I'm calling this my Hardin experiment.

ACROSS THE POLITICAL spectrum, people often use a morally loaded vocabulary around these issues. Market liberals dislike the collectivism of commons and jump on commons failures as evidence of freeriding, freeloading and laziness that they think can only be corrected through individualized private responsibility. Progressive liberals like the collectivism of commons as exemplary of the sociable and equitable character of humankind, which, at the extreme, they want to inflict regimentally upon everyone in every situation through disastrous schemes such as forced collective farms.

This moralism is unnecessary. Freeriding isn't usually a character defect so much as a structural consequence of not bearing the full practical and emotional load of a task – something that indeed can often be corrected by individualizing responsibility, but without making too much wider political capital out of it. Likewise, in their ultimately moralizing emphasis upon collective arrangements, progressives too easily underestimate the sheer hard work and mental load (what economists would call transaction costs) involved in negotiating effective commons – not to mention differences between individuals in how they prefer to work, some more collectively, others more individually.

All this is part of the larger and never-ending task of making flawed human beings better than they might otherwise be on a day-by-day basis, not least by designing pragmatically effective working arrangements, albeit inevitably imperfect ones. In this respect, I'd argue that orientations to collective work in left-wing politics too often overemphasize collective labour per se as a redemptive force and focus too much attention on moments of political catharsis, when power is equalized and the supposedly correct model of human social relations is implemented.

In the humdrum example I've given of firewood-making on our land, it might be possible for the other households to rise up against mine as the landholding power and institute their own arrangements (although the relevant people are far too nice to do that). But short of making me do it all for them to atone for my landlordly sins – at best a time-limited strategy – they would then face exactly the same commons problem. It's necessary to pay attention to the ongoing human power dynamics that always have to be managed in the long term.

No doubt some people can create and thrive upon genuinely collective arrangements along the lines of 'from each according to their abilities, to each according to their needs'. But it doesn't seem a great idea to base arrangements for society at large on what a handful of saints can achieve. A sober historical look at how low-input local societies have organized themselves to get work done via a sophisticated dance of carefully choreographed individual, household, commons and wider collective elements suggests the issues go far beyond just our problematic modern individualism.

For example, open field systems in premodern England were partly commons involving shared plough teams, but plots were cultivated by individual households. Likewise, in many Asian paddy rice cultures, the larger terraforming of the landscape was often done collectively, while the farming itself was a household matter.[12] In both cases, it made sense to manage the wider landscape collectively, and intensive arable cultivation privately. A lesson for the future, perhaps? It's possible to waste a lot of effort building unnecessary and over-complex forms of collective work.

Often when people talk about commons, they don't really mean a functioning resource commons like the examples of milk, firewood and cereal crops I've invoked, so much as a wider and more overtly political sense of land occupancy rights. Those rights are vitally important, and I discuss them further in chapter 6. But it's as well to think carefully about how to structure access to material resources like land in ways that are robust to failures, human flaws and mental load/transaction costs, because we'll need to be doing a lot more of that structuring in the future. Often, this will mean choosing private over collective property rights for much day-to-day livelihood-making, for most people at least, while preserving fair and distributed access to land for people in general. This is a different matter to collective political assertion by groups of people wanting access rights to land in the first place – the collective desire for open country is not the same as working open country collectively.

Looking at occupancy rights in the future from a commons perspective is informative, though. It's easy for a commons to be too closed around existing commoners' rights, preventing access by incomers – great, as Ostrom showed, for the longevity of the resource and the commons, but possibly not so great for the incomers. It's also easy for a commons to be too open to all comers – great, as Hardin showed, for the all comers at least in the short-run, but possibly not so great for the longevity of the resource and the commons. Resolving such conundrums is going to be critical for future wellbeing, and I'll come back to it in chapter 6.

Meanwhile, the willows are trembling.

CHAPTER 5

Home Economics: Caring

In the previous chapter, I avoided peeping through the curtains of the household to discuss who's inside. In one sense I think that's defensible – what matters most is that the model of the small household as a self-regulating economic unit of coresidents is in some kind of working order, and I believe it is. How the people within the households choose each other and divvy things up between them is less important – and isn't for me to say.

But I probably do need to bite the bullet, look inside the household and say some things about its structure. And when I do, I feel obliged to say that most – but not all – households in the dark-age future will be related by kinship. In other words, the main model for the coresident household group will be the family.

My guess is that most people would find that statement crashingly obvious, given that family relationships have been the main model for the coresident household group in almost every society worldwide past and present. But, like another well-known F-word, the idea of 'the family' is a controversial accentuator for sharply divided positions in modern politics. So I will try to set out a position as judiciously as I can.

Families

I begin, again, with a dark-age framing: the question is not how, in an ideal world, you'd prefer to fashion human relationships. It's how, in the far from ideal, dark and challenging world that's now upon us, you're likely to fashion them as best you can in practice with the cultural institutions to hand.

The question, also, is not about what kind of human relationships might work in a world of abstract monetary exchange that draws resources, products and the means of livelihood from distant places. It's about what kind of human relationships work in a world where you and those around you have to generate the means of livelihood locally for yourselves.

A few salient points against that background, and a definition. First, as in the case of households, the day-to-day coresidential family unit in many societies historically worldwide has been quite small, and often roughly in line with the structure of the familiar modern Western nuclear family, albeit varied in many details from place to place.[1]

Second, family or kin relations have some useful properties in situations of land-based livelihood-making where political relationships are thin. The small family group makes for an effective and relatable unit of day-to-day work (subsidiarity again), including care work, but kin relations extend outward beyond it. This makes them flexible and extendable in terms of creating additional relationships for work or political purposes.

These relationships – sister, brother, aunt, uncle, mother, father, daughter, son and so on – create roles that provide models for behaviour, roles that are available to others who don't 'really' occupy that role according to the local theory of family-relatedness. These roles also imply long-term relatedness that can't easily be broken, and this has a stabilizing effect on the household as a group oriented to long-term livelihood-making projects. Where politics is thin, known trustworthiness and reputation are important considerations, coming with transaction costs that kinship lowers (it's not a coincidence that the words 'hospitable' and 'hostile' share the same etymological roots). The same applies even where politics isn't so thin – there's a reason why so many farms and small businesses are still family run. Only where monetary and commercial relations are unusually strong do kin relations fade, and not always then.[2]

Kin relations are important, then, in low-input societies oriented to local land-based livelihood-making. In fact, they seem pretty important even in modern societies that aren't oriented to it, where the options for people to live however and with whomever they choose have probably never been greater. For example, in England and Wales in 2021, 98 per cent of people lived in a household, and only 2 per cent in a 'communal establishment' to use the official terminology. Among household dwellers,

63 per cent lived in a single-family household (i.e. a couple with or without children, or a lone parent).[3] Although a decrease from past patterns, kin-based household residence still looms large.

※※※

BUT WHAT DOES KINSHIP or family mean? Who is family, and who isn't? The answer to those questions is potentially long. To keep it short, let's turn to the discipline of anthropology, within which the study of kinship systems worldwide has been a key theme. And let's turn to a short book called *What Kinship Is–And Is Not* by one of the most eminent anthropologists of recent times, the late Marshall Sahlins. Kinship, Sahlins said, is about social relationships, a way that people model and structure their connections with others – hence, what kinship is *not* is something purely biological connected to shared genes. What kinship *is* is a set of systematic framings for the long-term co-presences that people have in each other's lives, what Sahlins called 'a network of mutualities of being'.[4]

Sahlins' student, the late, great and better-known David Graeber, wrote along similar lines that kinship is a:

metaphor for social attachments, in much the same way we'd say 'all men are brothers' when trying to express internationalism (even if we can't stand our actual brother and haven't spoken to him for years).[5]

The slight dismissiveness about family relationships in this remark perhaps reflects the fading interest in kinship of modern anthropology. As an undergraduate in the 1980s, I was probably among the last cohort of anthropology students who had to take compulsory courses on kinship and remember stuff for exams about things like matrilateral cross-cousin marriage (I don't remember it anymore). There were good reasons for de-emphasizing the kinship focus, one of them being the perils of getting overinvested in excessively formal models about how societies are supposed to work. One or two other social-science disciplines might profit from a similar new broom today, as well as other social-science concepts, like 'class'. Still, the fact remains that family and kin conceptions and relations continue to structure a large part of most people's lives – including in family farms and family businesses outside the charmed circle of corporate capitalism. The pendulum in anthropology has arguably swung too far.

As I see it, yes, it's quite likely that you can't stand your actual brother, just as you have your struggles with anyone with whom you interact closely for a long time (as they do with you). But maybe you also love your brother, partly for the same reason, and in any case his brother-ness and brother-ness in general are important metaphors for your in-it-for-the-long-haul implication in other people's lives, without the like of which a functional society would be impossible. No surprise that the well-named agony columns (*agōn* meaning struggle, contest) in modern magazines are full of people both wanting and not wanting to cut off contact with problematic family members, nor that reports from more traditional kinship-heavy societies likewise emphasize both endless obligation and endless frustration with kinsfolk.

Societies of the open country in the future will likely also be kinship-heavy in a similar way. And this may be problematic because the reasons I gave for why kin relations are functional for low-input, land-based societies are basically the same reasons that currents of liberal-modernist thinking give for why they're dysfunctional in a 'free' society – they can trap people, particularly women, in long-term and potentially oppressive, nonconsensual relationships.

The more extreme edge of that liberal-modernist critique calls for the abolition of the family, which it sees as fatally compromised by violence and complicity with existing power structures – as if the F-word itself has some autonomous and malevolent incantatory power to create flawed and damaged people who would otherwise be redeemed if only we dispensed with it.[6] Radical and liberatory as such thinking might seem, I'd argue it reprises one of the more problematic aspects of liberal-modernist thinking in viewing society essentially as an aggregation of self-creating individuals who can realistically aspire to breaking all potentially oppressive social bonds once and for all, rather than having to defuse and manage their enduring reality. This dualism of the individual versus the collective seems like something of a neurosis in modern Western thought that I imagine looks strange to other people. In the words of one Indigenous writer, 'Aboriginal people don't have to choose between the individual and the collective, left and right, because we are both at once. We are unique individuals with no boss, bound in dense and complex systems of relational obligation.'⁷ Many of those systems of relational obligation involve the idiom of kinship or family.

※※※

DISTRIBUTIST TRADITIONS also emphasize the relational obligations of kinship, drawing on subsidiarity and virtue ethics to suggest (paralleling Sahlins in some respects) the transcendent nature of kin relations.⁸ As distributist pioneer G.K. Chesterton put it, 'There is something in the family that might loosely be called anarchist', in the sense that it's a uniquely prior and self-reproducing form of community that's practically autonomous from the wider political community, notably the state. This idea is grounded in natural law concepts that I'll touch on in chapter 10, but that Chesterton frames in relation to kin relations thus: 'Marriage makes a small state within the state, which resists all such regimentation. That bond breaks all other bonds; that law is found stronger than all later and lesser laws.'⁹

Liberal-modernist critics of the family rightly fear that, left to itself, it's rife with potential for abuse and domination. But, pushed to its logical conclusion, this critique culminates in a world of cold individualism where people's capacities for abuse and domination can only be checked by the ultimate power of the state.¹⁰ This is problematic because the state itself isn't short of potential for abuse and domination, as evidenced often enough historically by state meddling in family matters, typically in favour of patriarchy. It's also problematic in the present historical moment because of the state's increasing inability to control political space, discussed earlier. If we forsake parenthood as a source of potentially beneficial social power and put the state *in loco parentis* just at the time when its powers are waning, we risk creating a lot of orphans – including adult ones.

But I won't further pursue that distributist line of argument here. To keep things more within a social-science framing, I'll merely observe that people's experience of abuse and domination indeed mostly does come from their mutuals, but one thing we know from cultural comparative work is that every society creates structured mutualisms – just as nature abhors a vacuum, so it seems does human society abhor an unstructured randomness to human relationships. In that sense, family abolition becomes meaningless because the family would be reinvented in some form as soon as it was abolished – especially in societies like the ones I'm discussing that have hard physical and political work to do. This is not, I'd stress, to say that 'the family' must meet some specific norm about exactly how people are to be and behave within it. I'm not advocating for such monsters as the patriarchal, the bourgeois or the biological family. I'm just suggesting there's little to be gained by approaching the challenges of the future through a family-free lens.

Another social-science approach considers family relationships in the context of their present, lived, socioeconomic reality, rather than how we might ideally want to reimagine family and gender relations. For example, Melissa Kearney has shown through detailed empirical work that rates of marriage have declined in the US disproportionately among working-class people with lower educational attainments because men in this group have lost out in the modern job market more than anyone else: 'In the past 40 years, the economic position of men without a four-year college degree has eroded, both in absolute terms and relative to women, making them less reliable breadwinners and less suitable marriage partners'.[11] Her point is not that marriage is some moral gold standard, but that socioeconomic forces have impinged on the tendency of women and men with lower income/education to form enduring relationships in respect of child-raising. The evidence she presents suggests it's harder on average for single/unpartnered mothers to achieve good outcomes for their children – particularly their sons – due to the additional structural obstacles they face, as well as to psychosocial factors in child development. Meanwhile men, in Kearney's words, 'continue to fall to the margins of economic and family life'.[12]

In the contemporary US, the remedies Kearney identifies include such things as tackling joblessness, mass incarceration, untreated mental illness, the opioid epidemic and, more implicitly, racism – modern burdens that rarely make it in the roster of our progress narratives. More generally, her analysis suggests a different framing for some problems of family and gender, especially the problem of (male) violence – not abolishing the family in the hope it will erase violence but instead supporting it economically and structurally to address some of the causes of violence. I'll come back to this and its relevance to the dark-age future shortly.

HOME ECONOMICS: CARING

A point that most people can probably agree on is that family isn't everything. Kith matters as well as kin – friendship, neighbourliness, localism, custom and the rich associational life of the localities within which families reside, and out of which can hopefully emerge a better ability to weather the future.

In these new circumstances, it's likely people will continue to challenge existing norms and experiment with new arrangements, as people generally do – one of humanity's more adaptive and usually likeable traits. Still, there are going to be enough challenges in the dark-age societies to come, enough things to be fundamentally rethought, without throwing perfectly usable kin relations into the mix as another thing to be torn down and reassembled anew. Kinship does a lot of work that otherwise requires the construction of elaborate politics, and the construction of elaborate politics will be a costly enterprise in the future, not to be frivolously undertaken in respect of institutions that are already in place.

So, to summarize a long argument with a short and perhaps obvious conclusion – family relationships are going to be important in the dark-age future, just as they've been important in every past.

※※※

CHILDREN – RAISING THEM, safeguarding them, teaching them, learning from them, is a vast issue in relation to questions of family and kin that I can hardly begin to address here but is obviously of vital importance – even more so in a future where other social institutions that support these aims may be weakening.

The cliché that it takes a village to raise a child has become a cliché because it's true. Whether in the form of official education systems or informal local kith, families can and must only be part-societies. Again, subsidiarity comes into play, as argued by distributist writer Andrew Willard Jones:

> The family is the place where the greatest happiness is possible because it is the place of greatest power. For the same reason, it is the place where the greatest misery is possible. There is no greater suffering than that of an abused child. In such a circumstance, a higher power must intervene.[13]

It's worth noting the language of 'greater' and 'higher' power here – a characteristic of distributism and its concept of subsidiarity that upends our conventional statist ways of thinking. *Greatest* power resides at the *lower*, more local, intimate and everyday level, whereas power at the higher and more abstract or distant level is weaker. Higher power may, as in this example, still be necessary, but 'higher' is not the same as 'ultimate'.

The devil is always in the detail of navigating these boundaries, and this may get harder in emerging 'dark-age' circumstances with so many past certainties crumbling. Still, in endless ways the societies likely to fare best are those able to define the contours of a rich community life, and this is another case in point.

At the same time, the benefits of childhoods spent in intimate contact with the day-to-day livelihood-making of the joint production–consumption household are immeasurable. These benefits arise not only in specific aptitudes but also in general attitudes. As Tennessee farmer Brian Miller puts it in his delightful memoir of agrarian life:

> *For many years and on many occasions, both personally and professionally, I've given the offhand advice, "Hire the farm kid." Sometimes it has been meant as a literal instruction, but at least as often it has been given as a more general recommendation ... Look for the person who learned a work ethic early and applied it often. The person who in the formative years wasn't given the choice of whether to pull his or her weight is the one you want.*[14]

There's a strong current of scepticism about this in contemporary culture – a kind of trade-union consciousness about improved wages and conditions, and against child labour, the exploitation of 'chores', and a critique of the apparent self-martyrdom of the family business. Which is all fine up to a point, although it easily flips a left-wing critique of corporate exploitation, commodification and the leveraging of monopoly advantage into a yet stronger critique of decommodifying and autonomy-seeking family businesses. The result is a brand of corporate-friendly quasi-socialism popular in the contemporary professional managerial class, which I believe is ill-suited to the coming future.

This corporate turn on the left fits oddly into the otherwise welcome re-evaluation of the wisdom of hunter-gatherer or foraging peoples and their lifeways in contemporary Western culture, now that that culture has largely obliterated them. It relates to what anthropologist Richard Gardner calls the 'adaptive-child-training' theory: 'While non-foragers tend to push children toward obedience and responsibility, foragers tend to press for self-reliance, independence and individual achievement.'[15]

When combined with corporate-friendly socialism, such thinking too easily generates a problematic ideological triad of freedom-loving foragers and wageworkers, as against miserable and exploitative farmers and family businesses, which seems to be a part of the contemporary zeitgeist. To paraphrase James Scott, foragers have never looked so good, while farmers have never looked so bad. Sometimes, parallels are even drawn between the opportunistic, happy-go-lucky lives of the modern wage-earning city dweller and our species' original gathering and hunting state, contrasting with the grim puritanism of the farmer – which works as a playful and thought-provoking conceit, but probably not as a punt on past or future human ecology.[16]

I dissent from that narrative. When we were building a house on our land at the end of our narrow and potholed farm track, we failed to find a logistics company prepared to help us with the heavy haulage required, on various bureaucratic if no doubt eminently sensible grounds – access, insurance, health and safety. Luckily, we knew a local farmer – I'll call him Bill – in possession of three priceless assets: a sense of neighbourliness, a hell-yeah attitude and a large telehandler.

As Bill unloaded an upright pallet of heavy and super-expensive triple-glazed windows, he knocked it with one of the telehandler's forks. It started teetering, and I jumped forward instinctively to steady it. Then I jumped backward as my body caught up with my brain's rapid cost-benefit analysis balancing broken windows with a broken head. Bill deftly repositioned the forks and got hold of the pallet, grinning mischievously out of his cab window at my save-the-windows-no-save-my-arse antics. To hell with insurance.

Telehandlers may be few and far between in the future, but a sense of neighbourliness and a hell-yeah attitude will still be able to do a lot of heavy lifting. All of which makes me cautious of overdoing the 'obedience and responsibility' narrative about farming and the corporate-socialist route to future wellbeing.

In other words, hire the farm kid. Or, better yet, as Brian Miller adds, 'If you have the opportunity, raise a farm kid.'

Of Patriarchs and Matrilines

Despite all this, a good dark ages will require defences from the more problematic aspects of family – not least in respect of patriarchy and an over-rigidity of roles.

One aspect of our self-satisfied modernism is the sense that only after the European Enlightenment and modernism generally have women been able to free themselves from the patriarchal subjection of past times. In earlier writings, I think I was a little too swayed by this view into worrying about how to 'modernize' local farm-based livelihood-making as a defence against patriarchy, as if local land economies of the future might replicate the gender relations of local land economies of the past simply by virtue of being local land economies. I'm now of the view that patriarchy is present and/or strongly latent in every society almost irrespective of its complexion, mode of livelihood and other features. Indeed, often enough modern (and colonial) regimes have actively buttressed patriarchal family forms.[17]

So, I don't see any special danger of 'slipping back' into past patriarchal ways due to land-based localism. Indeed, there's a body of research that suggests the kind of local economic activities oriented to the immediate livelihood of the household that I project in the future can sometimes be more supportive of women's social empowerment than world market commodification, which often involves the subservient commodification of women's labour and bodies.[18] Women are sometimes better placed to build social empowerment in the production–consumption dynamic of the household economy than in more commodified forms of production.

It's worth mentioning in that connection, too, the associations between patriarchy and heteronormativity in the long historical gestation of accumulative modern capitalist societies. Contemporary farm and rural landscapes can no doubt often feel like closed country for LGBTQ+ people. Some of these landscapes are now being painstakingly opened up, and part of that story involves queering the older history of the countryside.[19]

Still, these possibilities for the greater openness of household livelihood-making guarantee nothing in themselves, and the dangers of patriarchy darkening the future remain.

Smarter people than me have failed to entirely explain the origins of patriarchy, or how to overcome it, so I'm not going to claim I have any grand plan for a patriarchy-free dark-age future. Instead, I'll just submit four points that seem to me worth considering.

THE FREE PLAY of patriarchy within the household is arguably conditioned by the free play of patriarchy outside it. At the extreme, this involves a kind of untrammelled and predatory male collective violence – essentially the 'Viking' problem of a heroic-styled warrior culture or of what's sometimes termed 'masterless men'.

Many societies have recognized the dangers of this and sought ways to counter it. For example, Anglo-Saxon England emphasized 'hearth-fasting' men – linking them to a home and hearth, to the possibilities of local status and livelihood. In Edo Japan, the *wakamono-gumi* associations of young, unmarried peasant men mobilized them as nightwatchmen, firefighters and festival organizers, and linked them into wider local knowledges and systems. Age-set systems and initiation rituals have served similar functions in many societies. The emphasis is less on the man being the master of the household, and more on making the household the master of the man.[20]

But – as demonstrated by Melissa Kearney's work, mentioned earlier – we're not doing a particularly great job of this in contemporary liberal-modernist society. Education, employment and financial systems almost seem set up to fail and marginalize many young men, especially from low-income families. The erosion of kith, kinship and positive local associational possibilities adds to the risk they'll turn to misogynistic and violent ideologies to make sense of their situations. Models of society based on making widespread the possibility for men to become kith-and-kin connected, livelihood-making householders rather than atomized, internet-connected consumers of masculinist self-images adrift in a hostile job market can mitigate against this. Something to aim for, perhaps, in a postliberal dark-age future?

One part of this involves structural or class-based redress. Another involves building empathy between people in their flawed and biased but vulnerable and common humanity. *Improvable* humanity too – which brings me to my second point.

IN HER BOOK *Fair Play*, Eve Rodsky treats the average heterosexual marriage as a failed commons, typically with men freeriding on women's unacknowledged practical and emotional labour.[21] Like an Elinor Ostrom of the private modern home, Rodsky sets about systematically reconfiguring the usage agreements of the household commons so that the resource of women's time, work and overall commitment to it isn't fatally depleted. I'd recommend her book as an essential returning-from-honeymoon read – I only wish it had been available in the distant dark age when I returned from mine. The basic idea is that a careful audit of domestic tasks – not only who does them, but who thinks them through, plans them and takes ultimate responsibility (ideally the same person in each case, as with my earlier firewood commons example) – typically reveals disparities that can be corrected once they're out in the cold light of day.

Rodsky's 'fair play' title and her 'changing society one marriage at a time' strapline are interesting in their implicit challenge to the collective politics and emphasis upon binary, structural change typical of progressive liberalism and its taste for grandiose projects like abolishing families. Instead, an appeal to fairness, to some larger metaphorical court of appeal, and to the possibility of people (largely men, in this case – but not always only men) learning better forms of conduct, stake out different political ground. I'll examine that ground further in chapter 10. For now, I'll just reiterate the virtue of holding on to a model of people as flawed and potentially oppressive, but also as vulnerable and improvable – in that sense, not just people who are acting out predefined roles like female or male, but people who are really alive.

A word on gendered work roles is appropriate here, which I'll ground in my experience of my own farm and marriage. There are a few aspects of those that fit with traditional gender roles, and many that don't.

On one occasion, my wife came back from a stint regrading the farm track in the digger, fuming from a passing walker's words: 'Oh, well done

– but shouldn't your husband be doing that?' At least it gave me a flash of insight into the corrosive power of patriarchal assumptions.

Her husband was probably writing a book or something at the time. She's better than me at grading anyway, and digger use is one of several divisions of labour that we've painstakingly thrashed out over the years – generally, I dig the big holes and then she sorts out the mess I've made. Arguably, that works as a wider metaphor.

In any case, my point is that the possibly somewhat traditionalist emphasis I've placed here on marriage and family needn't imply traditionalist gender roles or hierarchies – nor need it imply they must be imposed on everyone. Given that generating a complete livelihood requires a suite of skills beyond the capability of any one person to perfect, historic gendered divisions of labour are perhaps understandable and may even have some advantages, provided they're flexible enough to accommodate people's individualism and don't mindlessly replicate ideas about the inferiority of 'women's work'.

But they don't seem fitted to present times. So, my advice to couples starting out together on a journey of practical livelihood-making is to begin figuring out early on who's drawn to what, and for men in particular to grow out of machine-machismo. Actually, for our civilization as a whole to do so.

※※※

GOING BACK TO OUR flawed but improvable humanity, improvability nevertheless requires a larger political field or community consciousness within which it can flourish. This is why founding moments, founding people, founding charters and suchlike are important, because they can cast forward historically and set the cultural tone long into the future. Hence, my third point. As we navigate the dark-age future there are going to be a lot of founding moments, new communities bringing themselves into being, new deals to be struck. These create opportunities for less patriarchal and more restorative relationships.

One inspiration here is the story of the landless workers' movement in Brazil – the MST (Movimento dos Trabalhadores Rurais Sem Terra). At a foundational meeting in Cascavel in 1984, the MST membership agreed to accord equal rights in the organization to everyone across the board. In the words of two later commentators, 'It was remarkable, in a society in which *machismo* was still so strong, and at a meeting at which there were so few women, that the *sem terra* gave equal rights to all members of the family – old and young, men and women.'[22]

Of course, this doesn't mean patriarchy was abolished from the households and communities the *sem terra* set up with that simple stroke. But it did help to establish a prerequisite: a political framework and a culture within which anti-patriarchal goals had social traction. And it seems relevant that this was shaped at a male-dominated meeting in the sense that it can be easier for people to work beyond immediate self-interest at foundational moments when their focus is upon grounding the wider good – perhaps especially in situations where community formation is defensive or addressed to a powerful enemy.

THE FINAL CONSIDERATION IS an intriguing longer-term possibility, namely the emergence of matrilineal kinship. Matriliny is not the same as matriarchy. The latter references rule or social power exercised by women, a subject much debated within feminism and social science that I won't pursue here. Matriliny by contrast relates to kinship and inheritance – specifically to situations where people trace descent or inherit goods or property on their mother's side only. Men may still enjoy more social power than women in matrilineal societies, but matriliny does usually help confer power to women and mitigate against the danger of social annihilation via disregarded domestic roles. Historically, it's been much less common than its patrilineal counterpart or the bilateral kinship familiar in Europe. But there have been many instances of it across the world nonetheless – notably in parts of India, the South Pacific, Indonesia, Western and Central Africa, and in Indigenous societies of North America.[23]

An interesting aspect of matriliny is its association with horticultural societies. Where livelihood rests heavily on small, intensively worked garden plots, usually associated with a home, matriliny is more common.[24] This contrasts with the patrilineal kinship more typical in livestock-herding societies where the boundaries of home or the home range are less clear. Whereas horticultural societies are typically organized through private property, patriarchal pastoralist societies tend to have more collectivist property arrangements, which are more readily arbitrated through violence.

My guess is that there'll be more of both kinds of society in the future, at the expense of the non-producer, bilateral, liberal-modernist households of today. But it's not hard to imagine an open-country world where small household plots increasingly take over from existing, extensive, high-energy commodity export cropping, and proliferate – perhaps a world where the key generational and property relationship is one of daughters inheriting mothers' gardens. This is one of several reasons why the kind of family abolitionist thinking that yokes patriarchy, kinship, private property and capitalism together as an unholy alliance requiring joint dispatch is misleading. Private property rights can mitigate patriarchy, while their absence can foment it.

Kinship resists change. Families won't disappear anytime soon (or at all), and nor will matrilineal systems appear with a snap of the fingers. Matriliny is more a long-term possibility – perhaps along the lines of the wisely low-tech, ecological and matrilineal Kesh people occupying northern California in structural opposition to the more industrial Dayao people in the far-distant, postapocalyptic future that Ursula Le Guin conjures in her novel, *Always Coming Home*. Le Guin's north Californian youth imbued with a knowledge of local Indigenous societies and cosmologies provides the real-world grounding for this possible future.

In the near term, finding ways to support women's access to and inheritance of land could be good ways to prefigure it. But to avoid the possibility of some future longhouse war developing between emerging matrilines and neo-patriarchs bearing the legacy of contemporary male supremacism, I'd argue it's wise to do this alongside some empathy for male vulnerability and nuanced attention to hearth-fasting men as well as women.

Communities

Finally in this chapter, we come to some face-to-face relationships not previously covered under the more tightly defined categories of households, commons and families.

Let's start with neighbours – those 'others' of kinship, who don't share family connections and don't share the household, but who otherwise are similarly a deep well of potential for mutual aid. Or else a pain in the arse. Sometimes both. It's no surprise that, alongside family disputes, neighbour disputes loom large in the caseload of therapists and mediators.

Another feature that neighbours share with kin is their givenness. Usually, you don't get to choose your neighbours, just as you don't get to choose your family. When this works out, its very randomness in the case of neighbours can sweeten its blessings. The unmotivated care of a neighbour sometimes counts for more than the dutiful care of kinsfolk, connecting with an uplifting sense that a wider benevolence exists in the world.

But when it doesn't work out, it can be hell. This is one reason why a lot of societies opt not to leave neighbourliness to chance and create codes of conduct to regulate local relations, sometimes with a cultural or religious emphasis on the connected local circle of relationships and care, mediated by powerful unifying forces like food and collective worship.[25]

Another reason why neighbourliness often wasn't left to chance historically, and in some communities still today, is that in land-based societies lacking the easy territorial mobility of modern times, finding a pool of potential marriage partners to fill the household wasn't always easy. A solution was, again, to regularize relationships between neighbours in the form of local territorial groups or villages as donors or recipients of brides or grooms, and/or to create kinship corporations (clans and lineages) that mapped kin-relatedness onto local settlement patterns.

How this plays out in practice can be vastly complex, with long scholarly books devoted to the local details. For my purposes here, I'll simply suggest it's wise not to get too hung up on the distinctions between households, kin, neighbours and community, and instead appreciate the numerous ways they can intersect and model each other.

❈❈❈

A WHOLE OTHER category under the generic heading of community is precisely that – a *community*, understood as a larger group of non-kin living together more or less as a single household. It's far beyond my scope or expertise to offer any historical summary of these intentional communities here. Historically, the hierarchical monastery has probably been the most common form, but no doubt there have been many others. Modern times have seen the growth of egalitarian intentional communities whose main distinguishing feature from the other kinds of community I've looked at is precisely their intentionality: the fact that their members actively choose each other.

The flipside of intentionality is the lack of mutuality of being associated with kinship, which perhaps is one reason for the notorious tendency of modern intentional communities to fragment. Still, a lot of experience has been amassed within them of establishing workable organizational structures and managing conflict.[26] My sense from a limited knowledge of this literature is that intentional communities face similar problems to non-intentional ones, such as challenging interpersonal power dynamics and patriarchy.

Those modern intentional communities that have geared themselves specifically around ill-paid, land-based livelihoods are perhaps of greatest interest as pioneers of the dark-age future. My six-word summary from reading a little of the literature around it and from my entirely non-systematic conversations with people involved in them is, 'It's hard ... but sometimes also joyful.' Pretty much the same as family-based production, in other words. Again, perhaps the take-home is not to overstress the difference between them.

A good deal of the contemporary back-to-the-land movement took place in intentional communities as a counterculturalreaction to the conformist individualism of the postwar bourgeois family that had stifled the childhoods of many of its pioneers.[27] That's likely to be less of a problem in the future, at least in open country, but the back-to-the-land communities didn't particularly escape the interpersonal power problems familiar from kin-based ways of living. To me, there's little virtue in advocating for one over the other. Hopefully, there will be experimentation and different structures that might suit different people. There are different ways to walk the path of our common flawed humanity.

Recent times have seen the development of various frameworks under labels like restorative or transformative culture and nonviolent communication geared to improving communication and resolution of conflict between people and within groups, building on older spiritual traditions.

Part of this involves connecting to people's needs and finding mutually acceptable workarounds to impasses without over-generalized labelling or who-did-what inquisitions – an approach that can build co-operation even in conflict-ridden and politically polarized situations.

On our farm, we've drawn on these approaches to try to create a more transformative culture between individuals and households. Something as simple as an explicit agreement for a 'no blame, no shame' approach to raising and responding to interpersonal tensions has been quite effective (though inevitably not perfect). But it's taken a lot of time and effort to build this culture (transaction costs, again). It's not a matter of paying lip service to an idea, but of developing relationships over time that embody it.

One impetus for it was that something of a 'them and us' culture had developed in respect of my wife and I being the ultimate owners of the land and therefore in a position of higher power. The power differential is real, and it isn't abolished by adopting a transformative framework.

But it's not the only fact that matters about interpersonal relationships in the community. Adopting a transformative framework on the basis that everyone's voice is equal in this group of people who are interacting in this moment here and now has generated a lot of positive, problem-solving community feeling. To some degree, the preceding 'them and us' culture was prompted by my wife's and my own apologetic approach to our owner/founder power and the undervaluation of the historical work we'd put in to making the farm productive and inhabitable.

In his interesting essay 'Of Torture in Primitive Societies', the anthropologist Pierre Clastres described some of the ordeals and painful scarring rituals in certain Indigenous cultures as a way of inscribing upon people, literally, what he called 'the law of primitive society ... *You are worth no more than anyone else; you are worth no less than anyone else.*'[28]

We're yet to take that radical approach to corporate branding on our farm. But however it's expressed, what I'm emphasizing is the benefit of living by a form of the liberalism that I criticized in chapter 1, along the lines that, within the groups that claim our allegiance, who's right or wrong is less important than the fact that we have to get along, that our voices all count in how we do that, and that this requires the cultivation of grace. I don't see this practical liberalism as contradictory to my larger anti-liberal position because I'm not proposing that society at large should be organized in this expansively neutral way – just that it's usually a worthy interpersonal aim with its face-to-face subgroups.

A possible criticism of this practical liberalism is that it works as a veil for power inequalities. The claim may be that no one's voice counts for more than anyone else's, but is that how things actually work? This is always a good question to ask, and the answer is usually no. However, there's a danger of proceeding too quickly from there to an uncritical utopianism – overthrow the hidden power structure to implement a 'real' equality that turns out to be another form of inequality with its own authoritarianism and ideological veiling. A gentler approach commends itself. The claim that everyone's voice is equal may be never fully realizable, but its public manifestation gives leverage for realizing it more.

Some of the more enduring modern land-based communities have been ones with a practical grounding in land work and a religious focus, often arising out of deep histories of radical religious communalism such as the Amish and the Mennonites. Though sometimes out of stranger and more complex histories, such as the Doukhobors, who delighted Leo Tolstoy with their communal peasant anarchism as an apparently living example and vindication of his political ideas, without the great man realizing that it had to some degree been imposed by their charismatic authoritarian leader's recent embrace of Tolstoy's very politics.[29]

A more recent example is the Bruderhof communities (again, the kinship metaphors – Bruderhof meaning place of brothers) with a radically collective ethos and ownership in common, although still with family-based organization. These Christian communitarians, who fled the blood-and-soil kinship extremism of the Nazis rather than submit to their nationalist education, have many similarities with the Catholic Workers in the US, the latter emerging out of the distributist movement I've been drawing on in this book. The Catholic Workers have a more radical and egalitarian edge than their distributist forerunners in England and have shown more historical endurance. Other distributist-minded/counter-cultural small farms can be found throughout the industrialized world.[30]

In common with older craft movements reacting to the onset of mass industrialism, these movements emphasize practical work, individual or workshop-based craftmanship, degrees of voluntary poverty and an ethos of shared community that distinguishes them from the market or state collectivism of mainstream liberal politics – the distinction I mentioned between communities and publics in the introduction.

Such communitarian thinking has long been subjected to the derision of industrialists and industrially minded socialists. Karl Marx and Friedrich Engels devoted a section of *The Communist Manifesto* to criticizing this kind of 'reactionary', 'feudal' or 'petty- bourgeois' socialism. Perhaps that was a forgivable mistake in the nineteenth century when mass industrial society seemed to be carrying all before it and the idea of 'scientific' social progress was less tarnished. I think it's less forgivable now.

A key practice of the more specifically religious variants of the communitarianism I'm talking about is worship. And, with that, a sense of the possibility of human redemption on Earth involving, as well as its religious elements, a re-enchanted sense of shared community free from the social antagonisms and instrumental economic relationships of modern life – the idea of the 'beloved community' popularized by Martin Luther King, Jr.

Some argue that such visions don't need to be specifically religious: 'Romantic sacramentalism has evoked communist, anarchist and artisanal visions, so pioneers of a postcapitalist future can draw on a rich imaginative trove of property forms and beloved communities.'[31] Alas, at present that trove has largely remained imaginative; it's struggled to realize itself in the face of Promethean mass industrialism. The same can be said of beloved religious communities, but the difference is that they're less susceptible to the Promethean temptation of worshipping the power of human industrialism and self-creation, because they orient to the transcendent as a gift emanating from a higher power (see chapter 10).

Either way, it's likely that all of this – our visions of the future, our sense of community, our sense of love, our sense of the transcendent – will be rigorously stress tested in the meta-crisis that's upon us. People will be obliged to ask themselves afresh – who are my people? Who is my community? What do I worship? Where is home? Through our sense of kin and family, and through our sense of community and politics, we find ways to connect with one another, and we find ways to distinguish ourselves from one another. The answers to these questions and the ways that we choose to unite and divide ourselves will, of course, be consequential for the shape of the dark-age future

CHAPTER 6

Land

In the future, more people will spend more of their time producing the necessities of life directly from their local landscapes, waterscapes and airscapes than is generally the case today. This activity will encompass the production of food and medicines, fibre for clothes, energy, construction and other material objects, and fertility to sustain all those other things.

This book isn't about the practical details of how that will be done. It's more about the social structures within which it'll be done, and that's the main focus of this chapter. There isn't a single best way to organize either the practicalities or the social structures worldwide. But I'd argue there are better and worse ways of thinking about the issues, and in this chapter, I'll try to highlight what some of those are.

To confront a worse one straight away, the problem we face and the problem that future dark-age people will face is not how to feed the world, how to save the world, how to cut the most carbon, how to produce the most calories on the smallest area, or other similar global-quantitative framings favoured by what I've called the 'world environmental problems framework'. Philip Loring writes, 'Only in the industrial, colonial way of thinking do solutions for producing food or managing environments need to be uniform, scalable and deployable to all corners of the map.'[1] Just so. A better way of thinking is to ask: how do we produce food or manage our surroundings *here*?

To begin answering that, it's always useful to examine how people produced food and managed their surroundings here in the past, before the uniform and scalable high-energy routines of the liberal-modern state imposed its world-conquering grids. That doesn't mean we should do exactly the same today, or in the future. There are some new skills and scientific knowledges we've gained. There are likely also – can we admit this? – some old skills and scientific knowledges we've lost.

Also, the surroundings have changed, the climate has changed, populations have changed. And, even in preindustrial times, colonialisms of more local or more global kinds still limited people's room to manoeuvre. Contemporary narratives of impoverished bygone peasantries invite us to celebrate our modern progress away from land-based livelihoods, but – perhaps deliberately – they divert the gaze from the people who were doing the impoverishing. It's not as if their type has vanished.

Yet even those narratives haven't been enough to extinguish a very modern yearning for land. For example, within living memory here in Britain, ordinary people organized to get access to land for food production and to create land-based livelihood communities against the backdrop of economic depression and the great imperial firestorms of world war.[2] Much of that social energy declined with industrial growth and suburbanization in the postwar years and, despite the present twilight of that postwar industrial age, organized activism around land-based livelihoods in Britain remains quite niche. I believe that will change.

Anyway, the wider point is that, in the past, people faced the problem of how to generate a livelihood locally using mostly low-energy local means and had to organize themselves accordingly. We face similar problems now. So perhaps we can learn something from them.

Imagine yourself, then, occupying open country and establishing your household as the high-energy, liberal-modern state loses its grip and we step more fully into the uncertain territory of the new dark ages.

Your main farming strategy will be gardening – by which I mean growing vegetables and fruits alongside grains and other 'staple' crops in garden or small-field settings – supplemented by livestock and woodland integrated into this horticultural ecology.[3] In places with low population pressure on land, there will be relatively more livestock and relatively less gardening. In places with high population pressure, the opposite will be the case. You'll need to find ways of maintaining the fertility of the lands you're working. Metals, plastics, high-tech electronics and many other farm inputs easily available today like manufactured fertilizer will either be unavailable or their prices will be spiking rapidly.

This is the context in which we must speak of issues like access to land and systems of ownership and land management in the future. A lot of the old debates – private or public, the state or the market? – will have fallen away, or at least will be framed very differently. But their underlying concern – how do we best create fair livelihood and prosperity alongside and along with other people – will be the same.

Let's look at land access and ownership in that light.

Owning the Earth

A couple of things to get straight at the outset. First, people don't own the earth. The earth owns us. This is a truth that's been known, among many others, by the Norse farmers of the post-Roman Dark Ages we met in the preface. A good deal of modern culture consists of attempts to deny this, which are ultimately futile. Still, for practical day-to-day purposes, societies need arrangements about who can do what with which resources, and this is what property or ownership pragmatically means.

Second, those arrangements imply some level of agreement within a society or community. There's no such thing as 'natural' property rights. Also, if property has to be continuously defended by force, it's not property – the property agreements have broken down. The agreements may not have been made on fair or equal terms, and they may be subject to continual renegotiation, sometimes backed by force. But to speak of property is to speak of a situation in which people usually behave de facto as if they agree with the arrangements.

Broadly, it's conventional to divide property into three types: common, private and public. Let's take a brief look at each.

I discussed common property or 'the commons' in chapter 4. A commons can be defined as a resource (like land) plus a community (the people with an interest in the resource) plus a set of social protocols (who is allowed to do what with the resource). The important thing about it is that no single person owns the resource.

In practice, commons can admit to different underlying ownership structures. Arguably, the wood commons on my farm that I described in chapter 4 isn't a commons because my wife and I ultimately own it. Actually, that's not quite true. To get picky about legal niceties, it's the king who ultimately owns it. But in practice, the king abdicates all significant property rights of freehold land to the freeholder. And, on our farm, we as freeholders in turn abdicate certain rights over wood in common to its residents, but not to other people.

Historically, a lot of commons have been structured in similar ways via agreed de facto rights of appropriation in respect of people who do not formally own them. Sometimes, this involves the remnants of older relationships where ownership was more definitive and unequal, as in the British example of freeholders and the king. There will probably be a lot of decayed remnants of older property relations like this in the dark-age future.

In other situations, there's no underlying 'ultimate' owner except the commoners themselves. But it's worth appreciating that historically commons often represented usage agreements between large-scale landowners and ordinary people. In Europe, many emerged in late medieval or early modern times as economies monetized and heated up. They weren't some original birthright of ordinary people reaching back to time immemorial, even if the idea of such a birthright remains an important narrative around which ordinary people can mobilize occupancy claims.[4]

It often takes a good deal of time and intimate local knowledge to figure out effective local commons around things like wood harvesting, grazing, hunting, fishing and irrigation. You need to know a lot about the local seasonal cycles of the relevant resource and about longer-term disturbances such as fire, flood and changing migration patterns of wildlife. You need to know a lot, also, about how this resource fits into local people's livelihoods and seasonal needs, and what kinds of tensions and rule-breaking may exist in the local community. But all this can be done. Sometimes it *has* to be done if the local community is even to survive. In other situations, the commons is more like a bonus or a safety net.

TURNING TO PRIVATE property, on the face of it this differs from a commons in that ownership and use isn't collective. Only an individual or a restricted group is permitted to use the resource.

But it's not quite so simple. In fact, the definition I gave above for a commons pretty much works for private property too – a resource plus a community plus a set of usage protocols. It's just that in this case the community structures the usage protocols around appropriation rights over the resource to a restricted group along the lines that 'we the community agree that this resource is yours to use in this way'. It's important to understand this. If I claim to 'own' something privately and expect others to take me seriously, then I'm saying that I'm in relationship with a community that's agreed to confer exclusive usage rights to me in respect of the thing I own. Private ownership is basically just a particular form of commons.

I'll caveat this again by saying that 'the community' doesn't necessarily speak with one voice. Some people usually have more power than others to organize property in their private favour. I'll come to that shortly, but the point remains that private property in principle simply involves a restricted right to make use of a resource – and numerous societies have accorded such rights historically worldwide in many different guises. It's virtually impossible not to.

Limitations can be put around private rights, so that ownership doesn't necessarily confer total power over a resource. With land, for example, there may be a private right to grow crops and derive the benefit from doing so, but not to build houses, mine for minerals or restrict other people's access. Property often involves a bundle of differently framed rights.

Liberal-modernist states have developed an extremist form of private property in land, in which rights over the owned thing are considered exclusive ('Get off my land!') and abusive ('It's my land and I'll do what I like with it!'). Not only that, but in this conception, property is aggregable: there's no theoretical limit on how much a given private property owner can have. And also abstractable, accumulative and speculative: land can be transformed into theoretical units like money and credit that can create relationships of power and dependency stretching into the future.

This extremist modern form of private property is built on the foundations of Roman law – a legal code befitting a predatory, patriarchal, colonial, expansionist, slaveholding empire. With the necessary amendments and updates, it's served modern capitalist societies, which have most of those characteristics, pretty well. But it's only one form of private property – unfortunately, an especially ecocidal and antisocial version that's come to dominate the world because of its ability to generate abstracted, quantitative wealth and create future dependencies.⁵

So, while it's often said that private property is an invention of, and exclusive to, modern capitalist societies, this isn't the case – only a particular extreme form of it. Even foraging (hunter-gatherer) societies that find little place for private property in everyday life, organizing most land use through wider commons, often organize sacred knowledge as private property, exclusive to subgroups within society.⁶

Individual or family private ownership of land is quite common in societies that depend heavily on producing food, fibre and other material necessities directly from the land through intensive forms of farming like horticulture rather than, say, foraging, especially when they organize themselves relatively equitably, without corporate-state power maintaining monopoly private landownership. For example, anthropologist Robert Netting described individual landownership, fixed land boundaries, inheritance and litigation of boundary disputes among the Kofyar people of Nigeria, and generalized from this example as follows:

> *Where land is a scarce good that can be made to yield continuously and reliably over the long term by intensive methods, rights approximating those of private ownership will develop.*⁷

This is corroborated by worldwide evidence. Here in England, for example, research suggests that farmsteads with private property rights over surrounding land go as far back as the Neolithic (the 'New Stone Age', when farming became predominant), persisting through the Bronze Age, Iron Age and Roman periods into the post-Roman 'Dark Ages', with the first documentary evidence of private property from the seventh century suggesting it was already a long-established practice.⁸

There's a world of difference between agrarian or horticultural societies like these based on widely distributed private property, and capitalist ones based on monopoly or oligopoly ('rule of the few') property ownership geared to the accumulation of liquid capital. The generic term 'private property' is too broad in that sense.

The word 'private' shares an etymological root with words like 'deprived' or 'privation', suggesting a lack. Private property rights are a good way of organizing a lot of day-to-day activity, but societies that organize themselves excessively through private ownership, especially accumulative private ownership, are lacking something. This is what's impelling us toward a dark-age future.

Therefore, there's a case for preventing the excessive accumulation of private property. This would place private property in the service of wider society – a sense of 'the common good'. As the name implies, the distributist approach I favour does this. It emphasizes distributed private property, along the lines of the kind of horticultural societies Netting describes.

One of the challenges such societies face – and distributist economic philosophy faces – is keeping property distributed, because it's easy for it to become less distributed over time. With a throw of the dice – bad health, bad luck or bad choices with unanticipated outcomes – somebody's land-based livelihood can fail. This may lead to loss of land and the means of prosperity for themselves and possibly for their descendants, while others accumulate property to their advantage and subordinate the losers to their landed power. The game of Monopoly was originally designed to demonstrate this. Everybody starts out equal, but throwing the dice of life means that one person eventually cleans up. I'll discuss some defences against this kind of concentration in the next section.

※※※

A FEW WORDS ON the third form of ownership – public. The ultimate logic of this is that instead of ownership by many (distributism) or ownership by few (oligopoly, capitalism) there is monopoly ownership by one single authority – the state. Calling this 'public' ownership suggests the monopoly is directed toward the interests of everyone, or at least of those citizens or publics entitled to claim rights against the state. One of the critiques of this is that, in practice, the state has its own independent interests and tends to ally with particular subsections of the population. So 'the public interest' is not necessarily the same as 'the common good'. Monopoly power easily becomes oligopoly power. The state-corporate nexus of contemporary global capitalism is a case in point.

The distributist argument in general is that we should strive to distribute ownership and control back to people and communities. My dark-age twist on that argument is that centralized states are and will be losing their monopoly powers of control and command, turning into more limited and localized power centres – the solar system or galactic model discussed in chapter 2. While it's hard to imagine dispensing with public ownership, or at least with tight forms of state control, in modern societies with massive, high-tech, multilayered systems for delivering services to vast populations who lack the means to furnish them for themselves, this is our direction of travel. It makes the case for distributism and building local powers and capacities all the more urgent.

Keeping Ownership Distributed

How, then, can we keep ownership in the hands of the many? I'll begin ground-up from my local setting, with the unlikely starting point of a tale about a freezer. In fact, two freezers.

When we upgraded the off-grid electricity supply on our farm, we decided we could probably run a second freezer from it. A freezer is a pretty high-tech, high-energy modern gizmo, which isn't widely available to many people worldwide today, and will probably be available to many fewer in the future. But meanwhile, it's a useful appliance on the farm for storing food and evening out the seasonal peaks and troughs of produce. In some ways, it's a technology of individualization. Without it, people would probably have to invest more in mechanisms of wider sharing to achieve the same result, although that's not always easy in seasonal climates where everybody faces the same peaks and troughs at the same time.

Anyway, one of the reasons we bought the extra freezer was because there were more people on the farm and we wanted them to have some storage space. Around the same time, we were doing some rethinking of our home economics. The freezer is one small thread in the farm's wider story, which, as I mentioned earlier, has involved my wife and I turning the place from a bare field into a residential and commercial operation with cropland, buildings and other infrastructure, all of which requires a mixture of money and time to establish and maintain.

Bringing other people into the project has been a trial-and-error process, always against the backdrop of the bad economics of food production. We briefly experimented with a two-year market gardening opportunity, involving in the first year working set hours for a stipend plus accommodation, some board and a learning curriculum, and then working as the main market grower/manager in the second year with a 90 per cent share of the market garden income plus accommodation. But our 10 per cent share didn't cover the costs of materials and our work in providing and maintaining the larger infrastructure and curriculum, so we moved to implementing a site residence fee to better cover this – though still not covering it entirely.

A tension arose with one or two of the young people on the programme in respect of this fee, or 'rent' as they called it. Part of this was around a sense that the fee was too high for the rather rustic and homespun nature of what we were offering. We discussed with them the costs of running the operation, and the small details of that, like using freezer space, came up in the conversation. From their point of view, the freezer was 'ours' and their use of it was no cost to us. However, somebody ultimately has to bear the time and money costs of providing infrastructure. Systems built on one-way responsibility usually breed ill feeling, and don't last.

We've changed things around on the site since that time and no longer offer the two-year opportunity – although currently we're in the fortunate position of being able to make the existing market garden available for others to run as their own business at zero rent. We've also, as I mentioned in the previous chapter, established a better framework for managing tensions. Perhaps part of the tensions arose from youthful naivety about the costs of running an off-grid household, business and farm, along with an understandable youthful resentment about the seeming impossibility of ever being able to afford to own a farm themselves.

Here we arrive at the bad economics of food, land and energy – in fact, the bad economics of modern society in general, which stacks the odds particularly against the young, and more generally against anyone who tries to swim against the current and provide most kinds of basic service (like food) in low-input, local ways. This bad economics manifests at the individual level in the form of tensions between people offering such services – tensions about freezers, for example – and at the ideological level in the form of misleading views about the 'inefficiency' of small-scale local enterprise.

The basics of this bad economics can be simply stated: food and energy prices are too low, while land and housing prices are too high. I've calculated, for example, that for a low-input agroecological market grower employing a worker at the minimum wage, that worker would have to produce and sell something like 60 kilograms of parsnips or 110 lettuces each day just for the employer to break even on wage costs. This is quite a tall order. And, oversimplifying somewhat, for the wage price of the physical work done by one farm employee, a diesel-fuelled small tractor could do the equivalent of nearly 700 people's work.[9] Meanwhile, when my wife and I bought our land, the price of agricultural land in our area was about £3,000 per acre, whereas now it's about £15,000 – an annual increase of about 9 per cent. Bare agricultural land with permission for volume housebuilding can sell for over £1 million per acre before a single brick has been laid.[10]

These figures hopefully help to explain in a nutshell why historically in Britain tractors have generally been getting bigger, lengths of hedgerows smaller, wildlife scarcer, horticultural work harder to find, fruit and vegetables more imported, volume housing poorer in quality and more cramped, greenhouse gas emissions higher and agricultural landowners richer – but only if they can cash out of farming. Maybe they also help to explain why, for different reasons, younger and older people who work the land get salty about things like freezers.

In a saner and more renewable economy, people would be able to earn enough from producing food to afford secure and decent housing, diesel use would be decreasing and so would stress levels in agriculture and wider society. Unfortunately, there is no trend or driver toward that kind of economy at present and those who want to live low-tech, low-input, land-based lifestyles have to find ways to navigate this, typically by decommodifying where possible, for example by emphasizing in-kind benefits and direct means of livelihood-making like growing their own food, rather than getting too wrapped up in the mainstream commodity price system. In the long term, most people will probably have to do this, hence the dark-age future. Hence also, perhaps, the light to be found in it. But, despite these benefits of more local futures, we'll still have to be clear about who's paying for the freezer, or whatever replaces it.

THE PROBLEM OF landlordism stalks the examples I've just given from my farm. Why is landlordism a problem, and so widely disliked? Not so much because the landlord charges fees to users who don't own the land or its appliances long-term – people rarely object to tool hire or car hire companies whose models exactly parallel this. But whereas a tool or a car (or a freezer) eventually degrades and becomes valueless, this doesn't happen to land. In the long-run, its value only seems to increase – and its owners seem to do nicely out of it without putting much work in.

This arises partly because land is limited – a fictitious commodity (see Fictitious Commodities, page 51) – usually enabling landlords to charge over the odds for it. Economists call this 'economic rent': an amount paid to a factor of production that's more than should be necessary to keep that factor in its present use. Tool or car hire companies find it harder to charge economic rent because other companies can bring other tools or cars into the market, whereas people can't really bring more land into the market locally. (Other people can often bring more agricultural land into food production somewhere else in the country or in the world where land is cheap and abundant, and export into your local food market. This creates many problems, including agricultural overproduction and needless expansion.) As the saying goes: 'Buy land, they ain't making it anymore.' But most people are priced out of buying land precisely for that reason.

One idea for dealing with this unearned advantage of landlordism is to tax away the economic rent via a land value tax. This was popularized long ago by Henry George (1839–1897) in his book *Progress and Poverty*.[11] George was careful to distinguish between the unearned, economic rent portion that landlords charge, what's usually known as ground rent, and the portion that more directly parallels the situation of a tool or car hire company – a fair recompense for services rendered.

Hence the flashpoint with the freezer in the case of our farm. The freezer is a good providing a service. It will degrade in time, and somebody has to pay for its lifetime costs. Paying for it does not involve economic rent.

A landlord owning residential property in a high-rent city earns mostly economic rent. The costs of maintaining the property – providing freezers and so forth – is low relative to income earned. Whereas if you set up a farm on more-or-less bare land, everything – access tracks, freezers, houses, outbuildings, tools, trees, cropland, water supply, energy supply – has to be set up from scratch and maintained at a cost.

I stress this because when you're the person doing the setting up this becomes obvious, whereas if you're a person in modern society accustomed to commercial rents then it's easy mentally to merge user fees with economic rent as exemplary of a generic and disliked landlordism.

This problem runs deeper than just landlordism. So many features of modern society and its high-energy material plenty involve economic rent and an unsustainable drawing down upon natural ecosystems and other people's labour when traced back to their source. Society is awash with surplus capital generated in this way, not least in the net fiscal transfer from the Global South to the Global North, nonrenewable drawdowns upon nature and in the financialized 'fictitious capital' that's generated in Wall Street, the City of London and the like.[12] The circa seventyfold difference I mentioned above between the price of farmland and housing land in my area reflects this overcapitalization or 'capital surplus absorption problem' – too much money looking for too few safe returns.

So, the issue isn't just landlordism as such. The circulation between salaried income, housing equity and consumer spending in which many people who aren't landlords are involved is part of the same problem. The relatively wealthy populations of the Global North float on a sea of economic rent. It's easy not to notice if you draw a salary for an apparently productive job (such as my previous one of university teacher), but it's there. Landlordism is only one especially obvious version of this wider overcapitalization problem.

This is why Henry George's single land value tax approach isn't an adequate solution to the problem of economic rent as a defence against our present dark-age economic and ecological trajectory, even if it could work well enough as a component of distributist fiscal policy for keeping landownership distributed. Land value tax only disincentivizes one form of capital accumulation – landlord's economic rent – but is relaxed about and, in fact, incentivizes other forms. Under a Georgist tax regimen, our market garden would have to try to pay its way by maximizing farm income, probably through such means as high energy and water use, heated polytunnels, mechanization and so on, or else through engrossment into a bigger and more highly mechanized cereal farm. There's no contradiction between land value tax and an accumulative and extractive capitalism.

LAND

THERE ARE VARIOUS other modern defences against speculation designed to protect land. Community land trusts and similar nonprofit vehicles can in principle also be used – though not always so easily in practice, because the temptation to turn land over to higher profits from residential rents and their equivalents such as eco-courses is strong. In more traditional agrarian societies, kinship corporations can have the same defensive function. Family land can't be easily bought or sold. It's kept in perpetuity as agricultural land for the benefit of the family.

The basic structure of land corporations like these is akin to a commons – with similar strengths and weaknesses. In practice, they often cede day-to-day land management to smaller units like households/families, but with larger collective responsibility and the power to sell/alienate the land vested in the corporate group. An important question from the point of view of any individual or smaller unit is whether the larger group's power becomes oppressive. Subsidiarity again is relevant, with its impetus to cede as much decision-making power to the lower levels and the higher levels charged with maintaining the wider common good.

As well as keeping land distributed horizontally within living generations, the distribution of land vertically down the generations demands attention. Inheritance is critical to the concentration of advantage. For example, if women are unable to inherit land in their own right, this obviously limits their economic power greatly in agrarian societies. The same applies when somebody accumulates economic advantage and can then pass this on to their descendants. Over time, this can lock in the advantage structurally.

Death or estate taxes are one way to limit inherited advantage. They have to be set high and made hard to dodge to be effective. They also require the tax-raising authority to support relative equality, and for taxpayers to judge the tax-raising authority as a trustworthy custodian of the wider good. On this latter point, ordinary people in agrarian societies – peasants, small farmers and so forth – are stereotypically untrusting toward government, often with good reason, preferring family autonomy and inheritance of small plots, with their own cultural markers concerning their identification with local land ('the property owned the owners').[13]

As I mentioned earlier (From Liberalism to Distributism, page 21), this is currently a lively issue in British farming politics arising from the government's recent imposition of inheritance tax on farmland above certain thresholds at a reduced rate. The problem with this is not the principle but the gross disparities between farm incomes and land values for the overcapitalization reasons mentioned above, making it hard to secure inheritance of an intact working farm. The likely beneficiaries will be corporations, which never die and which therefore don't pay the tax, and rich non-farming buyers who can still gain a tax advantage. For inheritance tax on land to work as intended, food and energy prices need to be higher, land and housing prices need to be lower, communities need to trust governments or tax-raising authorities, and corporations as well as individuals need to be disbarred from the over-accumulation of land and other resources.

Ideas like land value tax and inheritance tax are good as far as they go as ways of directing the flow of capital more fairly and beneficially within heavily capitalized societies. But where capital has melted away – as I've argued is likely to be the case in the future – they're less to the point. In that situation, people would have more of a free hand to generate what are sometimes called 'moral economies': worlds of livelihood-making based on a wider view of the common good than the quantitative bottom line of commodity prices. The lifehouses and kinship-structured societies I described in earlier chapters are versions of this, spreading land availability locally.

There's a danger in this situation that these local economies could be undermined by remaining footloose capital penetrating from outside.[14] If it's necessary to develop state fiscal policies to discipline incoming capital and prevent that, the battle has probably already been lost and the local moral economy will be gone soon enough. In this situation, there's already too much footloose capital in the system to sustain the moral economy. Besides, owners of capital are usually better at allying with states and co-opting their fiscal policies than small landowners. This is the equivalent problem in relation to economic regulation of private finances as the corporate-friendly quasi-socialism I mentioned in chapter 5 (Families, page 71) and its social regulation of family businesses. For better or worse, the defence of distributed landed economies has to be won in the sphere of kinship, as I've already discussed, and also in the spheres of political and moral communities, which I turn to in later chapters.

TO ANTICIPATE SOME OF those arguments, one approach is to press harder on the cultural inviolability of land. In modern legal thinking, this has been done by developing 'Earth rights' or 'rights of nature' frameworks to give legal teeth to the defence of species, habitats, Earth systems or entities like rivers. I see this as a modern example of Luddism – a word I invoke positively and not, as is usually the case, pejoratively. Like the medieval peasants who resisted the usurpation of community resources, or like the machine-breaking Luddites of nineteenth-century England, the idea is to protect existing ecologies, including human ecologies, from the blandishments of modern 'progress' ideologies that rarely benefit most people, still less the natural world.

The logic of Luddism says no, stop, enough, you can't destroy this valued thing on the basis of some quantitative and inherently questionable claim to be implementing something bigger and better, whether the valued thing is a local small-farm economy, a community of workers, a wild habitat and so on. But ultimately, it has to be something more systemic – and ideally something more systemically grounded in its local ecological base – than piecemeal legal victories or acts of sabotage that melt into the night.

A final approach is to spend capital quickly so that it can't accumulate and work its mischief. A calendar crammed with holidays, feasts and carnivals is one way this has been achieved historically. Another is to channel capital into low-carbon, human-intensive, socially useful ends – education and skills sharing, social support, healthcare and, of course, farming and gardening.

There's no great difficulty in dreaming up such schemes to keep destructive capital and abstraction in its place. The problem lies in whether they can be implemented: these are not projects of the centralized liberal-modernist state or those who would claim to run it for the benefit of the people. So, who will deliver them?

We'll consider that as we progress through the rest of the book. I'll just note that the dark-age optic I've been using, particularly in its 'open country' mode, may offset these difficulties a little. We're not talking about a situation in which confident nation-states with a growing command of resources and political power are calling all the shots.

CHAPTER 7

A Dark-Age Distributism

I've now laid out the basic elements for understanding access to land. It's time to put them in motion in relation to future scenarios.

Imagine some generic village community, maybe here in South West England where I live, trying to get by as the welfare-capitalist state and its supply chains orchestrated from London a few days' walk away slowly crumble.

The village, its households and its land – the vegetable allotments and horse paddocks on the edge of town, the farmers' fields and remaining patches of woodland beyond it, the gardens and little greens within, and the occasional smallholding dotted here and there – have become of increasingly intense interest recently as other sources of food, fibre and fertility from the wider world have grown scarcer and dearer.

There will be collaborative experiments in breaking ground, growing food and sharing resources. We've helped start something along these lines on our own farm now that we've handed the market garden onto younger hands, establishing a group of friends and neighbours to share growing a rotation of potatoes, cereals, alliums, squash and brassicas in small teams.

As with the wider farm community (see Communities, page 85), we agreed a 'no blame, no shame' culture around mistakes and failures. This proved just as well in my case after an unfortunate crop loss visited upon me by badger spirits. No blame and no shame is an easy game to play at the moment, since none of us will starve whatever the outcome. But as the stakes in producing a local livelihood get higher, the game may get harder. It will be interesting to see how our experiment unfolds.

On the one hand, multi-household sharing can operate as a form of insurance. On the other, history teaches us that agrarian societies generally merge the producers with consumers in the same household for the reasons discussed earlier. Substantially individual or household/family rights of resource or livelihood appropriation have been ubiquitous worldwide historically. Even heavily managed and rigorously egalitarian systems such as the Andean *ayllu* associations ceded day-to-day livelihood autonomy to the subsociety of the family – and according to some interpretations *were* themselves families in the form of kin corporations related by lineal descent. The notion that the individuated household/family as unit of production is some weird affectation of modern Europe and its offshoots must be laid to rest.[1]

In fact, managed egalitarianism transcending the immediate household/family unit also occurred in Europe, for example in credit-based commercial accounting with periodic 'jubilees' or equalization. But it was only extended to people who were locally known and considered skilled or trustworthy enough to bring something to the table – another kind of 'mutuality of being' (see Communities, page 85).[2] How do we build such distributed systems anew?

Well, certainly not by replicating the exclusive, abusive, commodified and accumulative property rights of the kind that *are* a weird affectation of modern Europe and its offshoots. For that reason, the residents of our future village would be well advised to ponder the issues I mentioned in the previous chapter to ensure that property rights remain distributed.

※※※

PRIVATE, HOUSEHOLD land is important, but so are commons. I argued earlier that commons can be hard to devise and require intimate knowledge of local ecologies and politics – the kind of knowledges often missing in modern settlements where people don't need to make a local, land-based livelihood. So, on the one hand, it's important to start building those knowledges straight away and developing commons geared to local livelihood-making. On the other, it's important not to rush it, or to overplay the importance of commons at the expense of private household access to land. People will save themselves a lot of time and tension if they focus on activities that particularly lend themselves to commoning (see the list in Commons, page 64) – for example, seed saving, grazing, firewood collection, hunting, fishing and river rights, postharvest gleaning and irrigation – and on resource protocols that fit both the activity itself and local culture.

In this context, Tyson Yunkaporta distinguishes between 'high-context' oral cultures, such as his own Australian Aboriginal one, and 'low-context' print-based cultures. The former, he says, 'have no isolated variables: all thinking is dependent on the field or context', while the latter focuses on ideas and objects in isolation, where reasoning 'is hierarchical, solitary and disconnected, making it possible for communication to be one-way in the form of rants, instruction and, most importantly, orders'.[3]

I'd argue there are ways that print-based cultures can become higher context, and the judicious creation of well-functioning local commons is one of them, involving high-context procedures such as, in Yunkaporta's words again, 'dialogue and complex agreements' that 'use a lot of non-verbal communication and leave many things unspoken due to common shared understandings and established consensus about the way things are done'.[4] But this is almost the antithesis of our present legalistic liberal-modernist world of the book and the law emanating from the sacred centre of the nation-state. So, it won't be achieved overnight. We need to develop those common understandings through livelihood practice rather than rushing to create commons and other collective arrangements at the outset and doing it badly because we're still operating in low-context ways that don't understand the complexities of the local ecology, including our own human one.

Hence there's a kind of hybridity to the dark-age distributism I'm proposing. On the one hand, bringing to light in 'low-context' ways the work and implicit debts we contribute or owe one another. On the other hand, aiming toward higher-context ways of relating to each other within the local culture of a functioning livelihood community.

Accessing Land

Imagine a scenario, then, where you're seeking occupancy rights in open country, like in the village setting with which I opened this chapter. Maybe it's the place you already live, maybe somewhere you've travelled to, most likely as part of a larger group, but somewhere where there are here-first landowners of uncertain strength relative to the powers of your group. You want land – how do you get it from them?

Obviously, much depends on the wider circumstances that have brought you together, but I'd suggest that a friendly attempt to negotiate fair terms would be a good starting point. Existing landowners are probably well aware of the advantages landownership theoretically confers and they may be keen to charge ground rent if they can. They may also be in a relatively weak bargaining position. Not only because of crashing financial systems and farm commodity supply chains, but also because – as I said earlier – private property is a property of communities, and in this situation who's included in the community and on what terms is suddenly up for grabs. Modern commercial farmers and landowners can't necessarily turn themselves overnight into the militarized landholding elites of bygone times. Therefore, existing landowners may have an interest in recruiting newcomers as potential local allies in the radically changing circumstances of the emerging dark-age politics.

In such situations, neat pre-existing theories about the evils of landlordism, the benefits of land value tax, the nature of class struggle or the war of all against all are less to the point than how you configure new relationships on the ground. Right now, you're unique participants in a complex drama of real human beings that you're helping to write, not rote performers of old lines.

Naturally, I can't say how these dramas will work out. What I can say is how I'd try to think about this as a local landholder mindful of the larger picture I've been sketching in this book.

The present realities mentioned earlier of low food prices, low energy prices and overcapitalized land prices, especially for volume housing development, will no longer be relevant. The global economy has crashed, volume housing developers have disappeared, farm input prices are spiking dramatically, wholesale markets for agricultural commodities have gone haywire, and there's a bunch of people on my doorstep wanting land to grow food and fibre for themselves.

I could resist their entreaties and carry on with my large-scale farming. Or I could accede and try to maximize my income from them as a landlord. Both options carry risks. What if I tried co-creating a local livelihood community with them? Also risky, but so is everything, especially now.

To develop such a community and its intensive horticultural infrastructures, people will need a long-term stake in the land and feel the arrangement is fair. Therefore, I'd be disinclined to charge them ground rent. The original capital endowment in the land arose out of a long-term history that's now melting away. Its value – £15,000 per acre, £1 million per acre, whatever – is becoming so much old hieroglyphics. Forget it. But my historical occupation and knowledge of the land counts for something, and I'm more inclined to defend that. I'd also want to think carefully about providing an endowment of land for my children.

In this new dispensation, I'd resist land value taxes and other charges levied by distant authorities in pursuit of lofty aims that forced me to monetize and commodify my land-based activities and to jump to somebody else's definition of productivity or efficiency. But I'd be intensely interested in supporting local political institutions that offered solidarity and services in my community and in paying my way into that as best I could.

I'd ask for rental payments (or at least a site residence fee) in whatever form I could agree mutually with the dwellers on the land to cover the costs of its buildings and infrastructure and my time and mental load in maintaining them, if that fell to me. I would want these dwellers to focus on producing food, fibre and other forms of material or non-material welfare locally, and not on earning income in the wider economy. So, if the present imbalance between low food prices and low incomes for care work on the one hand and high prices for land and labour in the wider economy persisted, I'd charge differential rents according to whether people were working in the former low-income, high-benefit sector or in the high-income, low-benefit one. In practice, these disparities would probably be fading rapidly in the emerging new world, so the differential rents would only be temporary.

Looking more widely, I'd contribute as best I could to developing effective local commons where they seemed the best way of improving the wellbeing of the community. I'd be guided in this by the thinking of the local people with the most experience of shared, local, land-based work, and more widely by whatever we could learn from elsewhere about well-functioning long-term commons. I'd also hope to support people with disabilities or want of various kinds – ideally through tangible access to the land and its resources, but if not then through supporting more collective local institutional solutions.

Writing as I have been here from the perspective of a local landholder, I must note that I've been assuming people who are seeking open country will be anxious to settle in *my* open country, and that we'll be benevolently disposed toward one another. I've also accorded myself a lot of power to call the shots in this scenario, not least in respect of addressing the social care needs of others I mentioned in the preceding paragraph.

Just to run a rule over those assumptions, I do believe that in the kind of challenging future I've been projecting, people will indeed be drawn to landscapes already terraformed to complex, small-scale, mixed-productive land uses. The predominant patterns of current land use that involve either a lot of asphalt and concrete (cities) or – their necessary counterpart – giant arable fields in the countryside terraformed to the proportions of large, fossil-fuelled machinery will be less attractive. Hence, some of the patterns I portrayed in our arc over future Earth in the introduction – relatively more people in east Kansas and New England, relatively fewer in west Kansas and New York. Relatively more in east Somerset, relatively fewer in London and East Anglia. Maybe my wife's efforts to grade our farm track in the digger that I mentioned earlier were a way of extending the welcome mat with the help of fossil fuels while they're still available.

The question of how benevolent the resulting social relations will be is something I already discussed in chapter 3. I freely admit it won't always be so. Even within the distributist movement, broadly conceived, there are forms of conservative distributism involving local landowner and business elites who are itching to give people a little land and have done with it. In this way, they stack the dice in the resulting Monopoly game in their own favour and set people up to fail. Ultimately, this generates a patron–client or neofeudal scenario with themselves in the patron role.

An alternative is some revolutionary overthrow of the landholders by the landless incomers. In that eventuality, the landholder power that I've been flexing in the foregoing scenario would be taken from me with the accusatory question ringing in my ears, 'Who do you think you are, trying to lay down the law about what's what around here?' The newly landed would then have the opportunity to lay down the law. If they did it wisely and justly, I'd suggest the result would likely be similar to the picture I just painted of my benevolent landholder society.

Either way, we're drawn into a world of village councils, voting systems, republican self-rule or Thomas Spence-style parishioner democracy. Or else of kinship and beloved communities. In all these cases, I believe there's little merit in trying to specify abstractly and ahead of time in a book like this, or a book like anything, the exact details of how I think it should work, which

– unlike the history of my own farm – isn't really my story to tell. In all of these scenarios, there's enormous scope for factionalism, power politics and tyranny. There's also enormous scope for co-operation, care and benevolence.

It seems likely that a lot of people will be facing questions of land occupancy and livelihood-making along these lines soon enough. Standard positions across the spectrum of liberal-modernist politics don't equip us to answer them well. What will matter will be defining a local politics of the common good with the real, complex people around us.

※※※

TO RUN WITH THE SCENARIO just mentioned of incoming landless people expropriating landowners, this is the situation addressed by the landless workers of Brazil – the MST –mentioned in chapter 5 (Of Patriarchs and Matrilines, page 80). The classic MST model is confrontational, involving 'cutting the wire' of large private estates and mass occupation of the land by groups of landless workers, the *sem terra*. The idea is partly about taking direct action to make land available, but also about creating various kinds of legal, political and media leverage.

For what it's worth, I support this kind of mass action to create land access where necessary and, as it were, to force open the country when it can't easily be opened in other ways. My hesitation isn't around cutting the wire so much as the way some political narratives romanticize the wire-cutting moment at the expense of specifics about how to create land-based livelihood communities in the long term after the wire has been cut.

Cutting the wire is symbolically important within the MST as a part of what it calls the *mística* of creating activist political communities.[5] I'm awed by the bravery of the people who do this in the face of often armed reaction – sometimes just bark, but sometimes murderous bite. Still, the larger lessons remain in what comes afterward. One plausible story that emerges from the MST's long experience of this is not to get overly caught up in modernist stories about collectivism, efficiency or beating large commercial operations at their own game, as propounded by some religious and political idealists within the movement, but instead to emphasize production for household needs, albeit set within a larger community of care and political action. 'We were not fighting for land to live out some rural idyll conceived by the priests,' in the words of one activist, 'but to grow food for our families and to improve our standard of living.'[6]

This is the key message I want to convey in this book. Effective, just and sustainable livelihoods revolve around semi-autonomous household production for its own needs within larger local collective institutions, whether this is achieved through polite negotiation, potentially violent occupation or through numerous modalities of taxation, landlordism or the creation of beloved communities. That's what needs to be worked out locally in fine empirical detail, starting right now.

Being Indigenous

A one-sentence summary of how people will orient to land in the dark-age future I'm projecting is 'learning to be indigenous' – or, as agrarian thinker Wes Jackson put it, 'becoming native to our places'.[7]

I'd emphasize the active verbs in those sentences: learning, becoming. As humans, we always have a degree of alienation from the wider natural world as a result of our ecology-disturbing methods of livelihood-making and our restless systems of symbolic thought – language, religion, money. We never really arrive at the serenity of just *being* indigenous or native. Perhaps the wise course is to treat this as both blessing and curse, neither trying too hard to overcome alienation and be at one with nature, nor overly embracing our alienation to worship ourselves as nature-transcending beings with limitless potential for reinvention.

What this means in practice is learning how to meet most of our needs for food, clothes, shelter, health and social connection adequately or abundantly, but not insatiably, not limitlessly. To a large extent, that means in turn learning to meet most of our needs from the relatively immediate surroundings that we and our local communities can act on directly as ecological agents.

All this raises questions about how it relates to existing Indigenous peoples.

Particularly in the anglophone world outside Britain itself, the historical context for this is genocidal processes of settler colonialism that parted Indigenous people from the land, typically justified by ideologies of settler superiority involving modern forms of racism.[8]

In progressive and ecologically minded thinking nowadays, that narrative has flipped, often positioning Indigenous people as having superior wisdom about living sustainably within local limits. There's a danger that this becomes another form of racism that presses Indigenous people into service as mere tokens of authenticity within an argument that liberal-modernism is having with itself rather than as real people living complex contemporary lives like everyone else. If this reversal is to have a critical edge that transcends this danger, it might be useful to home in on two specific components of contemporary Indigeneity, specifically: 1) low-impact, land-based livelihoods; and 2) self-determination.

Starting with the issue of low-impact livelihoods, there's a widely cited statistic that Indigenous peoples account for 5 per cent of the world's population and occupy 20 per cent of its land area, which is home to 80 per cent of its biodiversity. This, it turns out, is wrong, not least because it oversimplifies biodiversity into the idea of geographically countable units (again, we encounter the issue of spurious over-quantification).[9] Nevertheless, it seems likely that Indigenous peoples nominally occupy more land relative to their numbers than non-Indigenous populations, and that this land is disproportionately, although uncountably, biodiverse.

This is partly because many of the Indigenous people who haven't been physically or culturally obliterated by liberal-modernism live, not coincidentally, in places that liberal-modernism and its high-energy, growth-oriented, unsustainable economies haven't yet found a great deal of use for.

A more positive reason is that these people have generally done a good job of 'learning to be indigenous', of becoming native to their places. They've developed the kind of low-energy, low-input, low-impact local livelihood-making that I've been emphasizing in this book. It's complicated – not all Indigenous people necessarily follow what are regarded as indigenous livelihood practices, and there are political dangers involved in yoking 'Indigenous' as an identity tightly to 'indigenous' as a livelihood practice. Also, poverty mediated by racism can be another reason for low-impact lifeways. Still, we in liberal-modern societies can certainly learn from indigenous livelihood practices – not necessarily in terms of livelihood-making specifics that vary from place to place, but certainly in terms of general approach.[10]

A troubling aspect of much contemporary environmentalism, especially in its Promethean guises, is its odd dualism on this point. It usually embraces the idea that Indigenous people can or should follow low-input, local livelihood-making traditions, acting as land and biodiversity defenders. Yet the idea that the non-Indigenous global majority might also be land and biodiversity defenders, that pursuing low-input, local lifeways might also be an option for us, is widely dismissed as unrealistic – a view that's justified, if it's justified at all, via questionable Malthusian or neo-Malthusian assumptions about population or hunger.[11]

This dualism implicitly resurrects the old racism that low-input, local livelihood-making is okay for Indigenous (read: 'primitive') people, but isn't appropriate for we progressive, modern souls. And it puts a weighting on a binary concept of capital-I Indigeneity versus non-indigeneity that's surely heavier than it can bear. One way of life if you're capital-I Indigenous, another if you're not.

I don't accept this. Better, I'd argue, to try learning to be indigenous, to engage in the daily work of being an embodied, vulnerable human trying to create a livelihood as a protagonist within the wider local ecology. I believe this is the coming reality for most people in the world anyway, whether we like it or not. Might as well get started.

But that doesn't address the relationship between those many learning to be indigenous and those few who are already Indigenous by birth (not all of whom are 'indigenous' in the former sense). This relates to the second theme I raised – self-determination.

※※※

A LARGE ASPECT OF contemporary Indigenous politics concerns land rights, reclaiming land from settler-colonial appropriation and political self-determination as nations ('Land Back'). In other words, it's less about forming livelihood communities and more about forming publics claiming rights from the (settler-colonial) nation-state, to adopt the framing I used in the introduction.

This is well outside my area of expertise or local, lived experience. I'll just comment on a few aspects that are relevant to the wider themes of this book. Most importantly, Indigenous self-determination potentially represents an already-there example of the kind of political communities – republics, if you will – that I've been arguing must be constructed as alternatives to the liberal-modernist state. And although they're not necessarily livelihood communities as defined in chapter 1, they're probably closer to them than the standing start available to most of the communities that might be forged by non-Indigenous people out of the wreckage of the liberal-modernist nation-state. So, they contain important lessons.

If Indigenous nations stabilize themselves with respect to these declining nation-states, then they get to determine whether their country is open country to others, and to *which* others. Just as many liberal-modernist states have increasingly engaged in a lot of border-policing antics grounded implicitly or explicitly in ethnic exclusivity around who counts as a 'real' member of the nation, so that option may be available to Indigenous nations to close borders around 'real' Indigeneity. My hope is that political communities of all kinds will go easier on these narratives of authenticity. But my personal hopes are neither here nor there.

It seems likely in the future that some of the land inhabited by Indigenous people will be coveted by others seeking occupancy rights in open country. Although low population densities in Indigenous territories may stem partly from the fact that much of this land isn't easily made more productive and hence has survived in Indigenous people's hands, it's likely that some of it could support more people using locally appropriate, low-impact and people-intensive methods of livelihood production.

A bad outcome in this scenario would be a new wave of frontier settler-colonialism, overrunning Indigenous lands once more. I don't have great answers about how to prevent it. I'm not sure anyone does. But inasmuch as my arguments have endorsed an agrarian populism that, in North America particularly, is tainted historically by what some have described as a racist 'plain folks ideology', I reject that version of populism and seek other directions.[12]

One way to do that is to detach populism from wider cultural ideas about wealth accumulation and manifest destiny. Genuinely trying to be more indigenous, trying to build local livelihood communities, rather than embracing neo-Malthusian hero journeys and saviour narratives about rescuing the poor from their poverty would be a start. A Tsawout First Nation elder had this to say about *hwunitum*, a local word for white people, meaning 'the hungry ones',

My grandmother used to call them 'squati hwunitum.' Crazy white people. They wanted it all. They still do. Their greed is insatiable.[13]

We get back to the politics of 'just enough', and earning the right to consider ourselves indigenous, if not Indigenous.

※※※

HERE IN BRITAIN, there isn't anything that exactly replicates those settler-colonial issues in the wider anglophone world. There are parallels in Irish history and, closer to home, in Wales.

When my wife and I were looking for a little land to buy, I spent a while visiting properties in Wales, following the trail west pioneered by an earlier generation of English back-to-the-landers like John Seymour. I love Wales and have visited many parts of it countless times. But, back then, it didn't feel like open country to me. I didn't feel like it could be home, or that I'd feel welcome.

I may have been mistaken. In his superb account of Welsh culture and landscape, Carwyn Graves writes that in the Welsh-speaking world the idea that the Welsh are the native inhabitants of the land is the cornerstone on which the culture is built, but:

> *This is not an understanding that excludes others ... The primary barriers of inclusion and exclusion within this culture lie with language (rather than, for instance, race or ethnicity), a feature that anyone can learn and therefore be included. And this sense of nativeness manifests itself in a tendency to tie almost all parts of culture to place.*[14]

My guess is that the extent of this inclusiveness toward an English non-native Welsh speaker will vary from person to person and place to place, but nevertheless there's a plausible opening here into 'learning to be indigenous' or 'becoming native to one's place'.

That learning process requires some grace about what's already there. Since my prospective visit to Wales many years ago, a movement has arisen in Britain in favour of so-called 'rewilding' of upland pastoral land as an alternative to the overproduction of sheep. It's true that, in general, there's overproduction of sheep in the British uplands. But, as Graves shows, it's been imposed from without by the extractive modernist logic I've discussed elsewhere in this book. Associated government policies have created such monocultures of overproduction everywhere – too many sheep in upland Wales, too much wheat in East Anglia and Kansas, too much money in London and New York.

Rewilding has become a toxic idea in Wales, redolent of moneyed English people arriving as latter-day colonists with fixed 'low-context' visions about what's appropriate for landscapes seen as more or less a blank canvas. Graves shows that much greater agricultural and natural biodiversity persists in the Welsh countryside than meets the untutored eye, and lies as a wider latent potential if it can be liberated from the low-context fictions of land prices, money prices and generic ideas of wilderness.

Maybe that applies to culture more generally. In Manon Steffan Ros's postapocalyptic novel, *The Blue Book of Nebo*, a character reconnects with a Welsh-speaking heritage she lost as an adolescent when her starry eyes were fixed on the wider world and the global teenage culture of the Anglosphere. So, there are many starting points into learning to be native to place. Perhaps the most important thing is to choose one – and start.

CHAPTER 8

Making a Living

When my daughter was younger, I'd often walk with her to school. Often enough on these school-run mornings, I'd see a figure approaching along the footpath across the field, out for a run. Let's call him Cato. Cato was a proudly local man, who was usually looking to get one over me. He saw me as a kind of woke blow-in from the southeast, lacking any local authenticity. So much for not feeling welcome in Wales. Even in the village a hundred miles away where I grew up, I could hardly claim to be a 'real' local. This unreality is a fact of modern times that probably now applies to the majority of people worldwide. Which perhaps challenges the usefulness of real localness as a concept.

One morning, Cato effected his favoured path-blocking tactic. He had a question:

'Wood – good or bad?'

He knew we heated our house from the rainforest we'd planted, and the news cycle at that time was in quite a lather with the latest moral panic about the evils of wood-burning stoves, owned disproportionately by middle-class virtue signallers. Like me. Grist for Cato's mill.

Wood – good or bad? Well, there's a question. The kind of wood that's felled in forests across the world, pelletized and shipped by the millions of tonnes to England to be burned in the Drax power station to make 'sustainable' electricity that ticks government decarbonization metrics – yeah, that's quite bad. Whereas the ongoing cycle of thinning, replanting and pollarding of firewood on our holding is probably about as good a way of providing warm air and water as any, and better than most, even bearing in mind air pollution concerns.[1]

'Well, it's complicated,' I said. 'I mean, it's all about context.'

Cato waved dismissively, as if to indicate he'd expected nothing better from a mealy-mouthed smartarse like me.

The 'good or bad' binary somehow became a catchphrase in my family, to be appended jokingly to any topic of conversation: 'rain – good or bad?'; 'sparrows – good or bad?' I'm not totally comfortable about it, imagining it's the kind of thing that would only confirm Cato's views about my stuck-up ways. If we lived in an ideal world, I'd like to learn from his local knowledge and appreciate his sense of humour, and I'd like to be more than boilerplate in someone else's self-justifying story. Sometimes, our inability to see the real people in front of us troubles me, like a smudge on the horizon foretelling a coming storm. It happens across the political spectrum, and I'm not immune myself.

But I guess it's good to have a Cato appearing out of the mist on regular occasions to take you down a peg or two and remind you that not everyone's going to like you, no matter what. Anyway, this preamble illustrates three basic points that I'll elaborate on in this chapter as I consider questions of work and money.

First, we don't live in an ideal world. That's not going to change. Indeed, it's likely that in the future the raw material available – both physical and social – for building everyday life might be less ideal than now. Metaphorically, there will be many more Catos materializing to spoil our cherished self-constructions, and we need to be more prepared for them than I usually was when I saw him approach on my morning journeys with my daughter – not with smart rejoinders but with ways of building feasible local societies in spite of them.

Second, context matters. There are rarely simple 'good or bad' answers. Often, there's a case for prudence, judgement or balance, which is locally framed. Energy from wood may be bad as a general proposition for humanity, but good when judiciously used in a particular context. As with wood, so with most things.

But, third, if there's one area where present society has been erring to the bad, I'd argue it's in the way we've come to think about work, money and trade, which has seriously deformed the possibilities for living a good life and led us into the perils we now face globally. Here, I stand in the opposite to camp to those who believe they have the numbers to show that we've never had it so good. For reasons I touched on in chapter 1 and will amplify here, you just can't show this with numbers. In fact, overzealous number-mongering is often precisely the problem. Instead, I'll pursue a more cultural argument about work and money in the dark-age future.

Work

But let's start with a few numbers all the same. Taking waged and salaried employment in the US as broadly indicative of employment patterns in the wealthier countries, there are a lot of jobs connected with virtualized, abstracted, mediated and therefore necessarily bureaucratized relationships: 22 per cent of the workforce in professional, business, finance and information; 18 per cent in trade, transport and warehousing; 14 per cent in federal or state government.

There are fewer connected with more immediate production: 8 per cent in manufacturing; 5 per cent in construction; 1 per cent in farming, forestry, fishing and hunting; less than 1 per cent in mining, quarrying and oil/gas extraction; less than 1 per cent in utilities – although there's quite a lot of direct relationship work (private healthcare and social assistance at 14 per cent; leisure and hospitality at 11 per cent), which is commodified as paid work.[2]

In the future, it's likely that pattern will be more-or-less turned on its head. There will be a lot of jobs in immediate production and relationships, and fewer in the more abstracted sectors.

Is that good or bad? Well, maybe not entirely good – there's often something to be said for abstraction and mediation. But it takes a lot of social, political and physical energy to generate them, as with the global provenance of the supposedly low-carbon electricity from Drax. Those will be in shorter supply in the future. But not entirely bad either. Contemporary abstraction and mediation have gone too far, and we're reaping the consequences. In contrast to the abstraction of work and money in the state-or-market thinking of liberal-modernism that culminates in ideas like Universal Basic Income, here I advocate a more distributist approach in terms of the dignity of work grounded in access to land and/or livelihood that seeks autonomy from those modern forms of abstraction.

I'm not going to go down the rabbit hole of picturing how this future world of work and its different sectors might function in detail, but I'll provide some brief notes here.

※※※

THE IMPORTANCE OF farming in the future has already loomed large in this book and I won't say much more about it here. Presently, there's little agricultural employment in the world's rich countries like the US, while it's the majority sector in the poor ones, with levels around 70 per cent or higher in the ten countries with the highest employment in farming. The median level worldwide is 16 per cent.[3] In a previous book, I calculated roughly that the UK (currently employing 1 per cent of its workforce in agriculture) could feed itself using low-impact methods with about 15 per cent of the adult population employed directly in farming. Possibly that's something of an underestimate.[4]

The currently low figures in rich countries belie the fact that many of them import a lot of food, especially labour-intensive products from poorer countries. In the long term, that will happen less, and – in 'good' or 'bad' ways – patterns of human settlement will shift toward the more productive, agricultural regions. The current global median of 16 per cent will increase, and the current variability between the richest and poorest countries will narrow.

The modernist story we still tell ourselves that the route to prosperity lies in quitting farming will become palpably untrue. As I argued earlier, it was always only a partial truth, neglecting the vast hunger and suffering caused by the often-forcible incorporation of small-scale farmers into global commodity markets and transport networks. But inasmuch as it used to have some truth, that truth was borne on the back of high-energy, low-labour, unsustainable and destructive practices involving synthetic fertilizers and pesticides and fossil-fuelled traction and transport, essentially operating as labour substitutes.

The neo-Malthusian stories we tell ourselves about the future typically involve projecting more labour-saving innovations of this kind, only now less damaging ones. My argument has been that this is unlikely to happen widely, and more likely to reverse. Liberal-modernist states will try to hold on to low-labour arable commodity farming for as long as possible, but the wave of the future – for good or bad – will be job-rich, small-scale local forms of food production, especially horticulture.

❦

HEALTH CARE, SOCIAL CARE, education and human services collectively form a low-carbon, work-rich, pro-social sector. Whether the future is good or bad will depend a lot on how much this sector can be nurtured. This goes way beyond how many formal jobs it has – making care and learning culturally resonant as a local property of families, households and communities is more important.

The details of this could fill many books, and I'm not going to go there. The overarching idea I'd emphasize is Hilary Cottam's one that I quoted in From Liberalism to Distributism on page 21: 'As I stand beside you, how can I support you to create change. ... The emphasis is not on managing need but on creating capability.' The many ways of doing that must be front and centre of attention.

For now, I'll just identify a couple of ways of creating capability. One is the importance of retaining basic 3R literacy – something of a casualty of previous dark ages, which definitely wasn't an upside for ordinary people. And ideally of rebuilding universities at the centre of future civilization.

It might seem absurd to be talking about the role of the university in the new dark ages, and perhaps it is. But maybe we can learn something from the way our predecessors managed to retain or relearn knowledge and build such centres of learning out of earlier darkness.

That links to my second point about capability. It's critically important to retain as much science, technology, engineering and mathematics (STEM) knowledge as possible, and use it pro-socially, 'standing beside' people with it to help them improve their capabilities. Alas, this isn't for the most part how it's configured today. For all the benefits STEM knowledge has brought, it's also been thoroughly co-opted by the technological liberal-modernist state and used against ordinary people.

Earlier, I mentioned the philosopher Alasdair MacIntyre's book *After Virtue*, in which he attempts to make sense of modern times poised between past and future dark ages. At the start of the book, MacIntyre invites his readers to imagine a world in which a series of environmental disasters are blamed by the public on science. Scientists are persecuted, books and instruments destroyed, and a Know-Nothing political movement takes power and represses scientific learning. Later, people try to reconstruct scientific knowledge from surviving fragments, but lacking the deeper structures of understanding that have been lost, science becomes little more than a set of apparently arbitrary and contradictory precepts.[5]

The point of MacIntyre's exercise was to suggest that moral philosophy today has reached the same impasse – a point I touch on lightly in chapter 10. But to stick for now with the thought experiment itself, I don't find it hard to imagine scientific knowledge meeting that fate. The Covid pandemic almost felt like a dress rehearsal. Already, many educated liberals see themselves as engaged in a high-stakes battle for the truth against the first battalions of the Know-Nothings.

Much as I want to stand with them on the side of STEM truth, I'd suggest they should take a look at themselves to understand how we got here. In relation to agriculture, for example, there have been endless premature epitaphs for small-scale, low-input, local farming over the last century that vaunt romanticized views of 'scientific' agriculture as saviour technologies. The concept of science they invoke has less to do with any underlying science and works more as a kind of cultural metaphor for social progress.[6]

Meanwhile, the remaining farmers who haven't been parted from their land to swell the numbers of the precariously underemployed have increasingly become deskilled peons of top-down proprietary technologies – patented seeds, patented software, rising input prices and an ever-increasing thicket of often weakly validated regulation over which they have no control. If such people form part of a Know-Nothing revolt against science, it may be because they know something.

A better approach would make STEM knowledge available to farmers and other people in their daily lives as a voluntary offer geared to improving their capabilities as judged by themselves. This is the old idea of agricultural extension – as supported historically in the US by the land-grant universities as enablers of local farmers, not as enablers of corporate agricultural technology. Ideally, it would be accompanied by the re-ordering of moral inquiry that MacIntyre sought in the humanities, thus making universities more universal.

MAKING A LIVING

MANUFACTURING HAS BECOME a sector of labour-shedding overproduction and global monopoly in much the same way as agriculture. Capital and political collapse along with energy decline will hit it harder than agriculture, if anything.

A cautionary tale sometimes told about post-Roman Britain is that ceramic manufacture disappeared entirely along with the departing Romans. This is an exaggeration, but it does seem that the industry simplified and localized. What similar tales might be told of our own future?

Looking at the mass of high-tech manufactured products around my house and farm, I find a lot of reasons to be fearful about this. Perhaps we should get simplifying and localizing fast. As we head back unavoidably to the world of the local workshop, what's clear is that there won't be anything like the modern petrol or diesel car in it, still less electric vehicles, driverless cars and all the rest. But there may be a lot of useful stuff that local workshops and technicians can turn out with whatever energy they can muster, repurposing and catabolizing what's to hand from the prodigious material remnants of the dying high-energy economy.

Such local manufacturing enterprises would be priority energy users, since it's hard to de-energize or decarbonize them. That means that other sectors like farming and construction would have to bear the brunt of energy constraint – which is eminently possible if we change our optics of what these sectors should look like.

It's easy to see all this as some desperate return beyond even the dark ages into the Iron Age or beyond. But memories are short. As recently as the 1950s, blacksmiths in Western European countries, some of the richest and most 'developed' on Earth, were still plying their trade as general fabricators, menders and fixers of things.[7] As a child of the 1970s, I remember plenty of workshop-based local industry that looked jerry-built by modern standards.

In her book about the 'wilding' of her once-farmed estate, Isabella Tree describes its occupation by various wild species made rare by the previous destruction of their habitats through modern farming practices.[8] Yet here they are again. How did they survive in the interim? Where? When I visit the annual scythe fair not far from my home down on the Somerset Levels,

I'm likewise struck by the myriad of craftspeople who appear there, like rare species finding liveable habitat again – not only scything folk but traditional blacksmiths, woodturners, basket makers and many others.

I daresay I need to build a better account of how to restore viable local industries than this – perhaps a task for another time. The reality, I think, will be uneven, unpredictable, chaotic and strange – like the part-organic and part-industrial future worlds portrayed by novelists such as Rebecca Campbell and Claire North.[9] Meanwhile, I'm at least encouraged to see the craftspeople at the scythe fair, with their knowledges still waiting in the wings, like the mythical knights of an Alan Garner novel slumbering underground until their time comes around again.

In any case, we need to let go of the notion that the high-tech globalization of industry in modern times that kicked into overdrive around the 1980s is some non-negotiable grounding for a decent life.

Perhaps I'm at risk here of slipping into that fated endpoint of every anarchist rural utopia, which involves sitting around the campfire singing 'Kumbaya'. In my utopia, nobody has to sing 'Kumbaya'. But there are worse fates than that, and the socioeconomic world that's brought us more sophisticated entertainments is rapidly hustling us down the road toward them.

I'LL PASS MORE QUICKLY over some of the other sectors. Construction and utilities will command a greater proportion of the workforce. Less energy and water will be available locally, and more people will need to coax what they can out of the landscape and repurpose old infrastructure. There will be more work in job-rich construction and building trades, using local materials like wood and stone, as in the historic vernaculars of most places. A lot of rebuilding, reusing, recycling and repurposing. A lot of do-it-yourself home building in view of the costs of labour, energy and materials, with reams of building regulations long disappeared up the chimneys of woodstoves for fire-lighting, and the occupation of building inspector one of those strange job titles that reminds us how the past was a different country. Maybe more home and building site injuries, though maybe not – gas pipelines, high-voltage electricity and lofty scaffolds are from another country too.

There's always work in trade and transport, but there will be a lot less than the current US figure of 18 per cent. The number of traders and transporters must ultimately be tied fractionally to the ability of a local human ecology to produce things worth trading, just as the number of livestock must ultimately be tied fractionally to the ability of a local farm ecology to feed its people and its animals. In a world of distributed land access and household-based farming, traders have a harder time persuading farmers to part with their hard-earned money. But there are certainly many things worth trading and circulating around the local economy, provided it doesn't get out of hand.

This 'getting out of hand', the overinflation of trade, occurs with the overinflation of money as I'll discuss in a moment. One of the roles of government is to stop that from happening. But you probably don't need many people employed in government to do that, especially if you've built a high-context culture.

In fairness, some of the 14 per cent of government employment in 2023 no doubt refers to people working in education and other human services – work that, as I've already said, is very much to be welcomed and defended. But a good deal of government employment involves the bureaucratized aspects of the corporate-state nexus and the overinflation of money and trade. This is not to endorse old arguments about supposed public sector inefficiency, currently enjoying a new lease of life via the Department of Government Efficiency in the US, initially helmed by Elon Musk, wielding his metaphorically waste-cutting chainsaw – rather ironically given that the chainsaw is now only a tool of choice for underpowered artisanal woodsmen like me, with commercial forestry long converted to more 'efficient' large-scale machinery. The wider point is that within the parameters of the present system, there's no doubt that government employees as well as large-scale forestry equipment both do a good job. But those parameters are set to change, and with them the whole structure of how we define efficiency and necessary work.

There's a distinction to be made between record keeping and bureaucracy. Good science, good healthcare, good farm management and good business management involve measuring, counting and keeping a record of things. Bureaucracy, on the other hand, involves a state appropriating such records and holding them as a kind of potential power against every person's name, and possibly their descendants' names, in perpetuity. The career of big data in recent times is an acceleration of that.

The idea of the jubilee – cancel the debt, destroy the records, reallocate the land – had more hold over premodern imaginations than it does today. Often more dreamed of than realized, it was nevertheless implemented from time to time, either top down by enlightened rulers or bottom up by peasant rebels.[10] Constructing dark-age communities rather than publics, to use the terminology established in the introduction, involves another jubilee, whether top down, bottom up or else as a side effect of collapsing centralized state bureaucracies. Probably a necessary if insufficient condition for that is to have fewer people employed professionally in government, and more people working part-time in governing themselves.

Cancel the debt, destroy the records, reallocate the land, delete the database, turn off the computer.

Money

What is money? Printed on the £10 banknotes issued by the Bank of England you'll find the phrase, 'I promise to pay the bearer on demand the sum of ten pounds' (the same pledge can be found on the other denominations promising their respective values). On the face of it this seems odd, since we tend to think that the banknote *is* ten pounds. The Bank's website explains that the phrase dates from the time when banknotes were redeemable in gold. But this doesn't get us far, because people rarely want gold for its own sake any more than they want to collect £10 notes.

The real meaning of money is right there in the words on the banknote. 'I promise'. A £10 note is a promise to do something for somebody. More specifically, it's a promise to do ten pounds' worth of something for the person who gives you the note – a promise that only works if both parties consider themselves to be part of the community of circulating promises, of note-givers and note-takers. All the money in the UK has a picture of the monarch's head on it, which gives a sense of how that community is defined, although increasingly money can only be understood internationally.

The distributist thinker John Médaille gives the best short definition of money I know: 'a necessary power of the community'.[11] Turning that around, we could say that a community is an aggregation of promises

– real, specific, redeemable promises, not just vague affirmations of intent. Money isn't the only kind of promise that circulates in communities – we make other kinds of real promise, for example to family or to gods. But money promises are important.

They're also typically unequal or asymmetric. Médaille adds this to his money-as-community definition: 'As such, it will either be the democratic power of the whole community, or an oligarchic power of a few members of the community.'

Given the way the modern global economy works, it's invariably the latter. Central governments use their monopoly of sovereign power to enforce a monopoly of money, creating legal tenders and outlawing or sidelining other currencies. Their taxation systems create society-wide need for the monopoly currency.

This currency is created by private banks, to whom the government delegates its sovereign monetary powers. Essentially, the banks conjure money out of nothing (fractional reserve banking) and then charge interest to ordinary people and businesses, creating money debts that, as currency users rather than issuers, they can only pay off by effectively offloading the debt onto others. This is part of a vicious cycle of new money and debt creation, new offloading, and therefore new economic growth. It's good on paper in terms of increased gross prosperity, but it's a prosperity that most people don't see much or any of.

So, looked at from a purely monetary angle, political and monetary monopoly involves the creation of increasing prosperity, drawn from ordinary people and businesses, and placed into the coffers of governments, banks and other owners of capital by handing on debt to someone else like a hot potato.

Looked at from a social angle, it involves people being dependent on jobs and money over which they have no control. They're at the behest of powerful gamemasters and they often have few options for staying out of the game.

Looked at from a world-historical angle, this is colonialism. It's the scramble to expand economic frontiers, grab new resources and draw new people into the game on as disadvantageous terms as possible. Some argue that the callous violence of colonialism and capitalism arises precisely when human relations are replaced with monetary equations – the fury of paying off debt driving the pioneer colonizers, the implacable bureaucratic calculus of the algorithm or the bottom line, black-and-white figures in the ledger that can brook no argument as they lay waste to people's lives.[12] This is one reason I'm cautious about over-zealous number-mongering in political debate, because numbers are only intelligible within stories, and if our stories are violent – even if only implicitly – then the numbers we use will do violent work.

Again, looked at from a world-historical angle, this is also the mismatch between money or price and *value* in the sense of what human and natural ecologies can sustain in the long term – an increasing mismatch, as the controllers of money get inventive and amplify it through virtualized forms like derivatives, credit default swaps and the like. In John Médaille's words, 'Values are created only from human labor applied to the gifts of nature. There is nothing else.'[13] By that definition, exchanging, trading, raising credit, betting, hedging, insuring and many other such derivatives of money's power that a lot of people spend a lot of their time doing in contemporary society adds no value. But it often adds a lot of money.

Médaille's definition of value, and the idea of sustainable human and natural ecologies, keys us into the discipline of ecological economics and its insight that the human economy with its currency of money is merely a subsystem of the natural ecology with its currency of energy. The subsystem of the human economy can depart from the governing system of the natural ecology only temporarily until the latter brings it back into line. Seaborne global colonialism and then the availability of cheap and abundant fossil fuels bought many of us out of that truth for longer than cultural memory comprehends, but the bill is now coming due – and it's unlikely to be postponed through attempts to innovate new energy sources or other techno-fixes.

There's no shortage of ideas about how to redress the imbalance between money and value, making the economy work better for ordinary people. They all tend to founder in the face of the quantitative power of money, the political power of the oligopolies controlling it and the ecological power of the Earth systems controlling all of us. But somewhere within these ideas lie the best lights for the future, so a brief appraisal is in order.

I mentioned modern monetary theory (MMT) in chapter 1 (see From Liberalism to Distributism, page 21). Technical details aside, its basic idea is that governments can use their political and monetary sovereignty for the good of their citizens, unencumbered by conventional economic fears about budget deficits or trade deficits.[14] This can be true in theory, but MMT involves at root a vision of the state as benevolently oriented to citizen wellbeing, lacking an analysis of how the interests of the central state and the common good are structurally different. It also lacks much of a theory about how some states have more sovereignty than others – in other words, a historical understanding of the colonial foundations of the modern system of states that makes it harder for, say, Haiti to generate citizen wellbeing than, say, the US.

Most importantly, MMT theorists underplay the monetary and energetic imbalances in the contemporary global economy that I mentioned above. A sustainable MMT-style pro-citizen form of governance is certainly possible, but if it were truly sustainable it would be incompatible with the high-energy, urban-industrial economies taken for granted in most countries, certainly the wealthier ones. MMT or no, the bill is still due.

Socialisms of most kinds err in a similar way. They correctly note the unfair imbalance between the rewards to capital and labour in the economy (which ultimately have the same source in Médaille's 'human labor applied to the gifts of nature' and should therefore probably have more or less the same rewards). They rightly organize to redress it, again in a state-centred way. (They have a better theory about state power than MMT, if ultimately usually a naive one, involving the state working for the interests of ordinary people once they get control of it.)

But, again, they typically underemphasize monetary and energetic imbalances. Crudely put, the plausibility of the old socialist revolutions was in offering the possibility – if not necessarily the reality – of a fairer distribution of rewards in a growing economy. New socialist revolutions, or reforms, can only offer the possibility of a fairer distribution of rewards in an economy that will deliver materially less to ordinary people than at present. Notions of less work, more leisure, richer human relationships and post-growth hedonism are all great so far as they go. But the material paucity involved is likely to shock rich-country publics. It's not a palatable political sell.

Finally, a word about distributist approaches. Unlike MMT and socialism, distributism isn't state-centred. The place it finds for local autonomy – local currencies even – is appealing. Distributists would no doubt salute the Appalachian mountaineers who used their home-produced whiskey as a currency and in 1794 fought off a militia headed by George Washington and Alexander Hamilton raised to enforce payment of their whiskey tax, projecting state territorial power.

John Médaille argues, rightly in my opinion, that despite their surface differences, the various major economic doctrines that have shaped the modern world – including capitalism in its various guises, state communism, fascism and social democracy – have shared four basic features. They believed in an economy that: 1) followed science-like laws; 2) was global and universal; 3) was capitalist in the sense that it put great accumulations of capital in the hands of comparatively few bureaucrats (whether public or, as with corporations, private); and 4) should be managed by a technocratic politics. In Médaille's distributist alternative:

> *We could do worse than simply to take these four features of the prevailing ideologies, and* do exactly the opposite. *So then, in place of a claim of physical science, we should* re-moralize *the markets. In place of globalist claims, we should* re-localize the economy. *In place of capitalist claims, we should* re-capitalize *the poor, the small farm, and the small businessman. And in place of the sterile politics of technique and expertise, we should* re-invigorate and re-localize *the political order.*[15]

I agree, and I've tried to embody these arguments in this book. But distributism also lacks a nuanced theory of the state, or at least an explicit one (in chapter 11, I try to make its approach more explicit). It lacks an account of how to bring the global economy into monetary and energetic balance, too. The distributist impetus toward local livelihood autonomy as the economy tumbles back into balance with true value and with Earth systems is more appealing than hoping that a centralized government in the hands of MMT theorists or socialists somewhere far away will give you a job. But it doesn't have a great account of how to make that tumbling less painful or chaotic.

※※※

THIS IS ONE REASON why I project a dark-age future. Money in the global economy has become completely out of whack with sustainable value. It needs rebalancing, but it's hard to see how we can now destroy enough money in its present quantitatively excessive form quickly enough without also risking the destruction of Médaille's 'community power' – a more positive form of money, but one we've built unstably in recent history on the tottering edifice of historical usury. Few of our existing economic doctrines are much help.

Either we find a way to manage a calm and rational, but fast, descent to a more stable and sustainable world of work and value creation, or else we career uncontrollably downhill toward that same lower point in the landscape. Alas, this latter outcome – an economic depression that becomes 'the fucking dark ages', as described by the character from Stephen Markley's novel I mentioned in the introduction (The Hero Is You, page 11) – currently seems to me more likely.

I don't want that uncontrollable descent to happen, but nor do I want vain attempts to stave it off by shoring up the tottering edifice. This is partly because the edifice is now unsavable, but also because it's actively damaging while it lasts. Far from creating value, the way that we add money to the global economy reduces value by degrading both labour and the gifts of nature that produce it. This is why I said earlier that, in the present world, the answer to the question 'money – good or bad?' is often 'bad'. The challenge of the dark-age future is to try to make it good.

❧❧❧

WE HAVE ALL SORTS of gambits to try to duck this reckoning with nature and true value. But they don't really work. I'll briefly discuss a few, partly because they're myths that need busting if we're to have the conversations we need about how to reform work and money, and partly because understanding the myths helps ground those conversations.

Thailand has been a relative economic success story in recent years, increasing its GDP per capita well above the global average. Historically, it's had a large offshore fishing fleet, but with the country's economic success it's become hard to recruit Thais into the industry. Fishing is hard and dangerous work – who'd do it when there are better options in a growing economy?

Often, the answer is people from poorer nearby countries like Myanmar and Cambodia. Often, too, these workers toil in conditions of near or actual slavery. Slavery has been defined as a state of social death, and social death is easy to arrange on a boat in the ocean run by people from a different country and community.[16]

When accounting the benefits of economic growth to Thais, it's necessary also to account the price that's paid by others from surrounding countries. The story of money as a power of oligarchic community and money as usurious increase is a book of violence and social death written on a global canvas, with people enslaved on Thai fishing boats one footnote among many.

The alternative, when money is a power of the whole community and when the rewards to capital and labour are similar, is that a community has to assume the laborious and dangerous burden of offshore fishing for itself if that's what it chooses to do, and it therefore has to reward the people who do it accordingly.

Another fishy gambit relating to this story is the common argument that technological progress will eliminate workplace misery. The history of the Thai offshore fishery surely belies this. A modern offshore fishing boat is a triumph of technological progress, whereby a handful of people can land hundreds of tonnes of fish in a few days. Yet this isn't enough to eliminate enslaved labour. Which isn't surprising, since slavery bears no definite relation to technological advancement.

If you trace the origins of the prodigious energy resources needed to fuel new technologies physically, and the venture capital needed to fuel them economically, their environmental and social ledger is none too healthy either. This applies to supposedly pro-environmental food technologies such as manufactured microbial protein as well as to more obviously questionable ones like trawling.

Examples like this proliferate across the real-world economy, where bad money chases out good. In my book *Saying NO to a Farm-Free Future*, I argued that in existing market conditions it doesn't make economic sense for small farms like mine to produce staple crops like wheat commercially. To illustrate: with average UK wheat yields at around 8 tonnes per hectare (3 tonnes per acre), and wholesale prices at around £200 per tonne, I'd stand to make around £600 gross annually from an acre, the largest area I could feasibly grow – although in practice I'd be unable to interest a wholesale buyer in a crop that small. It makes more sense to grow vegetable crops that command higher prices. Note that the issue isn't about per-acre crop yields, which don't necessarily vary with farm scale or mechanization. The issue is per-labour income, which does.

It would be eminently possible to create a world of small, work-intensive farms, each growing crops like wheat along with a diverse range of other wholefoods on a few acres that could feed local populations affordably and well. But doing so would require radical changes to the economy, at root involving an end to usurious money as an oligarchic power of a few members of the community and instead making it a power of the whole community.

What we often get instead is misleading paeans to the supposedly superior efficiency of large, heavily mechanized farms in breadbasket places like Kansas that can (over)produce staple foods like wheat at low market prices and distribute them globally through high-energy supply chains, or even more misleading paeans to food supposedly from 'thin air' in the manufactured food narrative.[17] And a race to the bottom in food commodity prices that tends to clear small farmers off the land to the benefit of oligarchic power.

There's a fantasy in all this that the hard work of provisioning ourselves can be costlessly offloaded onto other people, other places, new technologies and exotic forms of energy. But we can't keep buying ourselves out of local ecological relationships with nature and with each other in this way. This doesn't mean that everybody has to produce every aspect of their own subsistence for themselves. But it probably does mean we somehow have to find ways of holding close economically to everybody who's producing those aspects for us and trying to make sure they're adequately rewarded in ways that represent the democratic power of the whole community.

※※※

IT'S CLEAR WE LIVE in an oligarchic economy from the prices of key necessities. Land (if you're a farmer) and housing (if you aren't) are eye-wateringly expensive, whereas food is cheap – although healthy wholefoods aren't cheap if you're poor. The energy that mobilizes the economy is cheap but getting dearer. And although some people are paid a lot, the labour that's devoted to creating the necessities of life is cheap (in other words, keyworker wages are low). Nature is also cheap – drawing down on it usually doesn't cost anything.

This would look different in a fair and sustainable livelihood community. Relative to present prices, land and housing would be cheap, while food and energy would be dearer (but affordable in terms of local ways of life). Nature wouldn't have a price but would be protected by the Luddism of local culture – you just don't do things that mess it up. And the price of labour would be – interesting.

We forget nowadays how weird and tyrannical wage labour seemed to people in the eighteenth and nineteenth centuries as it was becoming normalized. In removing autonomy or optionality over work, it was the 'very essence of slavery' according to a Philadelphia printer in 1826.[18] Or, if not of slavery, at least perhaps the essence of adolescence:

> *The first thing that "proletarianization" came to mean was that millions of young men and women across Europe found themselves effectively stuck in a kind of permanent adolescence. Apprentices and journeymen could never become "masters," and thus, never actually grow up.*[19]

Eventually, bottom-up trade unionism created considerable prosperity for these adolescents of the now normalized wage-labour market in the wealthy countries. And also top-down oligarchy – it's easy to neglect how much this prosperity rests on the historic labour of poorer workers in other countries, and on the unsustainable use of energy and nature. It's easy, in other words, to neglect how much it rests on colonialism, broadly conceived. It's now looking like that prosperity was always going to have a limited shelf life, as the costs of placating the systems of energy, nature and oligarchy increasingly propel the ranks of the waged back toward poverty.

The socialist strategy of trying to leverage more money for workers from oligarchic power is fine up to a point, but it ultimately founders in various dynamics of crisis. These encompass not only external issues, such as climate, energy and nature degradation, but also ones internal to the economy, like industrial overcapacity and monetary overcapitalization.

That leaves us contemplating other ways of generating prosperity. In the days before our permanent adolescence, this typically meant being a proprietor – becoming one's own 'master' or mistress.

MAKING A LIVING

I found it eye-opening when I quit my academic job many years ago – a reasonably well-paid one, resting as it ultimately did on oligarchic power, along with cheap energy and nature – to become a self-employed vegetable grower. I knew the returns would be low, but it's hard to really get your head around it until you actually do it. A lot of farmers and growers are quick to blame themselves for their inadequacies on this front – and if they're not, others are.[20] Of course, there are always more things you can do, more ways to try to increase returns. Usually, they involve using more fossil energy or other nature-degrading tricks. But that's another story. My main point is that the dismal economics of the self-employed vegetable grower are ultimately a reflection, if a slightly distorted one, of the real economy of nature and Earth systems, to which all of us are destined to return.

Proprietors in bygone times tried to work their way around this. A common approach to labour in preindustrial England involved young people working fixed terms as 'servants' for an owner-occupier farm proprietor. This had a learning element and – in an economy where liquid money was often scarce – payment in kind (food, clothes, accommodation). Often, the servant worked fewer hours than the farmer and enjoyed various fixed benefits. However, the farmer owned the business, the land and the social status, if also the ultimate risks.

Cash-strapped farms and small businesses today have reinvented this kind of relationship, with apprenticeships and internships of various kinds. It's even been semi-formalized via organizations like WWOOF (Worldwide Opportunities on Organic Farms). I mentioned the parallel arrangement we experimented with on our own market garden in chapter 6 (see Keeping Ownership Distributed, page 98).

One would-be worker at our market garden baulked at our 90 per cent profit share offer on the grounds that managing a market garden ought to attract a managerial wage – which would be a lot higher than 90 per cent of not very much. It probably *ought* to attract such a wage. But, in the present economy, the fact is it doesn't. And so here we come to the price of labour in the dark-age future. There won't be much money in the sense of coin or promises on banknotes to pay for it, leaving people looking at other promises, at various in-kind benefits, and ultimately a route out of adolescence and into proprietorship, into access to land. Non-monetized, kinship-based households are also part of this picture.

Possibly what was in the worker's mind is that my wife and I are sitting on a lot of unearned theoretical land capital derived from the speculative-oligarchic money system, and we are not poor. But you can't monetize land and farm it at the same time, and paying down capital isn't a sustainable business model. That seems to be pretty much what's happening at the moment in small-scale British horticulture, with a lot of wealthy people buying farms and running retreats and courses from them, with growers paid 'managerial wages' for running market gardens on the site at costs much higher than the market price for vegetables can cover. I don't think that route ends in politics that are as attractive as the distributist approach of making it possible for apprentices or wage-labourers ultimately to own their own land and grow food for themselves or others, but at lower 'wages'.

The real problem is that as a society we've foreclosed on the possibility for a lot of young people to get autonomous access to land, for the servant to become proprietor in the end. Again, we need to ride the downslope to a sustainable relationship between work, capital and value. Instead of a politics of labour agitation that hopes to summon greater riches for workers out of capital, we need to degrade capital so that we can interact with each other in community as owners of our own labour and necessary capital, including land. To invoke John Médaille one last time:

> *What is required is a strong sense of solidarity, not only with all other workers, unionized or not, but with the poor, and even with capital itself – in other words, what is needed is a commitment to the common good, not the particular interest.*[21]

UNFORTUNATELY, I CAN only see that happening now through dark-age circumstances, especially when you throw in all the other forces hustling us down that path. Those circumstances will be random and unpredictable enough to make worthless any detailed blueprint for exactly how an emerging society should organize its economic affairs. Any enduring arrangement would need to be worked out in detail on the ground, channelling the democratic power of the community, making it doubly inappropriate for me to lay out my own lofty vision of how it should be done.

Still, the preceding discussion establishes some pointers. A livelihood community establishing itself anew in open country would be well advised to make small plots of productive land (gardens, allotments, smallholdings) inalienably available to people at low or zero price. It would need to find a fair allocation method for such plots when they come available through death or desertion that prevents them concentrating in fewer hands. Maybe modernized versions of Thomas Spence's parochial self-management idea that I discussed in chapter 3 are worth considering (see Lifehouses, page 56).

It's unlikely that much established currency from the falling capitalist world would find its way into open country. If it did, it should be treated with suspicion – especially in relation to buying land entitlement or the other major means of creating local livelihood. More likely, it would be treated much as poor farmers have treated it historically – as a bonus that can buy occasional luxuries, not as the blood supply of everyday life.

But these livelihood communities would probably need some form of money-as-currency and money-as-capital to serve as that blood supply. Past agrarian societies have used such items as grain, cattle and – as we've seen – whiskey for this purpose, in some cases within the context of sophisticated modern economic theory. An example is the idea of government-backed granaries as 'subtreasuries' formulated by the agrarian populists of North America around the turn of the twentieth century. Whether grain, cattle or whiskey, all have interesting currency-like properties and inherent, though not foolproof, defences against inflation in respect of local value and the ecological base.

In small, dark-age livelihood communities more attuned to the importance of sticking together in the face of a wider hostile world, there may be more scope for subtreasury-type systems to work locally. Grain and granaries, or their equivalents, as currency and banks, creating opportunities to fund modest capital development and goods production when it's possible, and food security when it's not, always tied to the local ecological base and its ability to furnish value through labour.

CHAPTER 9

Working for Others

I've emphasized the need for a transition to low-energy societies of semi-autonomous local household production, but the 'semi' is important. Not only are households linked in all sorts of ways, but there will also be wider opportunities in these societies to work for others – the subject of this chapter.

To understand how that might operate, it's worth considering likely attitudes to work and life in societies of this future dark age. I've said quite a lot about the challenges of the transition, while trying not to neglect the positive aspects of past and probable future dark ages, but I'd like to flip that framing at least for a moment and lighten the mood around a dark-age future.

The virtues of sobriety and hard work loom large in modernist thinking. One critic of mine reserved his greatest scorn for my argument about the importance of the 'mysteries and passions' of life, as compared to the primary importance, in his view, of putting food on the table. Of course, the two needn't be mutually exclusive, although there are numerous ways in which people are willing to prioritize their cultural passions over the satiation of immediate wants.

Here, I'm minded to invoke as my patron saint and champion St Francis of Assisi. In contrast to the self-important, materialist, high-energy and high-tech conquest of nature for the greater glory of humanity associated with modernism, the way of St Francis involved, in the words of Eugene McCarraher, 'the rejection of vexing, burdensome riches – and hence of the disciplined frenzy to produce them. Fewer personal possessions would mean, not worry and pain, but a richer, more relaxed, more pleasurable life.'[1]

McCarraher adds that this Franciscan way was followed 'with exemplary inattention to the laws of the State' and 'beckoned toward a world without the governmental machinery of repression and violence'. An interesting point to which I'll return in the next chapter.

Of course, there's a danger here of taking a romanticized view of poverty. I'd argue that pursuing voluntary simplicity is a lesser danger at this point in world history, with our present need to bring the power of money back into balance with the ability of Earth systems to sustain our demands, than the romanticized views of technological solutions, wealth and the 'disciplined frenzy' of its pursuit associated with modernism.

There's also a danger of taking a romanticized or tamed view of Francis as a kind of chilled-out saint of simple pleasures rather than an innovator of austere apostolic poverty. Still, according to Mikhail Bakhtin, the pioneering scholar of medieval culture and carnival, St Francis was the figure who 'carnivalized Catholicism', helping to meld it with a popular culture of laughter that emphasizes collective renewal and rebirth in the face of life's travails.[2] Says Bakhtin: 'Laughter must liberate the gay truth of the world from the veils of gloomy lies spun by the seriousness of fear, suffering and violence.'[3]

But laughter isn't just about having fun. The collective laughter of the carnival, in Bakhtin's treatment, represents the fecund regeneration of the world out of decay and death. Whereas joyless elites invoke a fear of death and nature's overmighty powers to frighten those they rule, the populist spirit of carnival laughs at their pomposity, celebrates human powers over nature and scorns death, out of which comes rebirth.

This is a different sense of human power over nature to modern sensibilities based on historical progress through technology and our cyborg dreams of evading death and other natural limits. It's a purely cultural power, a power of the human will despite our bodily mortality. And it offers two cultural poles to inspire conduct that are celebrated and brought together in carnival. Both gluttony *and* austerity. Both Carnival and Lent. Again, this contrasts with the single pole of modernist redemption that ultimately mimics the single-mindedly gluttonous mindset of elites: escape poverty, escape nature, escape death, embrace progress, embrace technology, embrace wealth, embrace endless growth.[4]

There's a lot to be said for rejecting the humourless self-importance of this mindset as manifested in our various Promethean and neo-Malthusian forms of liberalism and environmentalism that promise this escape but actually deliver cultural alienation, climate breakdown, financial crashes and various other Frankenstein's monsters. As I see it, medieval Catholic popular culture (as distinct from the medieval Catholic Church, which variously elaborated, tolerated and repressed it) offers more sophisticated cultural resources for inspiring our conduct in the face of contemporary problems than this gluttonous modernism. Other religious traditions have their own versions of this.

Although I've avoided being over-prescriptive about how communities in the new dark ages should construct their economies, I'm taken by Bakhtin's claim that fully two months of every year were occupied with fairs and carnivals in late medieval Lyon. I'd like to suggest that every community in the new dark ages considers following its example, if only to prevent the excess accumulation of wealth. Instead of kumbaya in the dark-age future we get carnival! But ideally not as a pastiche of the old. Instead, we need to build new political and popular cultures out of present celebratory possibilities.

As is no doubt apparent from what I've said earlier, the economic structure of my farm isn't exactly Franciscan, although it is based on not being overly attached to the highest monetary yields obtainable from the land – and on a certain amount of festivity, as with our weekly shared farm meal. My hope is that somewhere between apostolic poverty and grim capital accumulation, between the disciplined labour of the farm kid and knowing when it's time to knock off work, there lie possibilities for future dark-age societies where money is a power of the whole community, and where the whole community sometimes has some fun.

Guilds

Guilds are one way of organizing work and professions in such societies, where money is a power of the whole community. A guild is an association of craftworkers – builders, for example. It trains people in the relevant skill by creating apprenticeships. It sets prices for its members' services, the idea being that the price mediates between the interests of the producer in receiving adequate compensation and the consumer in receiving an affordable service. It also regulates the quality of the work and stands surety for its members against claims of malpractice.

A guild is to a community of craftworkers what a commons is to a community of landworkers. It can be understood in relation to the same commons structure I discussed in chapter 6 (see Commons, page 64) – a resource plus a community plus a set of social protocols.

The resource might encompass the raw materials needed for the craft. It definitely encompasses the labour and skills of the craftworkers. The social protocols encompass the things I've mentioned like training, price setting and quality assurance. The community ideally refers both to the community of craftworkers and the wider community it serves. In practice, guilds can withdraw from wider collective responsibility and become more akin to trade associations or trade unions organized mainly around their members' immediate interests. But the idea of a guild, like a commons, is that it's generated bottom up by a community to serve that community, rather than being a professional body regulated top down by a government or a state to serve the needs of a public dependent on the state. In the latter case, it can be easy for large-scale professional bodies to co-opt and monopolize government patronage, closing out more local, bottom-up opportunities.

Another way of thinking about guilds is in terms of the rich associational life of the community that I discussed in chapter 5 (see Communities, page 85). In Europe, guilds arose in later medieval times and were organized around many aspects of life other than work, including education, charity, leisure and religious observance. Maybe carnival guilds could provide a better model for what we might bring into the working day than the joyless austerity around work of modernist thinking.

But the medieval connotations of the guild may be precisely the problem in thinking about it as a way of addressing contemporary problems. Along with other aspects of low-input localism like small farms, they can seem redolent of a backward-looking nostalgia. In some hands that can be true. For example, in his *Walled Towns,* the American gothic revival architect Ralph Adams Cram made guilds central to his vision of a conservative neo-medieval new order in which usury, capitalism and Protestantism had all been swept away in favour of rigid social hierarchy.

G.D.H. Cole, an English near-contemporary of Cram's, took a different direction in his *Guild Socialism*, in which he tried to thread a narrow route between the interests of consumers and guild producers in the new age of mass global industrial capitalism. Cole wrote:

We cannot go back to "town economy," a general régime of handicraft and master-craftsmanship, tiny-scale production. We can neither pull up our railways, fill in our mines, and dismantle our factories, nor conduct our large-scale enterprises under a system developed to fit the needs of a local market and a narrowly-restricted production. If the mediaeval system has lessons for us, they are not parrot-lessons of slavish imitation, but lessons of the spirit, by which we may learn how to build up, on the basis of large-scale production and the world-market, a system of industrial organization that appeals to the finest human motives and is capable of developing the tradition of free communal service.[5]

A century after Cole wrote these words, I think it's fair to say we did not learn those lessons as we built ever larger-scale production and the world market. Guilds, like commons, are communal or co-operative rather than collective – creatures of bottom-up local livelihood-making rather than the top-down control of states, corporations and political parties. They're not designed to thrive in world market conditions. But they might thrive in the world to come, after the eclipse of those conditions.

Cram and Cole were writing at a time in the early twentieth century when the destructive materialistic spirit of untrammelled mass capitalism seemed to be carrying all before it, and in their different ways were part of an intellectual rearguard trying to hang on to the importance of associational life. The mid-twentieth-century period that succeeded them brought world war, then decolonization, welfare capitalism and rapid economic growth, which further eroded local associational life but promised some kind of prosperity under the star of the gigantic market and state institutions now bestriding economic life. The neoliberal globalization of recent decades represents the death of that promise and another cycle of destructive mass capitalism. It's left us today with an ecologically damaged, economically over-leveraged and socially homogenized and levelled world.

Meanwhile, the idea of local guilds and commons sits quietly in the wings, waiting to be re-energized.

WHEN THE COVID pandemic came to our town, the fresh vegetable shelves in the supermarkets quickly emptied of produce. Our small market garden, which usually gets about one new customer query every week or two, was inundated with a couple of hundred. The team expanded production as much as was feasible, which wasn't much, and did their best to meet local needs. One innovation at that time was a solidarity veg box, whereby customers would pay more for a box, subsidizing prices for lower-income customers on a self-selection basis.

The disruption to the supply chain in the shops proved only temporary. Pretty soon, the shelves were well stocked again and our customer base dwindled. But in the future, it's likely there will be deeper, longer and harder supply-chain disruptions. The fact that supermarket shelves are usually full of food is a current side effect of global free market economics, not its purpose. The idea that global free trade in food mitigates hunger is badly mistaken. When shortages arise, it will have been a good idea to have built a local moral economy whose purpose *is* to provide people locally with food and other necessary services, no matter what.

As I've argued earlier, commons and guilds are good ways of doing that, provided they keep a double moral focus on their immediate members and on the local community they serve. But it can take a long time to build well-functioning, local, moral economies, guilds and commons – time we don't necessarily have. All the more reason to start now, with whatever baby steps we can make, and without being too hard on ourselves for our failures.

Ways of pooling local finance and decommodifying land, such as community land trusts and their equivalents, and ways of supporting producers and bringing more of them into local production, such as through Community Supported Agriculture ventures, all result in food that usually costs more in terms of checkout price than buying food via world market routes in the supermarket for the various 'race to the bottom' reasons associated with our current bad food economics that I've mentioned earlier. But they represent a wise form of selfishness in building the resilience of a local moral economy that might sustain you in the future, rather than the foolish generosity of giving your money away to corporate players that won't.

Developments of this kind presently are more widespread in the food system than any other sector, such as service trades like building or manufacturing trades like solar-panel production. This is because the economics of being a local farmer serving local markets are more dismal than those of being a local builder – food can be economically shipped across the world, whereas buildings can't. And because they're less dismal than being a local solar-panel manufacturer serving local markets, who simply don't exist.

It would be a good idea to extend the guild idea out from farming to other economic sectors as far as possible to prepare for the local future. It may be unrealistic to create guilds of local solar-panel or electric-car manufacturers. Maybe that suggests it's unrealistic to plan for futures based on such products.

In a well-functioning guild society, you'd be unlikely to buy services from a non-local guild member, even if they were cheaper. They're an unknown quantity and your treacherous patronage is undermining people from your own community on whose good faith your wellbeing ultimately rests – as theirs does on yours. It's not that you don't care about people in other communities and wouldn't be willing to help them in a crisis. But their day-to-day livelihood-making isn't your concern.

All of this represents a mountain to climb and a lot of perplexing local detail to sort out from where we now are. Maybe even more so in dark-age situations where people have to create new communities in new places from scratch. Or maybe less. Either way, it's a good idea to get started.

Trade

Dark-age societies can sometimes pull themselves toward the light by increasing the volume of trade. It does depend a bit on what's being traded – slave trades, for example, often helped to build what today we deign to call 'civilizations' but for that very reason hardly commend appreciation for lighting people's lives. Indeed, escaping the misery of such civilizations was one historical push behind the emergence of 'dark-age' societies involving less trade and more local autonomy (see chapter 1, page 17). Nevertheless, other kinds of trade can be a good thing. The problem is that you can have too much of a good thing. The challenge from where the global economy now sits is reducing the amount of trade and building greater local autonomies.

That last statement runs counter to received economic wisdom. But not quite as counter as you might think – past titans of economic thought such as Adam Smith, David Ricardo and John Maynard Keynes, whose analyses did so much to create that orthodoxy via ideas like the invisible hand of the market, the theory of comparative advantage and increasing aggregate demand – themselves pinpointed trenchantly the potential failings and hidden assumptions in these ideas that, as it's transpired, have led us to the present economic cliff edge. Contemporary heterodox economic thinkers have built on that legacy.

Take any kind of economic unit or livelihood community – a hunter-gatherer or foraging band, a peasant farm or peasant-farm society, a modern industrial country. None are ever sufficient unto themselves. They will always interact with other people and societies, and seek the exchange of useful things. Also, none are necessarily 'better' than any other or destined to grow into another one in accordance with some evolutionary theory of history. What matters is what people in each of those societies want and value. If I've singled out modern industrial societies for criticism in this book, it's mostly because what people tend to want and value in those societies cannot be sustained long-term from the ecological base – although many things they value, such as love, friendship, peace and adequate nutrition can be.

In all these societies, I'd suggest there's a lot to be said for trade when:

- it's based on what you've sustainably produced agriculturally or industrially by applying human labour to nature
- it gives you useful things that help you to live your sense of the good life, a good life that cannot be defined only in relation to material goods themselves (hence the importance of 'mysteries and passions')
- it does not expose you overly to the potential malfeasance of others, for example by relying on them to provide you with the basic necessities of life and therefore potentially holding you to ransom over them or charging you excessive economic rent, or by funding it out of credit-fuelled consumer booms.

The problem of trade in the contemporary world is that most people and all countries are a long way from meeting those criteria, with few obvious political routes for realizing them – or at least few that will be painless and likely to achieve mainstream political traction. Yet I believe they *will* be realized because they're not just items from my personal wish list. They're ultimately the resting place for sustainable economic relationships. This gap between present reality and sustainable reality, with no clear path between, is one reason why I think we'll find our way to sustainable reality by a dark-age route.

NEVERTHELESS, THERE ARE some things happening at macro and micro levels that may help to shift the needle. At the macro level, governments in some Global South countries are starting to think in terms of national food and economic security, losing their allegiance to the economic asset-stripping associated with global free-trade ideology.[6] This is probably helped by the increasing multilateralism of global geopolitics and the waning of hard and soft power associated with the US and Western Europe. I'm doubtful national governments will do an especially good job of managing their food systems from the centre, but such narratives of autonomy may at least prepare the way for more radical forms of localist thinking.

They also prepare the way for the idea of keeping capital at home – the working assumption of economic pioneers like Smith, Ricardo and Keynes, who never advocated for the virtualized monetary merry-go-round of the present global economy. This is a prerequisite for the three planks of sustainable trading that I mentioned above.

When it comes to discussions about migration in the contemporary world, the focus is usually on people rather than capital, but the two are inextricably linked – and the causality usually runs from movements of capital to movements of people.

Recalling Tyson Yunkaporta's discussion of high-context cultures (see chapter 7, page 109) like Australian Aboriginal peoples, such cultures make a point of placing people within established social grids. A stranger will be asked, 'Who are you? Why are you here? Who do you know? Who are your people/clan? What story brings you here?' These aren't necessarily hostile questions, but they demand good answers.

At their worst, which they often are, current mobilizations around migration by so-called 'populist' movements in the rich countries of North America and Europe are simply racist. At their best, perhaps they could be interpreted as trying to build something like high-context culture. But right now, if a migrant from a poorer to a richer part of the world is asked why they're here, a sufficiently good answer is 'because you were there, messing up my country' – or, if not you or your ancestors specifically, then extractive capital from your country.[7] A prerequisite for building the high-context cultures we need in the future is to stop those flows of capital and build trade relationships of mutual advantage from localisms securely grounded in their ecological base. Only then are we entitled to ask such questions.

In view of the enormous uncertainties of the present meta-crisis, it's worth everybody imagining themselves as a potentially friendless migrant. Worst-case climate scenarios involving the loss of Atlantic Ocean current systems suggest rapid and catastrophic cooling in European countries. Picture white folks desperately trying to make it across the Mediterranean in inadequate small boats and throwing themselves on the mercy of the authorities in, say, Libya.

In the coming decades and centuries, the geographic distribution of human settlement will change profoundly, in largely unknowable ways. Ultimately, we will need to build locally grounded high-context cultures, but there's a lot of work to do first, probably through a dark-age route. I've repeatedly emphasized the need for open country as a way to make that process as humane as possible. It starts with keeping capital at home and building as best we can local economic autonomies in respect of land, food, materials, infrastructure, education and care.

※※※

LOCAL MARKETING OF local produce in actual, physical marketplaces is one among many places to begin this process. In my own specialism of local food, it's not as simple as just reinvigorating local markets, for various reasons I've already touched on. Here in Britain, the problem isn't lack of marketing opportunities so much as land access, food prices, energy prices and so on. What really needs redressing is the lack of people with local things to sell, not the lack of places to sell local things.

Still, supporting local markets as opposed to 'the' global market, bringing producers and consumers directly face-to-face, is a great way of starting to build the high-context cultures we need. Farmers' markets and the like in Britain have a reputation for being high-end foodie preserves of the middle class and are subject to some derision for that reason. It's fair enough up to a point, but this is only a symptom of the wider malaise analyzed in this book – specifically the overproduction of capital and the high cost of land and housing. I'm minded to summon the ghost of Mikhail Bakhtin and his arguments about carnival and the people's laughter, whose natural home was the local marketplace. The idea that cheap, crap food via long, vulnerable, high-energy, exploitive supply chains better serves the interests of the poor deserves no more than carnival mockery. We need to build better and more inclusive local economies out from local marketplaces.

History has many lessons to teach about the possibilities and perils of developing and defending local markets in relation to middlemen and toll-collectors, to cities, towns and countryside. They're beyond my scope here, but it's to these economic levels that we really need to be looking if we want to ease our dark-age descent path.

In truth, for all the positive stories and good energies they involve, current localist efforts cumulatively aren't anything like enough to offset the destructive drive of the over-accumulative, over-virtualized and over-monetized Mordor economy – which, again, is why I believe a dark age lies ahead. Nevertheless, here is where the light in that dark age will be found. When our efforts to carve out local autonomy and livelihood community apparently fail, it's easy to blame ourselves for not devising bigger or better ones, or to blame other members of our communities for failing to step up. Yet once the Mordor economy is unleashed and allowed to propagate over time, its inhuman systemic power is always likely to defeat such organic local efforts, and this isn't the fault of local producers or consumers. That power is not, however, immortal, which is why we must keep on keeping on and looking for the light.

CHAPTER 10

Politics of the People

When I moved to Frome over twenty years ago, I soon got to know Peter Macfadyen. It would have been hard not to because there seems to be at least two of him, always hard at work on local community and ecological projects. Whenever I've first come across a cool idea like local micro-grids, transition towns, community composting, electric delivery tricycles or solar hot-water systems, it usually turns out that Peter's long been on it and has already set up a local nonprofit.

Peter was characteristically in the thick of rejuvenating Frome Town Council when he helped establish Independents for Frome – a group that took control of the council in the 2011 election, winning ten of seventeen seats. It's been returned in three subsequent elections, winning all seventeen each time. Peter's book *Flatpack Democracy* gives a firsthand account of the story.[1] As the name implies, it's also a mildly insurrectionary instruction manual for others wishing to rescue their own local politics from moribund party-political bunfights.

To briefly summarize some aspects of IFF's approach, they set out to work as a group while retaining their independent voices and avoiding a party line wherever possible, to listen to local voices and bring people together across the town, to increase the diversity of representation and to say yes whenever possible to proposals rather than burying new ideas under thickets of stifling bureaucracy. They also set out to keep it light and fun. When he served as mayor, Peter's regalia comprised his characteristic shorts and red shoes along with a series of comic homemade chains of office, including one woven out of vegetables grown on our farm.

All this might sound like I'm trying a bit too hard for an upbeat start to a chapter about the politics of our dark-age future, and possibly I am. There's nothing very dark age about present-day Frome, with its artsy boutiques and inflating property values – though its medieval origins as a Saxon Christian mission and the remnants of its old industrial base speak of grittier times.

'Medieval' is a word that doesn't get a great press nowadays. It's typically used as a synonym for backward, barbaric, violent or oppressive. As for the Middle Ages in general, so for the Dark Ages in particular. Our modern sense is that the Dark Ages were a time of lack – a time with no pleasure and no politics, a dark heart of chaos to be avoided at all costs.

The first necessary correction to this is that yes, there were politics in past dark ages, and there will be politics in future ones. Modern notions of mere medieval barbarism become an intellectual barbarism of their own with this facile take on a millennium of intricate politics and history across swathes of the earth.

Some political scientists talk about a 'new medievalism' in contemporary global politics. They're not referring to its barbarity, but to its complexity. Specifically, they're referring to a newly emerging multiplicity of political forms in the twilight of the modern 'Westphalian' system created from the Peace of Westphalia in 1648 – our familiar world of nation-states, where political sovereignty emanating from a state centre suffuses each country smoothly up to its territorial boundaries, as in the 'sun-polity' metaphor I discussed in chapter 2 (see Suns, Supernovas and Solar Systems, page 38).

This modern multiplicity refers to organizations like NATO, the EU, the UN, the WTO and the OECD, all with some degree of sovereignty that complicates the Westphalian system. I don't think we've seen anything yet. Medieval times saw a much more contested field of politics, variously involving kings, emperors, dukes and other aristocratic houses, popes and other potential theocrats, religious orders and reform movements, trading leagues, free cities and republics, bandits and pirates, free peasant landholders, pastoralist hordes and indigenous or tribal/kinship-based communities, all laying claims to territory or people, and often vying with each other in respect of them. It saw different kinds of law, too – in Europe, common law, manorial law, Roman law and canon law. Something akin to that complexity may return in the dark-age future.

All of which no doubt is a far cry from Frome Town Council and the group that Peter helped to form. Still, that experience raises questions worth pondering as I press a wider argument in this chapter about the new medieval politics of our dark-age future. Specifically, it helps us think about what happens when people self-generate sovereignty bottom up, with a degree of indifference to higher levels of existing power and with an emphasis on building local resilience and communication. It also helps us think about the role of comedy in politics, which is a very serious matter.

Peter is the first to acknowledge that the new-look town council, while punching above its weight, has barely scratched the surface of local needs and possibilities. And, reading *Flatpack Democracy*, I'm struck by the dedication, thoughtfulness and hard work that was required even to chalk up its modest successes – which is sobering in view of the larger challenges to come, and the low base to build from with our existing high-energy industrial consumer society.

All the more reason to start now in whatever simple ways we can, while bearing in mind that we may need to be reinventing the whole livelihood base of local society – all of it, encompassing food, energy, housing, social services and material production – sooner than we think. It may only be when the existing supply systems for those goods have reached an advanced stage of breakdown that enough people start thinking not only about the material/biophysical aspects of that livelihood base, but also the kind of politics best able to organize it.

There's political work to do.

Livelihood Republics

My home town and its localist experiment has sometimes been jokingly dubbed 'The People's Republic of Frome'. Casting the localist net a bit wider, some years ago I wrote a series of essays around the theme of 'The Peasant's Republic of Wessex'. 'Peasant' to emphasize this need for localism ultimately to be grounded in practical livelihood-making. And 'Wessex', invoking the name of King Alfred's old Saxon kingdom in South West England where I live, defended as we saw in the preface from the Vikings, to suggest a functional scale for politics and the economy a bit larger than one small market town.

But let's home in on the common keyword of the two phrases: republic. In the future, there will probably be a lot of peasant's republics, or at least local livelihood republics, along the lines of the livelihood communities discussed earlier in the book. Here, I'll briefly sketch what it means for them to be 'republican' – a term that's only loosely connected to modern nation-states that call themselves republics or political parties that call themselves republican.

For the moment, I'm not going to look beyond the boundaries of the livelihood republic nor discuss how it relates to the wider political world in the dark-age future. I'll get to that in the next chapter. For now, imagine a situation in the confusions of the new dark ages in which a group of people settle a place, start generating livelihoods from it and set about establishing political protocols by which to organize their common life. Or, perhaps more likely, a situation in which people already in a given place decide that existing political arrangements are no longer fit for purpose and set about reinventing them.

In both these cases, people could do worse than drawing on the tradition of civic republicanism – a tradition that in European history was formulated intellectually in classical Greece and Rome, then by Renaissance and early modern thinkers like Niccoló Machiavelli (1469–1527), and more recently by various contemporary thinkers wrestling with the problems of the present. Similar ideas have developed in other cultures too – and arguably influenced later European ones. Ultimately, there are only so many ways to construe politics.[2]

Political scientist Iseult Honohan gives a succinct definition of republican politics as 'enabling interdependent citizens to deliberate on, and realize, the common goods of an historically evolving political community'.[3]

To understand what this means, it may help to define republicanism against what it's *not* in relation to other characteristic political ideas. So, it's not communitarian. That is, it's not grounded in a sense of some pre-existing 'natural' community arising before politics, perhaps one based in kinship or traditions from time immemorial. Hence, it's a 'historically evolving community' that's political in the sense that it's self-consciously inventing its rules.

Nor is it libertarian. It's not grounded in an idea of individual rights. In practice, it can and hopefully would emphasize some individual rights – for example, in rights to legal process or private property. But, taking the example of private property, it's not *grounded* in individual rights in the sense that it doesn't consider property a right belonging naturally to the individual. Instead, as in my discussion of property in chapter 6, it sees property as a right accorded to individuals (and not only individuals) by the community – hence its emphasis on *common good* or *goods*.

It's not socialist in the sense that, although it emphasizes the common good, it doesn't necessarily pre-empt what that common good is. It doesn't define the common good as equality of outcomes or capabilities. It's not inherently committed to the doctrine 'From each according to his ability, to each according to his needs', and it's not committed to the idea of bureaucratic government as the vehicle for realizing the common good.[4] But it does emphasize a rough equality of citizens and the avoidance of great disparities in wealth as prerequisites for achieving the common good and preventing factionalism and corruption.

Finally, it's not liberal in the sense that its emphasis on realizing common goods politically means that politics is at least partly about defining the nature of the good life. Liberalism, on the other hand, specifically excludes that kind of discussion. In theory, if not necessarily in practice, it's a live-and-let-live politics grounded in the idea that we're never all going to agree on the nature of the good life, so we should rule this out of political deliberation and allow people to pursue their own projects as far as possible – the embodiment of each to their own or, in modern parlance, 'you do you'. In the kind of republican livelihood communities I'm discussing, we will only be able to 'do us' to a limited degree. We'll have to find a way to determine the common good and the nature of the good life so that the community endures.

Perhaps this all seems quite abstract and not the kind of thing that future livelihood communities in stressful circumstances would have the time to worry about. But there are a lot of aspects of republicanism that precisely commend themselves in those circumstances.

The 'interdependence' and 'historically evolving political community' aspects of Honohan's definition loom large here. Suddenly, a loose group of people find themselves having to figure out how to make themselves into a functional political unit to realize the aims of securing basic livelihoods locally. No single person or household will succeed alone – they'll have to work together. But 'together' doesn't mean some vast communal enterprise, which will run aground in interpersonal conflicts, informational inadequacies and political power plays. It just means minimally defining the common good.

That 'minimally' might indeed be minimal, involving a lot of practical libertarianism and liberalism. There isn't the time or resources to micromanage anything but the fundamental basics. Our common good will be on agreeing how to allocate the means of producing food and the other goods and services our community needs. Some of the issues I've discussed in earlier chapters around defining property relations, marketing, industry, money, guilds and so forth represent a broad-brush attempt to sketch a republican sense of livelihood good in dark-age circumstances.

Still, there's a danger that republics will degenerate into repressive socialisms, and a greater danger that they'll degenerate into repressive oligarchies or patron–client systems. Land and power concentrates over time into fewer hands unless you take active steps to prevent it. Historic republics have sometimes put ceilings on landownership and other means of livelihood to prevent this, although often the emphasis is more on education and instilling ideas of the good of the wider community so that grasping behaviour and the seeking of personal advantage is frowned upon and rarely happens. This can be successful up to a point. Nowadays, we tend to think it's a weak defence against individual self-interest mostly because we live in societies that consider individual self-interest the fundamental human motivator. This is an unusual view historically.

Republics can also succeed in holding fast to ideals of the common good because they usually emerge out of the disintegration of a previous society that failed precisely for the lack of such ideals, a lack that persists in the memory of people in the new republic. In premodern times, the model often involved an aristocratic reformer rebelling against the oligarchy that formed them and allying with the ordinary people in a new dispensation. The foundation of the Athenian city republic by Solon (c.630–c.560 BCE) with his reforms of 594 BCE that released people from debt bondage is a case in point. There's an echo of that in populist-inflected politics of modern times encompassing figures as disparate as Vladimir Lenin and Juan Perón. The idea is that to realize their true ends, the people require leadership from above, albeit rarely aristocratic as such. Within civic republicanism, the point is that the republic requires a founder or group of founders acting as law-givers – a founding moment when the republic, which is not a given or natural community, comes into being.

As economic, biophysical and food crises amp up, supply chains falter and our conventional modern political stories stop making much sense, I don't find it hard to imagine latter-day Solons arising to found their new republics, along the lines I mentioned in chapter 8: cancel the debt, destroy the records, reallocate the land, delete the database, turn off the computer.

Natural Law I

Even so, the danger of new dark-age republics degenerating into oligarchic patron-client relationships or tyrannies remains real. It's a danger that stalks every political structure, including modern liberal capitalisms and communisms. One of the strengths of the republican tradition is its hardheadedness in acknowledging this and actively trying to build in defences against it, rather than succumbing to the happily-ever-after utopias typical across the spectrum of modernist politics.

That doesn't mean it necessarily succeeds. The idea of 'deliberating on and realizing the common goods of the political community' in Honohan's definition sounds great in theory: let's all sit down and figure this out like adults. But what if that doesn't work out? Adults have previous form here, after all. Modern republicans have discussed at length the possibilities for realizing the common good. Their emphasis on deliberation and non-dominance can be liberating, but it can also involve a kind of grim, exhausting and ultimately unsatisfying politicization of every aspect of life. The suspicion also lurks that getting people's agreement is just too weak a tool.

It will probably be easier to overcome this problem and realize the common good in a dark-age future than in the liberal-modernist present. If you don't grow the garden, you don't get food. If you don't band together, you get overrun by other groups who band together better. Republics often emerge in this way as defensive, militarized political units in times of conflict and trouble. Think Sparta.

It's likely such republics will emerge in the future for exactly this reason, but it's worth at least trying to aim for a republicanism that's a bit more capacious and open-hearted. What are the resources for doing so?

I've mentioned the philosopher Alasdair MacIntyre and his influential book *After Virtue* a few times already. MacIntyre largely endorsed the ethics of Aristotle (384–322 BCE), the philosopher of classical Athens who, along with his teacher Plato (c.428–347 BCE), basically invented the Western philosophical tradition. Aristotle's ethics are based on the idea that there's an essential nature to being a person, a true end, that it's our goal as people to try to realize, and that this is expressed in right-behaviour-manifesting virtues that aren't merely conventional or historical but, as it were, 'natural'. MacIntyre argued that all modernist philosophies have rejected this goal-based idea of an essential nature to be realized. The result is our 'you do you' world that gives us no basis for grounding morality. Hence the difficulties of defining the common good in modern republicanism – indeed, in modern society generally, and its consequent pathologies of financialized growth, commodification and ecological destruction, which tragically embody the ultimate logic of 'you do you'.

Aristotle's writings were rediscovered in medieval Europe after their dark-age eclipse via Muslim sources and worked into a synthesis with Christianity by the theologian-philosopher St Thomas Aquinas (c.1225–1274). Aquinas's Dominican philosophy (known as Thomism) was later contested by Franciscan philosophers, most famously William of Ockham (1287–1347), whose 'nominalist' alternative began to lay the foundations for modern liberal ideas of individualism and natural rights – ideas that have ultimately and unintentionally led to the contemporary moral impasse and the economic, political and biophysical meta-crisis.[5]

Here, I'm just going to draw a couple of thumbnail points out of this long and complex tradition. First, modern political thought usually scorns medieval philosophy as obscure and dogmatic. But not only did medieval philosophy pave the way for modern thought, it also wrestled with issues that are absolutely relevant to contemporary predicaments – specifically, how can we form enduring political communities that enable us to live well in uncertain times when our resources for doing so are thin?

MacIntyre argued that this was achieved with some success in the high Middle Ages, building on slim resources inherited from the 'Dark Ages' by 'generating just the right kinds of tension or even conflict, creative rather than destructive ... between secular and sacred, local and national, Latin and vernacular, rural and urban'.[6]

Second, I'd suggest that we or our descendants would be well advised to follow this example (as an example, not an exact replica) in the future. I can't lay out programmatically exactly what that would look like – there are already enough ten-point plans to save the world gathering dust. It has to be built up over time and enacted culturally. Some of the structures I've explored earlier in the book – families, local polities, landholdings, commons, guilds and beloved communities – represent nodes of social power wherein creative tension with higher level and more abstract political principle can manifest. Below I sketch a few aspects of these higher-level principles.

✦

WE INHERIT THE IDEA of natural law from classical traditions in Greek and Roman thought, and from their revival through medieval figures like Aquinas – as well as through Hebrew, Confucian, Taoist and other traditions worldwide. As C.S. Lewis put it:

> *First ... human beings, all over the earth, have this curious idea that they ought to behave in a certain way, and cannot really get rid of it. Secondly ... they do not in fact behave in that way. They know the Law of Nature; they break it. These two facts are the foundation of all clear thinking about ourselves and the universe we live in.*[7]

So, natural law refers to a universal moral order prior to any positive laws passed by this or that legislature. The concept has taken a lot of knocks in modern times, and it can be treacherous if used crudely (for example, along the lines that it's 'natural' for some kinds of people to be inherently superior to others). Equally, it grounds claims for liberation from oppression and the idea that might is not necessarily right.

Out of medieval natural law traditions emerged more recent ideas of individual rights and protection from arbitrary governmental power. In the dark-age future, we will have to let go of some of this – the parts that expect government or state sovereignty to enforce whatever individual rights we believe we're entitled to, and the liberal-individual idea that we can be whoever we want to be. In future livelihood republics, it's doubtful we can be whoever we want to be – which may not be a great loss, since it doesn't necessarily promote happiness or flourishing. But we can remember the idea and try to find a place for its positive aspects.

Instead of being whoever we want to be, we will develop frameworks for living, critical traditions. These will ground the importance of community and its various components – individual-in-community, household-and-family-in-community and the various other associational groups discussed in earlier chapters like commons and guilds, as well as spiritual practices.

Another inheritance will be modern ideas of nature and ecology, and what happens when we treat nature essentially as a resource to further immediate human ends – hence the case for Luddism and rights of nature discussed in chapter 6 (see Keeping Ownership Distributed, page 98). Likewise with the over-abstraction of money and the economy. This knowledge will help us ground local livelihood communities that, as I've emphasized throughout this book, will involve local agrarianisms and material and spiritual cultures keyed to a renewable ecological base.

Ideally, through all this we will learn to generate positive and creative tensions along roughly similar lines to the ones MacIntyre identified in medieval times. One such might be a tension between hierarchy and popular egalitarianism. 'Hierarchy', as I mentioned earlier, doesn't mean who's top dog and who's bottom of the pile, like a football league table. It's about parts within wholes, and the various reversals possible within that framing.

For example, we can think of humanity as a part of a more holistic, wider nature. But in much of everyday life, we distinguish the human from the natural and place human interests above those of other organisms. It would be difficult to cope day-by-day if we didn't. Ultimately, however, nature and the totality of other organisms is above and more important than us – something we sort of recognize, without doing a great job of incorporating it into modern life. Alas, we'll find out the hard way soon enough if we don't learn fast – if we don't listen to the teachings of the salmon (see The Hero Is You, page 11).

I'm aware that all this might sound rather vague, as indeed can natural law principles and Aristotelian ethics with their emphasis on the cardinal virtues of prudence, justice, fortitude and temperance – great ideas, but what do they mean in practice? MacIntyre got to the point: 'There is no way to possess the virtues except as part of a tradition in which we inherit them and our understanding of them from a series of predecessors.'[8] The problem is that our predecessors are either modern societies caught in deep crises – biophysical, economic, and political crises, which, ultimately, reflect a moral crisis that's precisely what demands new traditions to transcend – or else non-modern societies that, whatever their merits and valuable teachings, are so far from present circumstances that it would be absurd to try simply grafting a new tradition for ourselves onto their old roots.

As I see it, the way to meet that challenge is to defend or build livelihood communities as best we can, drawing on civic republican ideas of realizing the common good within newly developing forms of local politics, which can be grounded in electoral approaches like Independents for Frome or in various more activist, campaigning, religious, festive, guild-based or agrarian forms. But doing so, too, with an awareness of the need to transcend what I called the grim politicization of life in republicanism and to connect these communities to virtue ethics. The emphasis here is not on conforming ourselves to 'virtue' as defined and constructed for us by political or religious leaders, but on connecting to the virtues – that natural-law sense of how we ought to behave, developed within a critical community tradition – which our leaders should themselves embody and be held accountable against.

A WORD ON THE CATHOLIC basis of the preceding analysis and my own relation to it, along with that of the wider world.

I've dwelled at greatest length in this book on the case of Western Europe. This is partly because it's where I live and know best and partly because in many ways the present global meta-crisis has Western European roots. It's also because the Roman Empire fell hardest in Western Europe – so if there are lessons to be learned about the new dark age arising out of Western European culture from past dark ages, Western Europe may be a good place to look. And Western Europe at that time was Catholic.

The big picture of political history here is that ever since the fall of the Roman Empire, all efforts to unify Western European politics have failed – from the short-lived Carolingian Empire of the ninth century to the probably short-lived European Union of the twentieth and twenty-first centuries. The best unifying contender across all that time has been the Catholic Church but, after the Reformation split Protestant from Catholic Europe broadly across a north–south divide, that candidacy dimmed. The Peace of Westphalia that I mentioned earlier brought the major pan-European theatre of the wars of religion to a conclusion. That was the genesis of the modern system of nation-states.

I'm not going to apply my opening question from chapter 8 to all this. A unified Europe – good or bad? The Catholic Church – good or bad? There are some broadly positive things we take for granted today, like the limited powers of the state and ideas of natural rights and freedom that emerged out of the church's tussles with secular rulers. There are other things like racism and the church hierarchy's periods of venality, repression and abuse that go in the debit column. For the purposes of this book, what matters most is the distributist idea of generating a functional local politics within a more-or-less defective larger political field.

Distributism has Catholic roots, essentially being a modern take on the complex of natural law, Aristotelian virtue ethics and Thomism I discussed earlier, and involving an emphasis on subsidiarity and autonomy from state or market dependence in favour of local livelihood community. It traces a lineage from Pope Leo XIII's 1891 encyclical 'Rerum Novarum' (or 'Rights and Duties of Capital and Labour'), through the writings of Hilaire Belloc and G.K. Chesterton in England and the more radical and enduring distributist tradition in the US through figures like Dorothy Day and Peter Maurin, founders of the Catholic Worker Movement. It also connects with influential dissident strands of counter-modernist ecological thought as represented by the likes of Ivan Illich and Wendell Berry, and Fritz Schumacher's pioneering eco-treatise *Small Is Beautiful*.[9]

I'm not Catholic or even Christian myself. My parents grew up in working-class English families espousing nonconformist Protestantism, which they rejected long before I was born. They embraced versions of the secular liberal-modernism that energized the upward social mobility and progress narratives of their postwar generation. Religion in general, Christianity in particular, and Catholicism even more particularly than that, was not highly esteemed in my household as I grew up. Initially opting for my own version of progressive secular liberal-modernism, it's taken me most of my life – spurred on by the increasingly evident failures of that creed – to seek rapprochement.

Maybe rapprochement isn't necessary. Distributism takes the kind of positions on family, work, property, community and money I've outlined in this book with a 'common sense' appeal that needn't be specifically Christian, Catholic or Thomist. There are other paths that can be travelled.

Still, mitigating against destructive rather than creative tensions in a republican community probably needs more than just common sense. The relatively short-lived militarized and commercialized republics of premodern European history like Sparta, Venice and Florence are cautionary in this respect – and the tensions within more steady-state land and farm-based republics in a new dark age would probably be greater. A persuasive case can surely be made that somehow we need to find some spiritual glue (some 'mysteries and passions' – see chapter 9, page 143), a new sense of a critical livelihood-making tradition, some sense of the common life and its goals, of the kind that Aristotle and Aquinas sought, but made relevant to new circumstances.

Natural Law II

Natural law is given an apparently different meaning by anthropologist Philip Loring in respect of ideas about the wild inherent particularly among the Indigenous people who tend it and make their livelihoods from it close up. Loring writes:

> *The Wild can be dangerous, but it is not unruly. Wild does not mean lawless. Natural law is the strongest set of laws that we will ever encounter, and wild spaces follow these laws unconditionally. Wild spaces thus offer rules that anyone can learn to follow, and if we do follow them, we can be empowered, healthy and affluent. They're just not laws that we can set, or even influence.*[10]

This rings true. It works as a necessary, embodied, ecological and livelihood-focused complement to more abstractly political ideas of natural law of the kind I was discussing in the previous section. It resonates with the ideas of thinkers like Gerald Vizenor of Indigenous 'survivance' through stories prompted by 'natural reason' arising 'from experiences in the natural world'. This involves, says Vizenor, 'not a mere romance of nature' but instead 'character by natural reason'.[11]

We non-Indigenous who lack these stories and this character by natural reason might be able to learn the rules of wild spaces that Loring describes.

But this doesn't tell us quite enough about how to orient to natural law in constructing livelihood communities as a means of our own survivance in the face of liberal-modernism's increasingly indiscriminate destructiveness. It's the same when people say that instead of God they worship nature. Fine, but how do relationships with this nature-god and with other people manifest on a day-to-day basis?

The answer is in many different ways across different cultures – but, to invoke a generalization courtesy of the anthropologist Marshall Sahlins, typically through 'immanence'. According to Sahlins, the worldviews of the great global religions like Christianity invoke a transcendent otherworldly realm where God resides, and a very material, unenchanted Earth or nature. This contrasts with immanent (meaning inhering, remaining within) cultures where people are accompanied here on Earth by a cast list of dead ancestors, spirits, ghosts and deities – what Sahlins called 'metapersons' – on a near daily basis: 'The cultures of immanence, enspirited cultures, know only one world in which people interact with the myriad of nonhuman subjects, from the deities to the dead.'[12]

Sahlins elaborated on the cultures of immanence in numerous ways, including the idea – chiming with Loring – that people aren't in control of anything, not even their own culture. He discussed New Guinea societies where individual people are conceived not so much as having a soul as having a share in the collective life force of the enspirited world, and other animistic ones where exclusive clan ownership of ancestors brings forth food such as yams and other objects of exchange regarded as a form of the ancestors themselves – an example of private property (that again!) shared for the common good in what Sahlins called 'a cosmic system of sublimated cannibalism'.[13] For this reason, as in many Indigenous cultures, there are strong defences against waste and wanton nature destruction.

All this seems utterly strange to modernist thought. But its basic building blocks of distributed property made both exclusive and shared at different hierarchical levels and of embedded 'economic' relations governing people's interactions with each other and with things aren't so different (even if the boundaries between people and things are much less rigid in immanentist cultures).

Still, I'm not sneakily trying to turn New Guinea animists into Catholic distributists. The larger point is that people need to connect to a natural law that governs their relationships with each other and with nature, to create a sense of limits and the common good. This is to go beyond some toothless paper law forbidding this or that bad behaviour, which will inevitably be flouted – almost the more so precisely for being made illegal, especially by a government otherwise committed to limit-busting increase. We need to construct natural law that isn't flouted because it systematically organizes the economic stories we tell ourselves through what Amitav Ghosh has called a vitalist politics.[14] Like the story of the salmon, this enchants and makes immanent our traffic with the wider natural world, making our transgressions culturally outrageous. As I said earlier, this has to be more systemic than piecemeal legal victories. It won't happen overnight, but it's a cultural direction to emphasize.

Sahlins' distinction between transcendental and immanent cultures is too sharp. There are variants of modern culture that are more and less immanent. Less in the case of liberal-modernism and Protestant nonconformism, more in the case of Catholicism (despite the church hierarchy's periodic violent clean-up acts). More also in the lives of a lot of ordinary people who, in my experience, are often at home invoking shamanism, ghostly presences and hidden spirit influencers. Possibly, that's only because my experience has been unusually warped by living on the ley line of South West English counterculture running from Totnes and Glastonbury through Frome and Stroud. But it's quite a widespread and uncontroversial modern practice to visit graves and talk with departed family members. It's hard to cut immanentism out entirely.

Most of this modern immanence is disconnected from the business of making an everyday livelihood from the land and locality. It's one of the advantages of distributism that it does make that connection. Although distributism doesn't have much mainstream influence today, one future direction it can help formulate is aligning immanent elements with local livelihood strategies. Looking back at the quotation from Loring above, how do we embody the 'rules that anyone can learn to follow' in wild spaces (or in our wildly farmed spaces) culturally around how we produce and share food and other gifts of the wild?

The obvious place to look for historical inspiration on this point in most of the world, including Europe, is peasant culture. Historian Patrick Joyce's *Remembering Peasants* is, among much else, a wonderful sourcebook for the immanent aspects of enduring peasant culture in Europe. For example, this from a Polish peasant culture of a century ago:

> *Every field knows its owner, the Earth is indignant at every crime committed on its face. The moon watches and prayers are still said to it. The stars answer a woman or man who knows the right way to ask them. Nothing bad should be said near water. The wind listens and talks ... While animals do not know as much as man they know things he does not ...*[15]

... and so on. Whereas once I'd have dismissed this as outmoded mumbo jumbo, I don't anymore. I don't think secular modernist thought is any less bewitched in its own way – witness our obsession with brands, the 'magic system' of advertising and the seductions of the technological sublime that even lead some of us to hug nuclear waste.[16] None of this is taking us to a good place.

Joyce's examples are almost entirely Catholic and, in the words of one reviewer, 'miserabilist'.[17] It would be interesting to compare them with Protestant agrarianism in Europe and the Americas historically – but, while I daresay it's more complicated than a simple Catholic–Protestant dualism, those Protestant examples have more the vibe of an acquisitive and market-savvy mobility out of agrarianism and into capitalism, that 'religion of modernity'.[18] Modern intellectual traditions consist largely in cheerleading the transition from peasant to moneyed farmer and ultimately prosperous urbanite. But if I'm right that that transition is ultimately a dead end, then we need to look again at enduring, immanentist peasant traditions.

There's a disjunction here in that modern people nowadays seem happy to celebrate the immanentist close-to-nature lifeways of Indigenous, primarily hunter-gatherer, people, but not so much the immanentist close-to-nature lifeways of our recent peasant forebears. It's easy to build a complacent progressive politics on this. We liberal-moderns often now acknowledge that Indigenous people – those who were colonized, brutalized and considered inferior – turn out to have greater land wisdom than we descendants of the colonizers. But we also rest a little too comfortably on the fact that 'we' cannot be or claim to be 'them', which safely distances us from Indigeneity. It's as if Indigeneity is another mysterious at-a-distance technology, not unlike alt-meat or nuclear energy, that somebody else can deliver costlessly to our benefit. The Indigenous forager and the scientist as the elemental people of a mature modernity, unlocking its mysteries to achieve progress on our behalf.

European peasantries, by contrast, don't make such good progressive heroes, largely because of the historical burden they bring – not something to progress toward in the aftermath of a racist colonialism, but something apparently to regress back to in the aftermath of an unsustainable capitalism.

The truth, though, is that the land wisdom of peasants parallels the land wisdom of Indigenous peoples. Indeed, many Indigenous people *are* peasants Both use low-input methods keyed to a renewable local human ecology, and both – as Joyce puts it – understand land to be a 'social rather than an economic entity', anchored by family and kinship, such that 'reproduction as well as production comes into the picture'.[19] Anchored, too, by immanentist nature-thinking like that of the Polish peasants in the quotation from Joyce. Immanentist culture comes in many forms.

The land wisdom of peasants and Indigenous people is ultimately the land wisdom we moderns have to learn, not by some magic process that delivers us benefits for free but by long cultural development, starting now. There are no shortcuts to it. We can't just import someone else's symbology and start talking to the stars like Polish peasants of old. There's no harm in embodying old traditions in our practice, like planting holly trees by gateways, as I did on my farm. But we need to go far deeper than that. To begin that learning, it wouldn't hurt to drop the whole misplaced temporal topology of 'going back' and 'moving forward' as we try to learn how to be indigenous to place. No more elemental people – neither of the past, nor the future. This is the natural law and the essential nature we need to find.

CHAPTER 11

Divine Comedy: Or, the Stranger King

The local livelihood republics and natural law ideas discussed in the previous chapter can easily sound like pie-in-the-sky. Take a look up from idealized local politics, the argument runs, and when the proverbial hits the fan the future reality is a more dismal dilemma: the authoritarian central state or violent chaos.

I've already devoted some words to explaining why the reality is more complicated. We're too easily indoctrinated by the authoritarian state's self-justifications, grounded in the political philosophy of Thomas Hobbes and his *Leviathan*. To use Hobbes's terminology (see Suns, Supernovas and Solar Systems, page 38), yes, the power of the sword is prodigious, but politics is much weirder than that.

What's certain is there *will* be authoritarian central state governance in the future. There already is. And there will be chaotic violence. There already is. But these don't exhaust the field of possibilities. It will help to complete the analysis of politics begun in the last chapter to probe this point and bring the previous discussion of livelihood republics into relation with the Hobbesian duality of the mighty state or chaos.

The modern centralized state has three elements. First, bureaucracy – its power to keep tabs on everybody and everything, to remember everything. Second, competitiveness – its need to fight its corner, mostly against other states but also against other potentially threatening non-state actors. Third, and most importantly, sovereignty – the ultimate power to command.

The first element is increasing via things like new surveillance technologies, big data and artificial intelligence – although these depend on energy, material resources and political structures that aren't guaranteed to endure. The second element is also increasing as twentieth-century superpower certainties decline. These increases in the first and second elements can easily lead us to think there's bound to be an associated increase in the third element, hence authoritarianism. But sovereignty doesn't really work like that.

States will certainly try, and are trying, to augment their sovereignty. Some will probably succeed up to a point. But most will tread an increasingly fine line between meeting their wider international obligations and maintaining the welfare of their citizens through securing supply chains and key services. No doubt they will try to square the circle, as many presently do, by co-opting parts of their populations to nationalist 'we're in this together' rhetoric while making scapegoats of supposed internal and external enemies – but this is unlikely to be a winning long-term strategy as the challenges grow.

It would be nice to think that states could get over themselves and govern without recourse to ultimate power – a bit like Independents for Frome writ large, bringing people together, troubleshooting arguments, building consensus, finding workarounds, all without claiming to be the final boss. But the whole point of sovereignty is that it's unable to get over itself. It has to be the boss. Nor can it laugh at itself, which is one reason it was such a delight to make Peter Macfadyen's mayoral chain out of our vegetables.

But higher up the greasy pole of politics, the tensions in state sovereignty are getting ever more obvious. The onerous responsibilities that states have toward feeding the wider international financial system – the consolidation state issue discussed in chapter 1 (see From Liberalism to Distributism, page 21) – catches it on the horns of ever more intractable dilemmas.

One such issue in contemporary English politics is the long-running comedy over building a third runway at Heathrow airport. It's impossible to justify in terms of climate policy or community priorities, and impossible to avoid in terms of consolidation state responsibilities toward economic growth. It will boost GDP but not many people's wellbeing. Ultimately, the proliferation of this kind of thing risks breaking the implicit fiscal contract between governments and citizenries, and even breaking the whole idea of a centralized state as a unified entity.[1]

The result, at the least, is likely to be local failures, insufficiencies and potential power vacuums – local collapses, so to speak, at various geographic levels within nation-states as central state legitimacy wanes and the fraught equation of taxation, representation and services disintegrates, challenging state power and claims to ultimate authority. No doubt this will happen along existing fault lines – in a UK context, for example, with Scotland, Wales and Northern Ireland pulling away from their ties to London, and with that pattern repeating itself within those countries according to economic geography and other dividing lines.

In that kind of scenario, London may try to shore up its damaged sovereign claims by strengthening its ties with higher powers like the US. This has long been a strand in British politics, but one that's now looking shakier in the context of US–EU–Ukraine–Russia and wider geopolitics. More so than the UK, other countries such as Germany are rapidly exiting the gravitational field of the US as their own international and subnational tensions amplify.

Generally, in all these circumstances, the central state emanating from capital cities would likely respond with greater authoritarianism and coercion of ordinary people into its economic projects, but with uncertain results. All the more so in future situations of declining energy and fiscal power. Our view of modern states and governments as almost impregnable fortresses of sovereign power owes a lot to the recent history of generalized economic and energetic growth worldwide, stretching well past living memory, that they've been uniquely able to tap. The road for them from here looks rockier. Where that leads is not no politics, but potentially a different politics grounded in local livelihood.

※※※

APPROACHING STATE POWER from the other end, of what happens in its absence, probably lands in much the same place eventually.

There's a general foreboding about a violent 'dark age' future in contemporary society. It finds no platform in mainstream political discussion, but it manifests in other ways – not least in the chaotically violent future dystopias available from the writers of fiction. In my sunnier moods, I feel this violent outcome is overemphasized. Perhaps it stems from a fear among elites and the comfortably off book-reading public that many of the niceties of life we take for granted are about to be stripped from us. It's a well-grounded fear, but not quite the same as being chased down the road by ravening cannibals. Perhaps the cannibals stand as a demonic projection of our own guilt about the poor and the wretched of the earth.

A more realistic and more organized kind of violence where the writ of the state runs weakly is banditry – something that's manifested in many societies historically. As banditry organizes itself, it adopts forms like the protection racket and distributes some of its proceeds to clients. In other words, it levies tax and provides social services – the structural similarities between bandits (or 'warlords') and states or kings are strong. Bandits tend to be less bureaucratic and more arbitrary, but they possess the other two main characteristics of the state.

So, whichever side of Hobbes' dualism we start with, it's likely that in challenging future circumstances we end up with at least locally collapsed states, people trying to piece together livelihood republics in the resulting vacuum and various forms of violent and/or authoritarian state or would-be state actors snapping at their heels.

A lot of left-wing libertarian and anarchist thinking around livelihood republics, autonomism and municipalism devotes itself to imagining collaborative worlds of representative councils, deliberative democracy and so on that builds a wider secular republican politics from the bottom up. I'm sympathetic to these efforts, although I share the sentiments of *Lifehouse* author, Adam Greenfield, (see States of Refuge, page 35) that most of this stuff 'can only really be worked out in practice by those directly involved, in response to their emergent needs and desires'.[2]

But I don't think this is how things will shape up in the main, even if there are widespread local livelihood republics with a lot of day-to-day freedom to manage their affairs. This is partly because it understates the power of the would-be state actors snapping at localist heels with their attempted sovereignty grabs, and partly because it overstates the ability of secular republicanisms to get along without either a greater authority or lapsing into factionalism.

So, I'm going to pursue a different line of argument: in the future, local livelihood republics might well choose to ally themselves with one of the would-be wider sovereign actors snapping at their heels to buy some peace, while trying to keep their sovereignty at arm's length. Enter the concept of the stranger king.[3]

Taming Kingship

To understand how this plays out, we first need to take a step back and think about present and future politics through the lens of cultural anthropology.

A lot of societies build their politics around three kinds of cultural characters – gods, kings and the people. Kings like to justify their rule on the grounds that they're effectively gods-on-Earth (the main difference between a king and a bandit is that the king does this more convincingly). The people don't usually agree, seeing the king as just another person – but one with an anointed role to intercede with the gods, wherein ultimate sovereignty, the power to command, lies. The model here is the sacred king, who at the most extreme may be killed (sacrificed, meaning made sacred) by the people to propitiate the gods.

This seems a far cry from modern politics, but we've now merely displaced the divinity of the king onto the idea of the sovereignty of the people. Witness TV pundits on election nights intoning that 'the people have spoken' with misty eyes. The misty eyes are important, because for its power to work sovereignty has to be taken seriously. And in the case of the all-seeing, all-commanding modern state, we've got used to a *very* divine form of sovereignty, even if it's supposedly in the name of us, the people.

The idea of the stranger king is that the people stack the odds in their favour by importing a non-local monarch. In the introduction, I mentioned King William III of England, but from Holland, a relatively tame version of a stranger king that's intelligible within European modernist politics. Having spent the previous century or so arguing about what brand of king or queen they wanted, or even whether they wanted one at all, no doubt the English saw the benefits of an exotic but relatively powerless import.

More generally, the advantage from the people's point of view of a stranger king is that the king is then very obviously not 'one of us'. This helps confirm our status as equals. It would be a much more dangerous move to allow one among our ranks to rise to power. By this stroke also, it helps defuse potential factionalisms in the de facto republicanism of everyday local life, and it mitigates against us, the people, taking our own sovereignty too seriously and succumbing to our own closed cults of local community power.[4]

To emphasize the disjunction, the mythology around stranger kings in premodern times is that they break rules that would be unconscionable for ordinary people to break – such as transgressing sexual taboos or committing acts of extreme and arbitrary violence. But societies with this structure work hard to contain the remit of this dangerous sovereignty – only in the king's court or the sacred centre of the polity are such outrages permitted. This connects with my earlier discussion of the solar system or galactic model of political power. The king's attention is mostly devoted to doing his sovereign stuff in the sacred centre. Unlike a modern welfare-capitalist technocratic state, he has little interest in how the people manage their humdrum day-to-day affairs. The people may not get much in the way of money or resources from the centre, and they do need to create structures of local self-government. But they don't need the king's permission in relation to how to organize and regulate, in a modern context, things like farming, landownership, local markets, highway use and so on. There's leeway to build local governance and strong local livelihood communities.

From the king's point of view, historically stranger kingship could be appealing because on home soil the king's main competitors are other kings or would-be kings – not least dead ones, whose enormous mausoleums represent a monumental challenge (in every sense) to matching their status. There's a lot to be said for upping sticks and heading off to be a king somewhere else, where the status contests are less challenging. Again, framing it in modern secular terms, our contemporary ideologies of progress very much take this form. It's important to us to grow the economy and proclaim ourselves richer, healthier, longer-lived and more technologically advanced than our forebears. This gets increasingly difficult in a finite world, just as kings struggle with the proliferation of their dead ancestors. Hence our tendency to latch onto increasingly improbable techno-fixes to keep feeding our modernist egos.

In any case, in the traditional stranger king setting there's typically a dual form of sacred–secular sovereignty: the people, the locals, are seen as the owners of the land, whereas the king, the stranger, is seen as the owner of the people. The king expects various kinds of tribute and ritual obeisance from them, but he doesn't interfere overly in their day-to-day affairs.

Hopefully, it's clear where I'm going with this in terms of local livelihood republics set within wider claims of sovereignty in the future. Doubtless you could argue it's wishful thinking on my part in the face of the fearsome military and technological powers of the modern state to expect it to leave us largely alone to get on with the local business of making a modest livelihood from our ecological base. Maybe it is, but the counterargument is that it would be wishful thinking on the part of states forced to engage in increasingly fierce interstate rivalry over political power and resources in an energy-constrained world to be overtaxing, co-opting or otherwise annoying land-based communities. Especially communities that can't contribute much materially to state enterprises and are probably better kept quiet where they are than being turned into costly wards of an already challenged state that's failing to keep its side of the welfare bargain.

NOWADAYS, WE HAVE very divine secularized state sovereignty in the form of modern bureaucratic welfare-capitalist states that supposedly govern in the name of the people, but don't really. Recently this seems to be weakening, with a series of comic reversals that take us into the weirder political world of the stranger king.

One minor (and almost literal) shot across the bows here in Britain occurred in 2016 with a public poll to choose the name for the British Antarctic Survey's new research vessel. And the people's choice was: Boaty McBoatface. But, as I said earlier, sovereignty is a serious matter and the powers that be opted instead to name the boat *Sir David Attenborough*.

Later that same year, the entire electorate was called upon to vote on the UK's continued membership of the European Union and returned by a narrow margin the more comic option of leaving – comic in the sense that it wasn't the 'sensible' result of established serious opinion in view of the economic self-harm involved. Troubled though I was by the referendum result, I have to confess that this comic option did involve an element of nose-thumbing at perceived elite opinion and a sense of popular sovereignty.

A year earlier, outsider socialist candidate Jeremy Corbyn had been elected to the leadership of the Labour Party through popular mobilization among members. Corbyn was widely seen by supposedly expert opinion as a non-serious and unelectable candidate. This prompted the Conservative government to call a snap election, in which Corbyn's Labour Party secured only 2 per cent less of the popular vote than the Conservatives, wiping out their majority and forcing them into coalition government. More comedy.

Corbyn's eventual ousting required a combination of dubious political gymnastics by the more 'serious' centrist elements of his party, a Brexit side-plot and the arrival to the leadership of the Conservative's own comedy candidate, Boris Johnson. Five years later, the Conservatives fell – outflanked on the right by the Reform Party, a vehicle for another comically performative politician, Nigel Farage, and slightly to its left by the Labour Party under the technocratic authoritarian centrism of Keir Starmer, who gained a large but politically fragile majority

In the same year as the UK's EU vote, the US electorate delivered the presidency to Donald Trump. Trump was hardly a stranger to the public, albeit a stranger to Washington politics. But the litany of his transgressions that would have torpedoed any normal political candidate's chances carry definite echoes of the stranger king. Whatever Trump is, he's certainly not a technocratic manager of the liberal-modernist status quo. His re-election in 2024, notwithstanding the events in the Capitol four years previously, represented another comic choice. Meanwhile, professional comedians have gained political traction in other countries, such as Beppe Grillo in Italy and Volodymyr Zelensky in Ukraine, the latter rising to prominence by playing the role of the president in a TV comedy before becoming the actual president.

In describing these events as comic, I don't mean to make light of what's involved. As I said earlier, comedy is a serious thing – a point that's also underscored in the discussion of carnival laughter in chapter 9 (see page 144). There are serious dimensions to these politicians' platforms with serious consequences for many people. Nor is my analysis incompatible with other interpretations, such as the power of dark money, divisive dog-whistling, malevolent media influencing or the ultimate triumph of postmodern, television-politics as empty spectacle. For various reasons, I don't think such interpretations alone are adequate, not least because they don't explain why these strategies work.

But one interpretation that I'd submit is that ordinary people are using the blunt tool of one-person-one-vote modern democratic politics to bring their politicians down to earth and try to make them more sacral than divine. It's a high-stakes game, and it can easily backfire – allowing comic politicians to meld the liberties of the stranger king with the power of the modern bureaucratic state to build divine-dictatorial authoritarianisms.

Here lies the fear of fascism, which, as I see it, is a genuine one even if progressives tend to over-apply it to all sorts of regimes, people and political positions that really aren't. Partly, it depends on the broadness of the definition. Franklin D. Roosevelt's view of it as ownership of government by an individual, group or another controlling private power might suggest that most governments of the world today are fascist, whereas views more specifically grounded in the authoritarian politics of early twentieth-century Europe would suggest otherwise. From my distant vantage point on current US politics, the main problem with the fascist label now being applied to the Trump regime is that it imposes a smooth narrative arc on a more jumbled storyline that hasn't yet been written.

New York Times columnist Jamelle Bouie writes that Trump's administration is taking 'an ax to any and every program that helps ordinary Americans' and is degrading 'the federal government's ability to deliver critical services ... There is no apparent rhyme or reason to these cuts, only a nihilistic drive to cause as much damage and to make it as irreparable as possible.'[5]

This looks less like the programme of a fascist than that of a stranger king who has less obeisance than he wants and more sovereign power than he should be allowed to have. The opportunity, as Trump's administration axes services, is to rebuild them locally outside the central state sovereignty that he's degrading, using low-input human resources and capabilities of the kind that's going to be almost all we have in the future anyway. This is something that people in many other countries have had to do in recent and more remote history. The arbitrariness and inexplicable violence of the stranger king in his sovereign centre provides a foil for we the people, the owners of the land, to unite among ourselves around a local sense of justice and order.[6]

I'm not saying more conventional avenues of political resistance aren't also relevant, but here is a moment when the totalitarianism of modernist politics – which is implicit even in its more benign versions – might just be turned into something else, a game that doesn't really apply to us, the ordinary people. Instead, contain the sovereignty of the king and give him obeisance if necessary, accompanied with some appropriate carnival laughter. The alternative is to surrender our powers of self-sovereignty and attach ourselves as camp followers to such pretenders. In a modern context, that easily does result in forms of fascism or other kinds of tyranny. So, the political choices ordinary people make at the moment are consequential.

I'd make the same recommendation in respect of more 'normal' technocratic politics across the liberal-modernist spectrum, such as the Starmer administration in the UK. It's less bull-in-a-china-shop, but its incoherence around economic growth, climate, land use and, ultimately, culture takes the slower road to the same outcome. There is no normal, centrist politics to revert to anymore.

Alasdair MacIntyre wrote, 'The shared public goods of the modern nation-state are not the common goods of a genuine nation-wide community and, when the nation-state masquerades as the guardian of such a common good, the outcome is bound to be either ludicrous or disastrous or both.'[7] As I see it, if a latter-day stranger king like Donald Trump successfully masquerades as the guardian of the common good, the outcome will indeed be both ludicrous and disastrous. But the same will be true of liberal-modernist technocrats. It's true of every politician who gets burned by the corrupting flame of claiming state sovereignty as a means of delivering the common good. We need to stop believing that state sovereignty is geared to benefitting ordinary people.

Every political game has high stakes – it's entirely possible that more traditional centrist parties like the British Labour Party or the US Democrats could fashion authoritarianisms in concert with their 'consolidation state' corporate allies which gradually pick off alternative bases of autonomy. Certainly, one of the problems these parties have is a public perception that they've abandoned their populist base among ordinary people and increasingly represent the concerns of corporate-managerial elites. The uneasy alliance between corporate power and populist elements within parties like the US Republicans may soon succumb to the same perception. The time is ripe for a new Solon. Failing that, the future descent of both the major US political parties to malevolently authoritarian forces depicted in Stephen Markley's novel *The Deluge* seems to me plausible – and this isn't a problem that's confined to the US.

The final redemption of the Democrats and thence the world in Markley's book I find much less plausible. Ultimately, no politician or party has the answers for staving off economic-political collapse and the emergence into dark-age circumstances that will probably result, because there aren't really any answers. So instead of seeking best-case scenarios we believe can rescue us, I think it's better to seek least-worst ones with the humbler aim of creating local resilience, refugia or 'lifehouses'.

A least-worst outcome that could emerge from contemporary politics in the West is the development of solar system or galactic-type polities of the kind discussed in chapter 2. A series of sacred centres in places like Washington, DC, and London involving performative and ineffectual rites of 'making America great again' or 'taking back control' while crumbling infrastructures, rising prices and faltering supply chains push ordinary people into creating de facto local livelihood republics while paying lip service to rule from the centre. That's why I portrayed the US capital in my arc of future Earth in the introduction as I did. Presidents Washington and Lincoln are still standing sentinel at the sacred centre of the nation, but the real politics is happening in places like Kansas or New England, under cover of the darkness.

'RENDER TO CAESAR the things that are Caesar's, and to God the things that are God's' is one of Jesus's many enigmatic assertions reported in the Gospels.[8] When I was younger, I saw it as a case of political conformity and empty otherworldliness typical of religion. I now see it as something much more subtle – in essence, an invitation to think about three questions. What do we genuinely owe to state power? How might that change? And how might we craft our politics accordingly?

It's significant that the occasion of the remark was a discussion about paying tax to the colonial Roman occupiers in its own money, with Jesus's interlocutors attempting to trap him into either supporting or opposing the regime. I'd suggest on the basis of my discussions about money in chapter 8 and politics in this chapter that a good answer to those questions should likewise avoid the either/or trap: What do we genuinely owe to state power? A bit, but not much. How might that change? It's diminishing. How might we craft our politics accordingly? Via local livelihood republics set within the lightening shade of modern states on their way to becoming postliberal galactic polities ruled by stranger kings.

I don't think it's possible to answer the questions much more specifically than that in the pages of a book. It needs to be worked out variously and locally with careful attention to limits and contradictions through hard politics across the various dimensions I've considered in this book – land access, money, markets and so forth. But I will try to put some of these ideas in motion in the next chapter.

Another aspect of Jesus's Caesar/God assertion is that it invites us to consider what exists transcendently beyond the state or secular rule. In other words, it asks what we owe to God as well as to state power. The liberal-modernist answer is 'nothing', and that there is no God, or at least not one that's relevant to politics and collective human affairs. The problem with this was well described by David Foster Wallace:

There is actually no such thing as atheism. There is no such thing as not worshipping. Everybody worships. The only choice we get is what to worship. And the compelling reason for maybe choosing some sort of god or spiritual-type thing to worship ... is that pretty much anything else you worship will eat you alive.[9]

We know this is true at the individual level – the worship of such things as money, power, human beauty and social status destroys the person who worships them. We know this from myths, stories, Shakespeare's plays, religious and ethical teachings. But we also know it for ourselves in our bones, even as we're tempted daily into these worships. This is the natural law basis for a life based on the virtues that I discussed earlier.

But all this is also true at the collective level of society. I've argued in this book that liberal-modern politics across the spectrum from left to right involves the worship of ourselves, of social progress, of state or political power, of technological mastery, of a kind of vampiric conquest of life itself via transhumanism, long-termism and other contemporary creeds, and that this worship has created monsters like over-financialization and climate change that put us on the brink of a new dark age.

For some of those who worship instead within the existing world religions or in immanentist traditions, these points may be self-evident, even if that doesn't necessarily make it easier to avoid destructive self-worship. An advantage of these religious traditions is that they've survived from older times. Not unscarred or uncorrupted, but at least they provide foundations to build on – it's harder to invent traditions anew and build on an empty throne vacated by the human self-worship of liberal-modernism. However, that may be what we have to do if the existing world religions, like existing world politics, have run out of energy for the work of renewal that's needed.

To be clear, I'm absolutely not arguing that secular rule should be replaced with theocratic rule. Constructed and imposed religions, whether secular ones like nationalism and capitalism, or religious ones from Byzantium to the Massachusetts Bay, are just other ways of eating people alive. What I *do* argue is that we need to move on from liberal-modernism and create livelihood communities oriented to the common good. This will be less a matter of 'choosing' what to worship, as per David Foster Wallace's remarks, and more one of grounding worship in a rich and lived local sense of the virtues and practical livelihood.

If that sounds vague, it's because our fundamental problems today aren't economic ones to be corrected with specific policy instruments or engineering ones to be corrected with specific new technologies, but cultural and spiritual ones that are inherently more open-ended and can only be corrected with the slow accretion of thought and practice. The thought that's most worth looking at encompasses things I've mentioned earlier like money and economy as a power of the whole community, natural law as among other things a Luddite sense of limitation imposed by the wider human and natural ecology, and a religious sense of immanence and worship. The practice that's worth looking at is the construction of new, distributed local livelihood communities as best we can in the current challenging circumstances. As I said earlier, there's work to do.

CHAPTER 12

Walking West

To colour the picture I've painted in previous chapters, in this final one I'm going to describe a fictional future journey in the part of the world I know best, sometime around the end of the twenty-first century. I'm convinced that human beings and human societies can thrive in agrarian localist – and immanentist – ways of being, but the problem is that the path to those ways of being is crooked, involving 'the complete destruction of business as usual' (see chapter 1, page 17).

Present circumstances resemble the old joke about the countryperson giving directions: 'You don't want to start from here if you want to get there.' But we do need to start from here, and it's hard to see how we get there without a perilous journey. What remains true is that people in the future will move in search of a better life, perilously if need be, just as they've always done.

The future I'm projecting fits within Michael Albert's darker age 'neofeudal' or 'breakdown' pathways mentioned in chapter 2 (see States of Refuge, page 35). But in keeping with my title, I try to portray as much light against that darkness as I feel I can.

What I write here is not a prediction.[1] I see it as a dark thrutopia embodying aspects of arguments made earlier in the book. A tale part cautionary and part hopeful about a future southern England from this social scientist turned small-scale farmer with a nod to the cautionary fictionalized tales increasingly told by scientists like Dave Goulson and Bill McGuire.[2]

As we saw in chapter 2, Henry David Thoreau remarked, 'in wildness is the preservation of the world' in his essay 'Walking'.[3] The essay made a resonant case for seeking 'wildness' by walking west, albeit a somewhat politically uncomfortable one in the context of his nineteenth-century

New England grounding. Let's take a late-twenty-first-century walk west in a different setting, asking ourselves as we go what it means to be wild or tame, and what it means to preserve the world.

❧❧❧

> One summertime, when the sun was hot, I dressed myself in the glorified rags of the working man and slipped out of London.[4] I'd heard from a kinswoman near Glastonbury that she would welcome my help on her small plot. She was a cousin or second cousin, or something. I'd never got my head around that kind of stuff. I'd met her only once, when I was a child. But her offer had started to seem no worse a prospect than the increasingly hardscrabble life of the city. Probably better.
>
> I was one of the lucky ones, really. I had a steady job as a compostman. It didn't pay well, but at least it paid regularly – not like those on the government dime who never knew when their next payday would be. But the street violence was getting worse, the heat and the water were getting worse, my squat was falling apart with little chance of repairing it, and it was shaping up to be another bad malaria season. Most people I knew were scraping by, but you heard about stuff happening. Friends of friends. Soon it might be friends. Soon it might be me. Life was getting cheaper. Not the cost of it – if only – but life itself.
>
> London has a long history, but it was never built for a couple of million people to live on the back of a farm society with the climate going haywire around us. The tunnels filled. The sewers. The mosquitoes. The Thames. People I knew were drifting away. Sometimes it was unannounced – suddenly they'd just be gone. Maybe you'd hear about them on the grapevine, or maybe you wouldn't. They might be dead for all you knew. But other people would talk about their plans, varying from the wise to the foolish, until the day came. You'd break open a bottle of precious homebrew and toast them on their way. And think about asking if you could go too.

I didn't know if my plan was one of the wise or foolish ones. Finding my way the hundred-and-something miles west from London to Somerset was a daunting prospect, but also an exciting one. It was time for me to wander abroad in the world, listening out for its strange and wonderful events.[5]

I'd queued for hours to get my name on a work detail for some big construction project near Dunstable, just out beyond London in the home counties, that green ring of steel surrounding the city. Green because it was still a pretty landscape, and leafy enough, mostly. And steel because it was where the rich folks, the movers and shakers who ran London, preferred to live. Not much happened there that they didn't have a hand in or turned to their advantage. And not many people went into or out of it without their say-so. Whereas Somerset – well, I wasn't sure, but it had the savour of another country. You don't really hear people saying 'London' anymore to stand for the country as a whole, except with an irony that's bitter when it's spoken by people from outside it. The city itself, these leafy counties around it, the ports and farmlands it commands, the remnants of old England, old Britain – that's 'London'.

I don't know what they were building out in Dunstable – obviously something important, but it's best not to ask too many questions. I had no intention of doing the work anyway, but the free bus ride was a boon to get me on my way. A poor man found loafing in the home counties could land himself in trouble. Some easy wheels to Dunstable across the green ring of steel suited my needs.

There was a buzz of expectation among the ragtag group on the bus. The prospect of money, the prospect of doing something different, the nervousness of an unfamiliar destination under the command of unknown superiors. As we made our way down the entrance ramp of the motorway, I spotted the parliament building on its repurposed site of an old museum. Relocating Her Majesty's Government from the sacred but now swampy precincts of Westminster to the waste land of Colindale must have seemed like sound common sense at the time, but with hindsight it wasn't the greatest move for maintaining national purpose. The queen does her best to strike a tone. But not many people hear her earnest exhortations about the country pulling together to beat the crisis, and even fewer care. Hard to take seriously when she's not even in the country anymore. Apparently, she barely leaves Balmoral these days. They say it's turning into Gormenghast up there.

The Americans have always been smarter about stuff like this. The Potomac defences cost a fortune, but it created jobs and it maintained at least some semblance of an old-style nation with a stable, sacred centre shining forth. Still, it's one thing to believe your own bullshit. Expecting others to is a different matter. Greenland had gone okay, but the whole Canada thing was still tying them in knots all these years later. Not to mention the financial downturn, and then the flu. Oh, and the storms and wildfires.

Still, we don't hear much news from the rest of the world these days. I try to stay informed. I learned a lot from my grandad. He was an embittered old academic, but not such a bad guy when you got beneath the grumpiness. In his youth, he'd visited exotic places like Chicago. My mum told me he wasn't too bothered when they shuttered the university for good, and he could devote himself full-time to his little smallholding on the edge of the city. I learned a lot about growing and farming from him, which has stood me in good stead.

I'm glad the old guy was too far gone to realize what was happening when they requisitioned his holding for the London Grows initiative and rammed that arable field through our land. The language at the time was all about the need to feed city populations with 'efficient, modern agriculture'. So, it was goodbye to his garden beds, food forest and foraging goats, a compulsory purchase pittance for me and my folks to seek a precarious fortune in London, and the land consolidated in the hands of some contract farming concern with corporate money behind it. For the 'common good' – ha! The public enclosure of our little bit of private property. I daresay my grandad is still spinning in his grave. He used to mutter darkly about 'the liberal-modernist state' and its nonsensical metrics. How it would all end in tears.

A lot of his patter went over my head as a kid. Still does, really. But as I watched stressed-out civil servants hurrying to work in Colindale, it felt like they were trying their best even though the whole thing was deflating. A few generations of upward mobility built on fossil fuels and colonial plunder, and now we were sinking back into the normal state of things – the water, the earth, the people around you, getting by. But at least most of us were on the downhill journey together. Instead of a warlord aristocracy to worry about, the great and the good were more like some rudderless focus group trying to get their heads around an impossible problem. People who still couldn't quite understand what was happening around them, badly orchestrated by these grey technocrats in Colindale.

True, there were political chancers trying to ride the wave of the mob. The latest version on that front is Mayor Kingman, yet another 'colourful' politician promising to drain the swamp and crack down on the criminals and the other evildoers from his London base. It amazes me that anyone still believes this shtick when there's an actual swamp around Westminster that nobody knows how to drain.

Some still get drawn into these tall tales, but fewer. When everything kicked off years ago, there was a lot of clamour about blaming the immigrants, stopping the boats, pointing the finger at France, pointing the finger at anyone but ourselves. There's less of that now. And not much immigration. Some are still drawn here by the myth of the old West, but the idea of England as a sceptred isle was an early casualty of the crisis, here and elsewhere. Besides, when things are unravelling it's not so easy just to hitchhike over from the Sahel or wherever. It's hard enough to get from London to Somerset. On which note, take a look at this Londoner dreaming of a better life. Who's the migrant now?

Anyway, it felt good to get out of London and see a bit of countryside from the relative comfort of the bus before I had to strike out on my own. After I got my lunch ration, I slipped away from the worksite as soon as an opportunity arose. This was a moment of danger. Years before I was born, they'd finally succeeded in implementing the national ID card scheme that the Labour government had first floated at the beginning of the century. I don't think anybody cared much about ID cards further west, and the whole system was falling apart anyway. But in the green ring of steel around London, things could go badly without the right documents. The forgery in my pocket wouldn't stand much scrutiny. I don't think London could decide whether it wanted to keep the poor and needy in the city or disperse them. Where would they cause the least trouble? There was a resettlement scheme to seaside places like Margate. A lot of poor people jumped at the option of a one-way ticket out of the city and a few pounds in their pocket, but you didn't have to be a genius to see that London was going to get the better of that deal.

Meanwhile, ID cards meant that the powers that be and their eyes on the ground could process you whichever way the wind blew. And, generally, it blew favourably for these rich shire folks. Crisis or no crisis, some things don't change, I guess. Money, energy, policing. Especially policing. You didn't have to put too much of a foot wrong. If the face didn't fit, a unit might pick you up and chances are you'd get a five-year sentence for vagrancy to be served as a so-called 'apprentice' to a Parishioner. Thomas Spence – now there's another old guy turning in his grave.

With a mixture of stealth and brazenness, I made my objective by nightfall – the old Ridgeway Path that cuts out west along the backbone of southern England. As the name implies, it mostly runs along ridgelines where there isn't much water. Not much water means not many people, and that suited me fine. But if you know where to look, you can find just enough to keep from parching. I walked at night a lot to keep my thirst and my encounters down, lying up during the hot days. Sometimes I'd climb a tree and hide in the foliage. It's amazing how rarely people look up. Dogs can be more of a problem. The ones with people. More so the ones without.

A lot of the country as you head west is good arable land. The London Grows scheme is still very much alive. Its clammy fingers reach far out from the city, giving farmers and corporations access to whatever diesel the government can lay its hands on, or credits for making their own biodiesel, and contracts for selling grain to processors in the city. Nobody really knows what crops will work these days. As I walked, I saw a lot of wheat for bread and barley for beer – nobody grows row crops for livestock anymore. Also, rye as a banker for the hard winters and sorghum as a banker for the hard summers. Throw it up in the air and see what comes down. Then repeat next year, and every year as far ahead as you dare to think.

Most of the giant farm machinery of the 2020s was melted down long ago, leaving only landfills of LCDs and valueless semiconductors, but you see more than a few old Massey 135s and the like puttering around the fields. They don't have any software to go wrong, and they're a better fit. The fields are smaller than way back then, with more room for hedges to try to dull the knife of the winter storms. Goodness knows if the wildlife prefers the hedges or would like the old climate back. I don't think anyone's counting anymore.

There are more farm animals visible in this landscape than back then, too. Dual-purpose cattle and lowland sheep breeds like Wiltshire Horns. Traction and fertilizer costs something crazy, so you see all sorts of experiments. Mixed farming, grazed leys, draft teams, sheep grazing the rough downland by day and driven down at night to dung the arable fields like they did in the times before fertilizer. In the old days with the big tractors, people mocked the kids' books with farmyard pictures full of hens, cows and horses as just so much romanticism. Ha! There's nothing romantic about it now. Just the hard graft of making mixed farms work on thin margins and wild weather. Government scheme or going it alone, the burden's on the farmer, as always.

As I got further west, I moved into Wiltshire's Neolithic landscapes. The White Horse, Wayland's Smithy, Stonehenge to the south, Avebury. The things those tombs and circles must have seen in their time. The things they're seeing now.

The solstice had passed a couple of days before I passed through Avebury. There were still bustling encampments there, temporary outposts of the new religious wanderers who'd emerged from the nucleus of New Age, spiritual, Aquarian types that had long made Glastonbury their home. Well, it was certainly a new age now – they'd got that right. Wild-looking people with unkempt hair, but mostly harmless I thought. Shamans and seers preaching and begging. People arguing and crying. All human life. With some of them it felt like they were there because there was nowhere else for them to be. You could feel their stress. Others seemed in their element – people emanating a kind of wild power and freedom. Also, horses and wagons, bicycles and motorbikes – even the occasional van. I don't know how they kept those things on the road. Not so many roads to drive on these days anyway. Feeling out of place, I tried to saunter confidently through the crowds. They soon thinned out and I headed down into the plain.

Warminster still has its military, but it's more of an outpost now. I'd heard they share quarters and weapons with the police. Ammo is hard to find, I guess. Anyway, I gave the place a wide berth. Crossing the boundary from Wiltshire into Somerset through some well-coppiced woodland, it felt like more than an old line on a map I'd passed over.

The countryside was different, I'd known that from before – an older countryside of small fields and scattered hamlets that had avoided most of the hollowing out of the enclosures three hundred years ago, and was still plain enough to see. As well as the fields and hamlets, a denser tracery of broken country lanes, odd little blazes of woodland with willows, field maples, hazels and other trees I didn't recognize, all as well worked as the coppice I'd first passed through. But it wasn't only that. The arable fields with their row crops that spread everywhere further east had dwindled away. Here, there were gardens and tiny fields, mixed with orchards and copses. Goats and cattle were grazing along the lanes. Old, tattered fencing was missing in long stretches where it had been taken for some other use. The best fencing was around the gardens, where there was usually a ramshackle house cobbled together out of wood, stone and junk as more people had moved to occupy the countryside. Finessed with breeze blocks, roofing tiles and mock-Tudor ornament liberated from the now mostly derelict suburbs of the volume house-building phase that came to an end just a few decades ago when the pull of the money system came to its inevitable defeat from the gravity of the land.

So there were more people around here, then. They often looked curiously at me as I went by, but I'd lost the fear I'd felt further east. I didn't look so out of place here, and the vibe had less of that eastern suspiciousness and aggression. I asked around for Jane. Some kept tight-lipped, but I obviously wasn't from the government or some other potentially hostile force. I mentioned a few things I knew about the village, and the people here. That opened things up. The universal currency of place and kinship coming back to life.

Jane didn't seem surprised to see me. 'You came, then.' A quick hug and a tired smile, then she was bustling with practicalities.

Her place is a handful of acres and a few ramshackle cabins on some nicely sloping ground above the river. It's got four polytunnels, only one of which has any plastic, which isn't long for this world. The rest is more for hope, and trellising. The place is a riot of crops. Mostly veg, but there are fruit and nut trees. Patches of wheat, rye and sorghum, again. Potatoes. Jerusalem artichokes. Don't put all your eggs in one basket. Oh yeah, a few chickens too. The more I poked around the place in the days after I arrived, the more I found. Flax. Medicinal herbs. Clover. Reeds and willow pollards by the sink outflow. Mounds thick with mycelium. Hazels. A mixed firewood coppice laced with squirrel traps. An outhouse and compost heap, right up my street. Rural utopia? No, a lot of work, which I guess was why Jane was glad to have me. And a daily life without much backup. But that's true of almost everyone these days. The price we pay to past generations. Our glorious dead.

Jane's gran Kate had come to this place years ago for a vegetable growing job. The global economy went into what they called 'the downturn' soon after. A downturn that keeps turning down. At least it spared the climate a bit. There was no money to pay for jobs growing vegetables anymore, but growing vegetables was still a job worth doing.

I think people back then were amazed at how quickly things unravelled, like they didn't realize they'd already run off the cliff long before. Energy prices, food prices, climate shocks, the financial sector imploding into its own nothingness, the Americans and the Chinese defining their spheres and, all of a sudden, those layers of complexity that people needed to get fertilizer from A to B and plastic from B to A were washing away like sand on the tide. Everyone had had a theory about modernization, but nobody had one about de-modernization. My grandad told me people used to say 'this is the twenty-first century' when they were shocked about bad stuff happening. Now we say it like an amen when it does.

When Kate's friend and erstwhile employer Eve died, her daughter ran the place with Kate. They had five kids between them, three girls and two boys. One of the boys married into a local dairying family, and the other one got the spirit and went off with the wandering people. Maybe he'd been there at Avebury – I hope he was one of those wild ones. Anyway, that left the three girls to grow up and run the place – Jane being one of them, alongside Amy and Ruth. They were known affectionately in the village as the coven. Affectionately, I think.

Jane's filled me in on some of the local history around here. About how Bristol fronted up to London and detached its police units from the national system. Some of them are now based out at Warminster, which it turns out is a sort of rough boundary between the two cities' unofficial jurisdictions. Stay your side of Warminster, don't poke your nose in national affairs, and we'll leave you alone is roughly how it goes, with a few bumps now and then.

Like London, Bristol did the carrot-and-stick job with local farmers, leaning on them to feed the city. But the lefties in Bristol were a bit smarter than in London, where they still had grand delusions about economic growth, international politicking and all their steampunk techno-fixes.

In Bristol, they quickly realized that it's about making the land itself work, and no harder than it can sustain. Lots of education and knowledge-sharing about gardening and crafts. Lots of little green community spaces springing up in the city – more trouble than they're worth by the sound of it, but I suppose it sets the tone. Civilian service for the youth. You'd think they'd run a mile, but times are different now. Plus, there's not much else for them to do and the whole green localism thing started to catch the mood.

A lot of them went out on service to the farms here in the sticks. It suited everyone if they stayed, so all the parties tried to sweeten the deal as much as they could. Not like the Parishioners near London. You might think there's no space in the countryside but, believe me, when you're one family on a five hundred acre farm and you're at the far end of such a long global supply line that red diesel is only something you've heard about from your parents and your tanks are now storing human urine for the garden, then suddenly you look at the land in a different way. You have to work it differently. You have to find more people willing to do that, and you don't hold all the cards.

Out toward Frome, it's all very organized and rational – a real love-in between the republicans of Bristol and their spin-offs in the smaller town. Or is it the other way around? They've got a good thing going really, but it's hard to get a foot in the door. I think they're playing a long game, trying to reel in us outliers with their weekly markets and little luxuries, the remnants of civilization. Their taxes, too. But we're still a bit too wild west for that out here.

Jane told me some of the ways this played out. There's still the odd large-scale farmer here serving urban contracts, Bristol's version of the London Grows approach. In the early days they swaggered around with their fancy tractors and diesel deliveries, but the low prices they get and endless input shortages mean most of them want out, especially in these parts with the transport costs. Time to climb down from their high tractors, and muck in with village life?

Better to be a big landlord than a big farmer? Well, I've heard there are places like that, but that's a hard road too. Turns out you need more than just a couple of rifles in the gun case to be a feudal boss or lord it over sharecroppers. It takes a lot of practise and a surprising amount of politicking. Most of the farmers around here are happier talking about ley mixtures than servile tenures. Plus, it's a risky game to play, setting yourself up as a local potentate while London and Bristol have their guns nervously scanning the horizon on the lookout for rival power. And you don't want local people who know what an upstart you are plotting and scheming behind your back, either.

They did try over at St George's some years ago, I heard. It ended up in a big tenant revolt and a land occupation – that estate is really wild. Bristol and London have more to worry about than saving some rich family's arse from the mob out in the middle of nowhere. I think they moved back to London. Maybe the likes of Mayor Kingman will start piecing together some kind of big landowner alliance, but for now the Peasants' Republic of St George's has the run of that place.

There's an old saying that possession is nine tenths of the law. Make that ninety-nine hundredths these days. But 'possession' doesn't mean some name on a title deed anymore. It means being there, being the sower, the reaper, the builder. I still don't really understand how it works. I'm not sure anyone does. People inherit. People turn up and ask around. People camp out. For sure, there are a lot of arguments. Sometimes it feels like there's nothing to talk about in the village apart from bad health, bad weather and bad neighbours.

I'm exaggerating. People get by. Apparently, Bristol and its outposts like Frome tried to map it all out a while back and impose tithes and whatnot, but they don't have the feet on the ground for it. Maybe someday. But most people want a quiet life and are too busy anyway. Figure something out, get on with your work, don't get the busybodies from Frome or Bristol involved. The vicar and some of the old locals are a help. For sure, people covet this or that bit of ground, but in the end land disputes are people disputes and we're all neighbours. We all have to earn a crust.

You do hear talk about village assemblies and the like, modelling ourselves after Frome and Bristol. It's mostly the newcomers pushing for it, the ones with less power and connection round here. Nothing much has come of it so far. With my 'in' to the coven I don't have that newcomer anxiety. What I hear is more like, 'Who does so-and-so think they are trying to tell us what we should do?' Like I say, people generally seem to figure things out. But that's just my perspective, I guess.

You hear a lot of stories about strange goings on in the wildlands to the west of here – the watery flatlands of the Somerset Levels, now more watery than ever, beyond our little perch here on the edge of the Mendip Hills. And then the moors of North Devon beyond. There's one story about Women's Island, a now-stranded village where years ago a group of local yobs, drunk on the misogynistic algorithms of the dying internet, had tried to go full *Handmaid's Tale*. It ended with a stand-off outside the pub, until a young woman stepped forward. She hadn't been living there long, but the rumour mill about unnatural goings-on was already at fever pitch. When she aimed a shotgun at the ringleader, the story goes, he'd laughed at her and said she didn't know how things worked around here – a pervert like her had best get back to the city. Said she wouldn't have the balls to pull the trigger. But she did.

'Oh, that story's quite true,' Jane said. 'The women live pretty well out there now, organizing the fishing and fowling between them. It's all a bit pagan, though. The old queen lives off their tribute in a little palace with her brother. There are only a few other men there, I'm told. Every month the young women without children dance naked in the moonlight.'

She must have seen something in my expression. She laughed.

'I wouldn't, if I were you. They'd eat you for breakfast. You know about bees, right? The drones only have one purpose. Kings for a day, and then ... well, there we have it. Here.' She handed me a bucketful of food slops. 'Be a dear and take this down to the pigsties.'

I headed to the pigsties, musing politics – Mayor Kingman, the real queen in Balmoral and that strange old queen in the Levels.

Especially the one in the Levels. I still don't know if Women's Island really exists. But I wouldn't be surprised. There's a lot of weird stuff that happens out on the Levels and beyond. The republicans up north tried to draw the area into their oh-so-rational map-and-tax schemes, but it was no dice. All the farmers, together with the van people and the Aquarian types, came out in force and sent their delegations packing. They called it the Battle Between Bristol and Crystal.

Nowadays, the floods are nibbling away at it. I guess it's good to be Aquarian when you live that close to sea level. But there's still good summer grazing out in those parts. In the winter, a lot of the farmers drive the cattle up into the Mendips to overwinter on the higher ground and live there on the commons for the season, doing hedging and suchlike when they're not drunk on cider brandy or arguing over field boundaries. Some of the Aquarians go up there too, helping to mediate the arguments and blessing the hawthorns and the herds in return for a morsel of cheese or beef. There are little shrines all over the place on the cattle routes. Those Levels people always were a superstitious lot. If they ever get organized, who knows what they might achieve.

Along with the church and its hall, the pigsties are the main buildings in the village that everybody takes care of. It's almost a game as you walk around the place, keeping an eye out for anything tasty the pigs might like, as long as it's not tastier for people. It's a good job a few of the old-time folk kept these tough old breeds going. The local villages share boars around and try to keep an eye on the bloodlines. After the hog roast at autumn carnival, the fat is shared out. Fat for winter food and preserving, priceless stuff.

I'm not sure what's more important, really – the pigsties or the church. I'm joking. I was always an irreligious man. But people need spiritual food too. Before the bad times, the Church of England was almost dead on its feet. But people have drifted back. Probably for the community, the weekly togetherness as much as anything. There's a scattering of other faiths who come for that too. I'm not saying it's an oasis of religious tolerance around here. On second thoughts, I pretty much *am* saying that, compared to what it could be.

The vicar is old now, one of the last to be ordained before all that stuff fell away. She travels around the local villages, taking the young ones under her wing and teaching them Bible stuff. Organizing the school, too. I've been helping out with reading classes. I wonder how all that's going to pan out. I don't think the vicar's too fond of the autumn carnival. It's a bit wilder than the ones they used to have around here back in the old days with their tractors and floats. But there's food and cider that's best made use of than trying to keep it all through the winter, and at least the carnival date helps the midwife clear her diary for the spring.

The weirdest thing out west is the nuclear power station. Some say it's still running. If it is, goodness knows how, but it might explain why life in London is less horrendous than it might be. Others say it's an accident waiting to happen and will blow any day. Not much I can do about that. Whatever the case, a working grid in this little place is a distant memory. People do stuff with turbines, water wheels, ancient solar panels they're coaxing through old age, ram pumps and the like. There's a woman in the village who's great with all that stuff. She knows what she's worth. But I wonder what'll happen when it's past even her skills to keep the lights on.

Occasionally, somebody turns up with a new solar panel, or plastic sheeting, or stuff like that. I don't know if it's still getting made somewhere or just gets 'found'. There are the old dump sites, but Bristol keeps a tight rein on most of those. Anyway, there's a weird dance here that I'm still trying to learn. Kind of 'finders keepers' but only so far. Hoarding stuff and throwing your weight around doesn't look good. And not looking good matters.

When we can't get hold of hand-me-downs from the old glory days, there's always the smith. Sometimes a group takes a cart over near Radstock and scavenges coal for him when he has a job on. It's a precious cargo, so a potentially dangerous journey home. There's talk between the communities of carriage rights and tolls, but it's only a little cart of coal. Otherwise, it's a tight rope we walk with the land here. Land for food, land for timber and firewood, land for fertility, land for fibres, land for medicines. Medicines, there's a thing. We're relearning old skills, but I try not to think too much about getting ill.

A lot of people grow flax and hemp for fibre. Some of them are great weavers. They're getting pretty tight, building their own workshop. Most of us try our hand, but we're not so good at it, and it's a lot of work. So much to teach ourselves anew. Sheepskins are easier, but there's only so many sheep the land will bear when there's so much else you need from it. If you're a good-enough hunter, you might catch a roe deer. Skins are the high-end currency around here. Then apple brandy, the stuff that's not better put in the tractor, anyway. Old Jethro has a tractor that works off ethanol and will plough a row for you. He's one to watch. Anyway, then there's fat, then whatever else. Everyone wants to go to Frome with something to sell so there's some coins in the pocket, but you have to be careful flashing the cash in the village. Those moneyed, urban ways spell danger. Nobody pays anyone money here and nobody sells anything. That's the way of social death. But people are good at keeping count.

When I got a sheepskin, I felt like I started to belong in this place. That, and getting friendly with Amy's daughter, Meg. Part of the coven's plan all along, maybe. Or perhaps I'm just flattering myself. Anyway, I wear the sheepskin in winter – the habit of this unholy, hermitical life.[6] I wonder what it felt like when people first started wearing these rough animal skins here. From cotton cornucopia to *Robinson Crusoe* in two generations. Who knows how it'll all pan out? It's not the kind of life many expected just a while back, but it feels like a charmed one compared to what might be. You never know who else is out there, though, what new footprints we might find on the sand. At least we're getting by for the moment. We're all Crusoe now. We're all Friday, too.

AFTERWORD

The Distributist Moment

I've argued that the world we've inherited and the one we inhabit is effectively a Viking world, based on an accumulativeness born of predatory violence. That world is coming to an end from its own contradictions, pollutions and excess accumulation. It can't be patched up by any of its existing mainstream technologies – political technologies, economic technologies and material or engineering ones.

So, we have to try building a new world. If we fail, we face the axe-age and wolf-age described in 'The Seeress's Prophecy', hinting at the dawn of the Viking era, that I quoted in the preface. But hopefully we'll succeed and, like her, will be able to foresee another green Earth rising from the sea.

The future that I portrayed in chapter 12 was neither an axe-age nor a green Earth. It had the potential to devolve to either. 'London' had become a remnant of the current British multi-nation 'sun-state' that was turning into a weaker 'corporate quasi-state' of the kind described by political scientist Michael Albert in his future 'neofeudal' pathway (see page 38). Bristol had become in turn a city state of secular, civic republican form, semi-independent from London, and with Frome a smaller satellite in its sphere.

Within this new political landscape, attempts to create what Albert calls 'feudalized rentier capitalists and warlords' hadn't really got off the ground. It remained a longer-term possibility, perhaps even a likelihood, but – as I suggested in the last chapter, and elsewhere in the book – feudalized capitalism or warlordism isn't some natural state of affairs to which societies automatically gravitate. It's an outcome that requires a lot of political work. Just as with past low-energy agrarian societies in Britain and elsewhere, where the dominance of the many by the few is 'surprisingly difficult to explain', so in our low-energy agrarian future will warlordism or feudalized capitalism be one among several possible outcomes whose realization is not foreordained.[1]

My focus in chapter 12 was instead on what Albert called 'communities of surplus populations left to develop their own survival strategies'. One of these was the village near Glastonbury where my protagonist walked to, which was trying to generate a self-reliant local society bottom up – and where a tension existed between kin-based and more rational/republican or village assembly kind of approaches. Another was the religious nomads at Avebury – a historical brew-up of medieval-style mendicants and modern New Age or 'Aquarian' people. In the future I portrayed, various new religious forms were beginning to coalesce – the church in the village, the nomads in Avebury – but weren't yet fully formed, because this takes time.

Another 'surplus population' I mentioned in chapter 12 was built around the stranger kingship discussed in chapter 11 – or, in this case, stranger queenship. I don't think humanity has superseded such apparently strange and mystical forms of politics. In fact, our totalizing modern view of political sovereignty seems rather less sophisticated. As the grip of liberal-modernism weakens, more plural political forms that play more inventively with the idea of sovereignty seem likely to emerge.

The republicanism of Bristol and Frome I portrayed in the future continues a strand of their present politics in the new 'dark-age' circumstances. In this future, their outward reach into their hinterlands was patchy. They were trying to draw outlying people into their networks, using sticks but also the carrot of their access to residual prosperity and resources bequeathed from the present. The populations of their now more heavily peopled rural hinterlands were tempted, but they were also suspicious and were guarding their autonomy. In this world, the further away from an urban power centre you are, and/or the weaker the power centre, the easier it is to evade central power and do your own thing – one version of the solar system or galactic model discussed in chapter 2.

I portrayed a future involving what I see as almost inevitable hard times ahead, but nevertheless ones with some possibility to lead onward into a merrier dark age (see page 19) or even a green Earth rising from the sea, perhaps with eagles over fells and salmon thronging in British rivers again, teaching us how we should treat them (see page 12). If we and our descendants succeed

AFTERWORD

in realizing this new green Earth, I think it will result from ordinary people sharing and distributing what they need locally to generate renewable communities oriented to practical livelihood. And it will result from doing the sharing in the kind of considered, structured ways I've discussed in earlier chapters, drawing broadly on distributism and similar traditions.

To a large extent, it will also result from improvisation – from people of goodwill figuring things out on the ground in difficult circumstances as they go along, without necessarily fully recognizing what they're doing (see MacIntyre quote, page 28). It will not be achieved by people implementing grand plans to save humanity or seizing the reins of existing power to deliver 'solutions'.

Still, good improvisation is always built on an underlying order. I hope I've given a sense of where to look for underlying order in this book, and that this might help inform some of the work of figuring out local livelihood-making and other necessary structures. In this respect, I've come to think that older ethical, spiritual and practical frameworks have more to teach us about finding another green Earth than modern technologies, both social and material – which isn't to say that there's nothing to be learned from modern technologies. This is not a romanticism, except in a technical sense (see The Hero Is You, pages 11–14), but rather an anti-romanticism on my part directed against modernist culture and its romanticization of technology. Yes, older frameworks hark back to the past, but their age is unimportant. They've never really gone away, in part because they're timeless. But we do need to reconfigure them for present times.

Possibly the most important of the verses I quoted in the preface from 'The Seeress's Prophecy' are the last two lines: *bearing corpses to Hel, where I must go too*. Scholars remain uncertain about how to interpret the intricate Norse cosmologies of pre-Christian times and their ideas of the afterlife.[2] But it seems that Hel, unlike its Christian near-namesake, probably isn't a place of eternal torment for wrongdoing. It's just ... a place.

This is important because there's a kind of fury behind so much of the moral architecture of the modern world – a fury to improve, perfect, solve, revolutionize and transcend – which ultimately looks like a fear of death, and a misplaced attempt to evade it. Ironically, the consequence is only to make the chances of premature death and suffering, the darker side of a new dark age, all the greater.

At its best, this improvement ideology is well intentioned. It wants to lift people out of poverty and progress them out of hard lives working the land. Too often, though, this is just a smokescreen for business-as-usual activities that primarily reward the already wealthy.[3] It's better to make the rich more poor and the lives of people working the land less hard while they continue to work the land. Which is why the Norse idea of Hel is appealing. Even if we find a new green Earth, as I hope we do, we will still spend ordinary lives working, and then we will die – which is an okay place to be.

That seems an appropriate note on which to end this book. Thank you for reading it. I've written it over the course of a winter, staring often for inspiration out of my study window onto the brown grass of my farm, which is now turning green with the approaching spring. It's time for me to go outside and start some other journey. It's time, some might say, for me to go to Hel.

ACKNOWLEDGEMENTS

Special thanks to Sean Domencic, Paul Hillman and Jake Smaje for conversations and commentaries beyond the call in the writing of this book.

My thanks also to Allen Abramson, Mike Albert, Anna Alves, Bernadette Alves, Rebecca Collins, Rachel Donald, Ashley Fitzgerald, Anthony Galluzzo, Brianne Goodspeed, Carwyn Graves, Taras Grescoe, Dougald Hine, Alex Jensen, Paul Kingsnorth, SL, Peter Macfadyen, Brian Miller, Helena Norberg-Hodge, Rupert Read, Nick Richardson, Alexandra Rowlatt, Manda Scott, Vandana Shiva, Dan Smaje, Oliver Smaje, Jason Snyder, Jay Springett, Jim Thomas and Colin Tudge.

Appreciation to:
Gill Barron, Simon Fairlie and Mike Hannis for giving space to my writing in the excellent *Land Magazine*, and likewise to Kristin Sponsler at Resilience.

Everyone from the Vallis Veg community, through its many seasons and manifestations.

Muna Reyal for her editorial wisdom and patience during the writing of this book, Susan Pegg for getting it into shape and the rest of the team at Chelsea Green for bringing it to fruition.

The fantastic commenters on my small farm future blog at chrissmaje.com and its other online incarnations who, more than ever, have been a fount of wisdom, and of yet more things for me to read.

When I started writing this book I didn't realize how indebted it would turn out to be to two great thinkers and writers who are now among the metapersons. Here's to Marshall Sahlins and David Graeber, and to the walk out west to Chicago that for better or worse I never took with you.

My debt to Cordelia Rowlatt will be clear from these pages – with thanks and love.

It's customary in the acknowledgements pages of books to absolve all those acknowledged from ultimate sovereignty over it, and to reclaim local authorial autonomy. In this case, it's especially apposite.

NOTES

Preface: Ragnarök Revisited?
1. These are excerpts from: 'Völuspá: The Seeress's Prophecy.' In *Poetic Edda*. c.1270. Translated by Nick Richardson. The Junket. 6 January 2014, https://thejunket.org/2014/01/archive/voluspa-the-seeresss-prophecy.
2. Richardson 2014.
3. Christiansen 2002, quoted in Price 2020, 109, Price 2020, 528.
4. My account of the Vikings draws primarily upon Price 2020.
5. Compare Asafu-Adjaye et al. 2015 with Shepard 1998.

Introduction: An Arc of Future Earth
1. Finding the right words to describe my homeland of the British Isles presents some quandaries. The 'British Isles' refers to the whole archipelago, encompassing the two main islands of Great Britain and Ireland, along with numerous smaller islands. Great Britain is divided into the three countries of England, Wales and Scotland. Ireland is split between the Republic of Ireland and Northern Ireland. The latter, together with England, Wales and Scotland, form the single modern polity known as the United Kingdom or the UK. These boundaries and aggregations have changed over some of the historical periods discussed in this book and seem likely to change again in the future. The politics around all this have been, to say the least, contentious – particularly in Ireland, but also in Scotland and Wales. I'm loath to use the term 'United Kingdom', especially in a book so focused on political fragmentation and bottom-up politics. Besides, 'United Kingdom' lacks the specific geographical reference that 'Britain' has. My uneasy compromise involves referring explicitly to the UK, the British Isles or any of their constituent countries only when that's exactly what I mean, otherwise using the term 'Britain' – a word whose fuzziness at least reflects the fuzzy political reality. 'Britain' is anachronistic in some historical contexts before its various constituent countries were formally united – I beg the reader's indulgence for any haziness regarding this history and geography.
2. This section is my own speculative dramatization, not some rigorous modelling enterprise. It draws on various sources, including Albert 2024, IPCC 2021, Kim and Newman 2019, McGuire 2022, Sayers et al. 2022 and Xu et al. 2020.
3. Eliot, T.S. 1963. *Collected Poems 1909–1962*. Faber & Faber.
4. Mackie, David and Jessica Murray (2020), 'Risky Business: The Climate and the Macroeconomy', J.P. Morgan Securities, 14 January, https://extinctionrebellion.uk/wp-content/uploads/2020/02/JPM_Risky_business__the_climate_and_the_macroeconomy_2020-01-14_3230707.pdf.pdf.

5. For some overviews of the climate crisis and/or the financial crisis see IPCC 2021, Malm and Carton 2024, Keen 2017, Wallace-Wells 2019.
6. On which, see Hine 2023.
7. Smaje 2020, 2023. See also, for example, Albert 2024, Heather and Rapley 2023, McGuire 2022, Rees 2023, Streeck 2016, Wallace-Wells 2019.
8. For a variety of perspectives on this see Albert 2024, Ghosh 2021, Heather and Rapley 2023, Keen 2017, Zeihan 2022.
9. Lindsey, Rebecca (2023) 'Climate Change: Global Sea Level', National Oceanic and Atmospheric Administration, 22 August, https://www.climate.gov/news-features/understanding-climate/climate-change-global-sea-level.
10. Graeber and Wengrow 2021, Tainter 2019.
11. Figures from Smil 2017, 458 and calculated by the author from Energy Institute 2024.
12. Energy Institute 2024.
13. Fressoz 2024, Energy Institute 2024.
14. For a range of views on transition see Albert 2024, Christophers 2024, Fressoz 2024, IEA 2021, Smil 2022. I've explained my reasoning further here: https://chrissmaje.com/2024/08/off-grid-further-thoughts-on-the-failing-renewables-transition. There's much more to say!
15. See White et al. 2008.
16. See, among others, Schumacher 1974.
17. McCarraher 2019, 135.
18. Markley 2023, 716.
19. Loring 2020, 55.
20. Todd 2018.
21. Smaje 2023.
22. McCarraher 2019, 17.
23. Malm and Carton 2024, 188.
24. Stone 2022. See also Kallis 2019.
25. See Paprocki 2021 for a critique.

Chapter 1: Dark Age Ahead

1. Malm and Carton 2024, x.
2. Jacobs 2004; MacIntyre 1981.
3. Gabriele and Perry 2021.
4. See Graham 1979.
5. Oosthuizen 2019.
6. Graeber and Wengrow 2021, 442–3.
7. For various accounts of this see Albert 2024, Heather and Rapley 2023, Streeck 2016, Zeihan 2022.
8. Deneen 2019.
9. See Quilley 2024a.
10. Kelton 2020 provides an accessible introduction to MMT.

11. Streeck 2016.
12. Hagens, Nate (2023) 'The Mordor Economy', The Great Simplification, 27 January, https://www.thegreatsimplification.com/frankly-original/23-mordor-economy; Kingsnorth, Paul (2018) 'Life vs The Machine', 15 November, https://www.paulkingsnorth.net/machine.
13. See, for example, Sayer 2016; Hickel et al. 2024.
14. See, for example, https://www.cla.org.uk/news/family-farm-tax-could-leave-hard-pressed-farmers-paying-tax-bills-that-wipe-out-their-annual-profits; https://www.nfuonline.com/updates-and-information/an-impact-analysis-of-apr-reforms-on-commercial-family-farms.
15. Orrell 2010, 93–4.
16. See Smaje, Chris (2022) 'A Neo-Distributist Proposal', *The Land* 31: 44–7; Fairlie, Simon (2014–15), 'A Cautionary Tale', *The Land* 7: 52–5. See also Boyle 2019 for an overview of English distributism.
17. Quilley 2024b, 65.
18. Cottam 2018, 15 and 38.
19. MacIntyre 1981, 263.
20. MacIntyre 1981, 222.
21. Machado de Oliveira 2021.

Chapter 2: Building New Structures

1. See Smaje 2025.
2. Thoreau 1851.
3. Further explained in, for example, Holt-Giménez 2019 and Stone 2022.
4. Klein 2023, 342.
5. Albert 2024, 229.
6. Anderson 1974.
7. Brown 2022.
8. Scott 2009, 2017.
9. Author calculations from FAOSTAT: FAO (2025) 'FAOSTAT: Crops and Livestock Products', https://www.fao.org/faostat/en/#data.
10. Greenfield 2024.
11. Tambiah 2013. See also Graeber and Sahlins 2017.
12. Graeber and Sahlins 2017, 359.
13. Hobbes 1651.
14. Smaje 2020.

Chapter 3: Open Country

1. Stoll 2017, 211.
2. See for example Branford and Rocha 2002, Gilbert 2024, Handy 2022, Netting 1993.
3. Guldi 2021, 394.
4. Albertus 2025.

5. See, among others, Lipton 2009, Netting 1993, Stone 2022.
6. Davis 2001.
7. Davis 2001, 9.
8. Sen 1981, Guldi 2021, 322.
9. Schumacher 1974, 204.
10. Gilbert 2024, 12.
11. Monbiot, George (2023) 'The Cruel Fantasies of Well-Fed People', 4 October, https://www.monbiot.com/2023/10/04/the-cruel-fantasies-of-well-fed-people.
12. Smaje 2023, 154.
13. Scott 2009, 173.
14. See, for example, da Silva et al. 2022, Paprocki 2021, Scoones 2015 and https://chrissmaje.com/2022/04/a-further-note-on-gender-families-and-households-in-a-small-farm-future.
15. Jim Thomas tracks some of these issues here: https://gmwatch.org/en/106-news/latest-news/20310-the-many-problems-with-george-monbiot-s-bullish-backing-for-biotech-brewed-bacterial-banquets.
16. RetroSuburbia, https://retrosuburbia.com; The Simpler Way, https://thesimplerway.info.
17. Rees 2023. See also Taylor and Tainter 2016.
18. Polanyi 1944. See also Quilley 2024a.
19. Hagens, Nate (2023) 'The Mordor Economy', The Great Simplification, 27 January, https://www.thegreatsimplification.com/frankly-original/23-mordor-economy; Kingsnorth, Paul (2018) 'Life vs The Machine', 15 November, https://www.paulkingsnorth.net/machine.
20. See Stone 2022.
21. Netting 1993, Stone 2022, Ploeg 2008.
22. Graeber and Wengrow 2021, 442–3; see also Siedentop 2014, 171.
23. For a critique of microcredit see, for example, Paprocki 2016.
24. See as an example some of the projections in https://projects.propublica.org/climate-migration.
25. Subedi et al. 2022, Ortyl et al. 2024.
26. Spence, Thomas (1793) 'The Rights of Man', London, https://www.marxists.org/history/england/britdem/people/spence/rights_of_man/rights.htm#lecture.
27. Dreher, Rod (2005) 'Crunchy Cons', *National Review,* 1 May, https://www.nationalreview.com/2005/05/crunchy-cons-rod-dreher.
28. On all this, see Albertus 2025, Jones 2023, Smaje 2023, 2025; Rebanks, James (2024) 'The Farmers March on Westminster: Labour's Budget will Destroy Rural Life', UnHerd, 18 November, https://unherd.com/2024/11/a-farmers-revolt-is-coming.

Chapter 4: Home Economics – Producing

1. British and US household data are available respectively at: https://www.ons.gov.uk/peoplepopulationandcommunity/householdcharacteristics/homeinternetand

socialmediausage/bulletins/householdandresidentcharacteristicsenglandandwales/census2021; https://www.census.gov/topics/families/families-and-households.html.
2. Bradbury et al. 2014, Graeber and Wengrow 2021; Laslett 1972.
3. Laslett 2000, 95.
4. Albertus 2025, Linklater 2014, Lipton 2009, White 2018.
5. Netting 1993.
6. Chayanov 1924–5, Sahlins 1972.
7. Soper 2020.
8. Defoe 1724–6, 259. Fairlie, Simon (2007) 'A Short History of Enclosure in Britain', *The Land* 7: 17.
9. Bollier 2014, 15.
10. Hardin 1968.
11. Ostrom 1990, 63.
12. See Allen 1992, Bray 1986.

Chapter 5: Home Economics – Caring
1. Laslett 1972, Kuper 2003.
2. See, for different contexts, Faith 2020, Rofel and Yanagisako 2018, Strange 2008, Whittle 1998.
3. Office for National Statistics (2022) 'Household and Resident Characteristics, England and Wales: Census 2021', ONS, updated 13 December 2022, https://www.ons.gov.uk/peoplepopulationandcommunity/householdcharacteristics/homeinternetandsocialmediausage/bulletins/householdandresidentcharacteristicsenglandandwales/census2021.
4. Sahlins 2013, 20.
5. Graeber and Wengrow 2021, 280.
6. See Lewis 2022.
7. Yunkaporta 2023, 41.
8. For historical and/or distributist perspectives on the primacy of the family see Chesterton, G.K. [1920] 2024. *The Superstition of Divorce,* https://www.gutenberg.org/ebooks/62680, Laslett 1972, Quilley 2024a, 2024b, Siedentop 2014; Jones, Andrew Willard (2020) 'What States Can't Do', New Polity, 24 July, https://newpolity.com/blog/what-states-cant-do, Waldstein, Edmund, O.Cist. (2020) 'Short Notes on the Family and the City', The Josias, 18 November, https://thejosias.com/2020/11/18/short-notes-on-the-family-and-the-city.
9. Chesterton. *The Superstition of Divorce.*
10. See Blond 2010, 148.
11. Kearney 2023, 100.
12. Kearney 2023, 151.
13. Jones, 'What States Can't Do'.
14. Miller 2023, 21–2.
15. Gardner 1991, 543.

16. Scott 2017, 10, Eisenberg 1998, 364–8.
17. See, for example, Hadler 2013, Oldenburg 2010.
18. See, for example, Federici 2014, Rigg 2001.
19. See, for example, Grayson 2024, Jones 2023.
20. Brown 2022, Faith 2020.
21. Rodsky 2019.
22. Branford and Rocha 2002, 23.
23. See, for example, Agarwal 1996, Hadler 2013.
24. Johnson, Jessica. [2016] 2023. 'Matriliny'. In *The Open Encyclopedia of Anthropology*, edited by Felix Stein, http://doi.org/10.29164/16matriliny.
25. See, for example, Hess 2007, Ott 1981.
26. Christian 2003.
27. Ingram 2025.
28. Clastres 1987, 186.
29. Woodcock and Avakumovic 1968.
30. See Ingram 2025.
31. McCarraher 2019, 676.

Chapter 6: Land
1. Loring 2020, 177.
2. See, for example, McKay 2011; Worpole 2021.
3. I discuss this further in Smaje 2020 and Smaje 2023.
4. DeMoor 2015.
5. See, for example, Bhandar 2018, Linklater 2014.
6. Graeber and Wengrow 2021.
7. Netting 1993, 158.
8. Oosthuizen 2019, 102–3.
9. See https://chrissmaje.com/2023/12/food-land-work-and-rent-the-real-story-of-vallis-veg/, https://chrissmaje.com/2024/11/tractor-man-speaks.
10. Land Site, https://www.landsite.co.uk/landprices.html.
11. George 1879.
12. See Durand 2017, Hickel et al. 2024.
13. See preface, page xii. In more commercialized societies, peasants readily took a more instrumental view of land and land sales – see Netting 1993, Whittle 1998.
14. Steven Stoll's analysis of Appalachia provides an interesting historical case study – see Stoll 2017.

Chapter 7: A Dark-Age Distributism
1. See Mantha 2020, Graeber and Wengrow 2021, 424.
2. See Graeber 2011, 237, Graeber and Wengrow 2021, 598.
3. Yunkaporta 2019, 172–3.
4. Yunkaporta 2019, 173.

NOTES

5. Branford and Rocha 2002, 65.
6. Branford and Rocha 2002, 91.
7. Jackson 2011, 81.
8. Bhandar 2018.
9. Fernández-Llamazares et al. 2024.
10. Anderson 2005, Kimmerer 2013 and more generally Yunkaporta 2019 provide much inspiration.
11. I'd argue such assumptions are apparent in, among others, Asafu-Adjaye et al. 2015, Monbiot, George (2023) 'The Cruel Fantasies of Well-Fed People', 4 October, https://www.monbiot.com/2023/10/04/the-cruel-fantasies-of-well-fed-people/, and generally in much popular food journalism. For alternative perspectives see Kallis 2019, Stone 2022 and Thomas, Jim (2023) 'The Many Problems with George Monbiot's Bullish Backing for Biotech-Brewed Bacterial Banquets', GM Watch, 28 October, https://gmwatch.org/en/106-news/latest-news/20310-the-many-problems-with-george-monbiot-s-bullish-backing-for-biotech-brewed-bacterial-banquets.
12. Dochuk 2011.
13. Grescoe 2023, 273.
14. Graves 2024, 10.

Chapter 8: Making a Living

1. On Drax, see https://www.drax.com/wp-content/uploads/2022/03/Drax_AR2021_2022-03-07.final_.pdf, Fressoz 2024, 126. On the issues around wood-burning see Barron, Gill (2024) 'What's So Wicked About Wood?' and Fairlie, Simon (2004) 'Is Air Pollution Worse in the Countryside than in the City', *The Land* 34: 48–55.
2. Author calculations from US Bureau of Labor Statistics (2023) 'Employment Projections: Employment by Major Industry Sector', US Department of Labor, updated 3 September 2024, https://www.bls.gov/emp/tables/employment-by-major-industry-sector.htm.
3. Author calculation from the World Development Indicators, https://databank.worldbank.org/source/world-development-indicators/preview/on.
4. Smaje 2020.
5. MacIntyre 1981, 1–2.
6. See Smaje 2020 and Stone 2022.
7. See, for example, Mak 2010.
8. Tree 2018.
9. Campbell 2022, North 2021.
10. Graeber 2011, 219.
11. Médaille 2010, 88.
12. See Graeber 2011, 314; Davis 2001, Robbins 2003. Or, for something more literary, John Steinbeck's *The Grapes of Wrath*.

13. Médaille 2010, 66.
14. See Kelton 2020.
15. Médaille 2010, 238–9.
16. On slavery in the Thai fishing industry, see Urbina 2019. On slavery as social death, see Patterson 1990.
17. On which, see Smaje 2023.
18. In Lasch 1991, 203.
19. Graeber 2011, 351.
20. See, for example, James, Liv (2024) 'Money Really Doesn't Grow on Trees. I Know, I'm a Market Gardener', SSAW, 12 November, https://www.ssawcollective.com/post/liv-james-money-really-doesn-t-grow-on-trees-i-know-i-m-a-market-gardener.
21. Médaille 2010, 134.

Chapter 9: Working for Others

1. McCarraher 2019, 356.
2. Bakhtin 1984, 57.
3. Bakhtin 1984, 174.
4. Galluzzo 2023 provides an extended meditation on the issue of modernism and death. See also Hine 2023.
5. Cole 1920, 33–4.
6. See, for example, Soo Wern Jun (2023) 'Malaysia Needs "100pc Self Sufficiency", Food Security Ministry Official Says Amid Soaring Global Prices for White Rice', *Malay Mail*, 9 September, https://www.malaymail.com/news/malaysia/2023/09/09/malaysia-needs-100pc-self-sufficiency-food-security-ministry-official-says-amid-soaring-global-prices-for-white-rice/89843.; Wicks, Noah (2024) 'Mexican President Unveils Agricultural Plan for Food "Self Sufficiency"', Agri-Pulse, 22 October, https://www.agri-pulse.com/articles/mexican-president-unveils-agricultural-plan-self-sufficiency.
7. Patel 2021.

Chapter 10: Politics of the People

1. Macfadyen 2014.
2. See Graeber and Wengrow 2021
3. Honohan 2002, 1.
4. Marx, Karl ([1890–1] 1999) 'Critique of the Gotha Programme', Marxists Internet Archive, https://www.marxists.org/archive/marx/works/1875/gotha/ch01.htm.
5. See Siedentop 2014.
6. MacIntyre 1981, 171.
7. Lewis 1952, 8.
8. MacIntyre 1981, 127.
9. See, for example, Freyfogle 2007, Quilley 2024a.
10. Loring 2020, 53.

NOTES

11. Vizenor 2008, 11.
12. Sahlins 2022, 37–8.
13. Sahlins 2022, 81.
14. Ghosh 2021, 235–44.
15. Joyce 2024, xiii.
16. On which, see Cavanaugh 2024, McCarraher 2019, Williams 1980, https://www.weplanet.org/post/how-i-came-to-love-and-even-hug-nuclear-waste.
17. Fairlie, Simon (2024) 'Remembering the Downtrodden', *The Land* 34: 56–7.
18. See McCarraher 2019.
19. Joyce 2024, 23.

Chapter 11: Divine Comedy: Or, the Stranger King

1. See Graeber and Sahlins 2017, 22; Heather and Rapley 2023, 158–9.
2. Greenfield 2024, 197.
3. I draw in this section mostly on Graeber and Sahlins 2017, and also Milner 1994.
4. On which, see MacIntyre 1999, 142.
5. Bouie, Jamelle (2025) 'Trump Promised Retribution', *New York Times,* 5 March, https://www.nytimes.com/2025/03/05/opinion/trump-revenge-american-people.html.
6. See Graeber and Sahlins 2017, 6.
7. MacIntyre 1999, 132.
8. For example, Mark 12:17.
9. Wallace, David Foster (2005) 'This Is Water by David Foster Wallace (Full Transcript and Audio)', Farnam Street, 29 May, https://fs.blog/david-foster-wallace-this-is-water.

Chapter 12: Walking West

1. It draws on various themes discussed in earlier chapters, as well as Langland 1378–9 with some inspiration from Rankin-Gee 2021 and Scott 2024.
2. Goulson 2021, McGuire 2022.
3. Thoreau 1851.
4. With apologies to William Langland – see Langland 1378–9, 1.
5. Langland 1378–9, 1.
6. Further apologies to William Langland – Langland 1378–9, 1.

Afterword: The Distributist Moment

1. Faith 2020, 1.
2. Price 2020, 262–4.
3. Malm and Carton 2024, 224–5.

BIBLIOGRAPHY

Agarwal, Bina. 1996. *A Field of One's Own: Gender and Land Rights in South Asia*. Cambridge University Press.
Albert, Michael. 2024. *Navigating the Polycrisis: Mapping the Futures of Capitalism and the Earth*. MIT Press.
Albertus, Michael. 2025. *Land Power: Who Has It, Who Doesn't & How That Determines the Fate of Societies*. Basic Books.
Allen, Robert. 1992. *Enclosure and the Yeoman: The Agricultural Development of the South Midlands, 1450–1850*. Clarendon Press.
Anderson, M. Kat. 2005. *Tending the Wild: Native American Knowledge and the Management of California's Natural Resources*. University of California Press.
Anderson, Perry. 1974. *Lineages of the Absolutist State*. Verso.
Asafu-Adjaye, John et al. 2015. *An Ecomodernist Manifesto*. https://www.ecomodernism.org.
Bakhtin, Mikhail. 1984. *Rabelais and His World*. Indiana University Press.
Bhandar, Brenna. 2018. *Colonial Lives of Property: Law, Land, and Racial Regimes of Ownership*. Duke University Press.
Blond, Phillip. 2010. *Red Tory: How Left and Right Have Broken Britain and How We Can Fix It*. Faber & Faber.
Bollier, David. 2014. *Think Like a Commoner: a Short Introduction to the Life of the Commons*. New Society.
Boyle, David. 2019. *Back to the Land: Distributism and the Politics of Life*. The Real Press.
Bradbury, Mason et al. 2014. 'Long-Term Dynamics of Household Size and Their Environmental Implications', *Population and Environment* 36: 73–84.
Branford, Sue and Jan Rocha. 2002. *Cutting the Wire: The Story of the Landless Movement in Brazil*. Practical Action Publishing.
Bray, Francesca. 1986. *The Rice Economies: Technology and Development in Asian Societies*. University of California Press.
Brown, Azby. 2022. *Just Enough: Lessons from Japan for Sustainable Living, Architecture and Design*. Stone Bridge Press.
Campbell, Rebecca. 2022. *Arboreality*. Stelliform Press.
Cavanaugh, William. 2024. *The Uses of Idolatry*. Oxford University Press.
Chayanov, A.V. [1924–5] 1986. *The Theory of Peasant Economy*. University of Wisconsin Press.
Christian, Diana Leafe. 2003. *Creating a Life Together: Practical Tools to Grow Ecovillages and Intentional Communities*. New Society Publishers.
Christiansen, Eric. 2002. *The Norsemen in the Viking Age*. Blackwell Publishing.

Christophers, Brett. 2024. *The Price Is Wrong: Why Capitalism Won't Save the Planet.* Verso.

Clastres, Pierre. 1987. *Society Against the State.* Zone Books.

Cole, G.D.H. 1920. *Guild Socialism: A Plan for Economic Democracy.* Red and Black Publishers.

Cottam, Hilary. 2018. *Radical Help: How We Can Remake the Relationships Between Us and Revolutionise the Welfare State.* Virago.

Davis, Mike. 2001. *Late Victorian Holocausts: El Niño Famines and the Making of the Third World.* Verso.

Defoe, Daniel. [1724–6] 1971. *A Tour Through the Whole Island of Great Britain.* Penguin.

DeMoor, Tine. 2015. *The Dilemma of the Commoners: Understanding the Use of Common Pool Resources in Long-Term Perspective.* Cambridge University Press.

Deneen, Patrick. 2019. *Why Liberalism Failed.* Yale University Press.

Dochuk, Darren. 2011. *From Bible Belt to Sunbelt: Plain-Folks Religion, Grassroots Politics and the Rise of Evangelical Conservatism.* Norton.

Durand, Cédric. 2017. *Fictitious Capital: How Finance Is Appropriating Our Future.* Verso.

Eisenberg, Evan. 1998. *The Ecology of Eden: Humans, Nature and Human Nature.* Alfred Knopf.

Energy Institute. 2024. *Statistical Review of World Energy*, https://www.energyinst.org/statistical-review/resources-and-data-downloads.

Faith, Rosamund. 2020. *The Moral Economy of the Countryside: Anglo-Saxon to Anglo-Norman England.* Cambridge University Press.

Federici, Silvia. 2014. *Caliban and the Witch: Women, the Body and Primitive Accumulation.* Autonomedia.

Fernández-Llamazares, Álvaro et al. 2024. 'A Baseless Statistic Could Harm the Indigenous Peoples It Is Meant to Support', *Nature* 633: 32–5.

Fressoz, Jean-Baptiste. 2024. *More and More and More: An All-Consuming History of Energy.* Allen Lane.

Freyfogle, Eric. 2007. 'Wendell Berry and the Limits of Populism.' In *Wendell Berry: Life and Work*, edited by Jason Peters. University Press of Kentucky.

Gabriele, Matthew and David Perry. 2021. *The Bright Ages: A New History of Medieval Europe.* Harper.

Galluzzo, Anthony. 2023. *Against the Vortex: Zardoz and Degrowth Utopias in the Seventies and Today.* Zer0 Books.

Gardner, Peter. 1991. 'Foragers' Pursuit of Individual Autonomy'. *Current Anthropology* 32 (5): 543–72.

George, Henry. [1879] 2006. *Progress and Poverty.* Robert Schalkenbach Foundation.

Ghosh, Amitav. 2021. *The Nutmeg's Curse: Parables for a Planet in Crisis.* John Murray.

Gilbert, David. 2024. *Countering Dispossession, Reclaiming Land: A Social Movement Ethnography.* University of California Press.

BIBLIOGRAPHY

Goulson, Dave. 2021. *Silent Earth: Averting the Insect Apocalypse*. Jonathan Cape.
Graeber, David. 2011. *Debt: The First 5,000 Years*. Melville House.
Graeber, David and Marshall Sahlins. 2017. *On Kings*. Hau Books.
Graeber, David and David Wengrow. 2021. *The Dawn of Everything: A New History of Humanity*. Allen Lane.
Graham, A.C. 1979. 'The *Nung-chia* "School of the Tillers" and the Origins of Peasant Utopianism in China', *Bulletin of the School of Oriental and African Studies* 42 (1): 66–100.
Graves, Carwyn. 2024. *Tir: The Story of the Welsh Landscape*. Calon.
Grayson, Jennifer. 2024. *A Call to Farms*. W.W. Norton.
Greenfield, Adam. 2024. *Lifehouse: Taking Care of Ourselves in a World on Fire*. Verso.
Grescoe, Taras. 2023. *The Lost Supper: Searching for the Future of Food in the Flavors of the Past*. Greystone.
Guldi, Jo. 2021. *The Long Land War: The Global Struggle for Occupancy Rights*. Yale University Press.
Hadler, Jeffrey. 2013. *Muslims and Matriarchs: Cultural Resilience in Indonesia Through Jihad and Colonialism*. Cornell University Press.
Handy, Jim. 2022. *Tiny Engines of Abundance: A History of Peasant Productivity and Repression*. Rugby: Practical Action.
Hardin, Garrett. 1968. 'The Tragedy of the Commons', *Science* 162: 1243–8.
Heather, Peter and John Rapley. 2023. *Why Empires Fail: Rome, America and the Future of the West*. Allen Lane.
Hess, Andreas. 2007. 'The Social Bonds of Cooking: Gastronomic Societies in the Basque country', *Cultural Sociology* 1 (3): 383–407
Hickel, Jason et al. 2024. 'Unequal Exchange of Labour in the World Economy', *Nature Communications* 15: 6298, https://doi.org/10.1038/s41467-024-49687-y.
Hine, Dougald. 2023. *At Work in the Ruins: Finding Our Place in the Time of Science, Climate Change, Pandemics and All the Other Emergencies*. Chelsea Green.
Hobbes, Thomas. [1651] 1968. *Leviathan*. Penguin.
Holt-Giménez, Eric. 2019. *Can We Feed the World Without Destroying It?* Polity.
Honohan, Iseult. 2002. *Civic Republicanism*. Routledge.
Ingram, Matthew. 2025. *The Garden: Visionary Growers and Farmers of the Counterculture*. Repeater.
IEA. 2021. *Net Zero By 2050: A Roadmap for the Global Energy Sector*. IEA.
IPCC. 2021. *Climate Change 2021: The Physical Science Basis. Contribution of Working Group I to the Sixth Assessment Report of the Intergovernmental Panel on Climate Change*. Cambridge University Press.
Jacobs, Jane. 2004. *Dark Age Ahead*. Vintage Books.
Jackson, Wes. 2011. *Nature As Measure*. Counterpoint.
Jones, Anna. 2023. *The Divide: The Relationship Crisis Between Town and Country*. Octopus Books.

Joyce, Patrick. 2024. *Remembering Peasants: A Personal History of a Vanished World*. Allen Lane.
Kallis, Giorgos. 2019. *Limits: Why Malthus Was Wrong and Why Environmentalists Should Care*. Stanford University Press.
Kearney, Melissa. 2023. *The Two Parent Privilege*. Swift Press.
Keen, Steve. 2017. *Can We Avoid Another Financial Crisis?* Polity.
Kelton, Stephanie. 2020. *The Deficit Myth: How to Build a Better Economy*. John Murray.
Kim, Youjung and Galen Newman. 2019. 'Climate Change Preparedness: Comparing Future Urban Growth and Flood Risk in Amsterdam and Houston', *Sustainability* 11 (4): 1048, https://doi.org/10.3390/su11041048.
Kimmerer, Robin Wall. 2013. *Braiding Sweetgrass: Indigenous Wisdom, Scientific Knowledge and the Teachings of Plants*. Penguin.
Klein, Naomi. 2023. *Doppelganger: A Trip into the Mirror World*. Penguin.
Kuper, Adam. 2003. 'What Really Happened to Kinship and Kinship Studies', *Journal of Cognition and Culture* 3: 329–35.
Langland, William. [1378–9] 1992. *Piers Plowman*. Translated by A.V.C. Schmidt. Oxford University Press.
Lasch, Christopher. 1991. *The True and Only Heaven: Progress and Its Critics*. Norton.
Laslett, Peter. 1972. *Household and Family in Past Time*. Cambridge University Press.
Laslett. 2000. *The World We Have Lost – Further Explored*. Routledge.
Lewis, C.S. [1952] 2012. *Mere Christianity*. Harper Collins.
Lewis, Sophie. 2022. *Abolish the Family: A Manifesto for Care and Liberation*. Verso.
Linklater, Andro. 2014. *Owning the Earth: The Transforming History of Landownership*. Bloomsbury.
Lipton, Michael. 2009. *Land Reform in Developing Countries: Property Rights and Property Wrongs*. Routledge.
Loring, Philip. 2020. *Finding Our Niche: Toward a Restorative Human Ecology*. Fernwood Publishing.
Macfadyen, Peter. 2014. *Flatpack Democracy: A DIY Guide to Creating Independent Politics*. Eco-logic Books.
Machado de Oliveira, Vanessa. 2021. *Hospicing Modernity: Facing Humanity's Wrongs and the Implications for Social Activism*. North Atlantic Books.
MacIntyre, Alasdair. 1981. *After Virtue: A Study in Moral Theory*. University of Notre Dame Press.
MacIntyre, Alasdair. 1999. *Dependent Rational Animals: Why Human Beings Need the Virtues*. Duckworth Books.
Mak, Geert. 2010. *An Island in Time: The Biography of a Village*. Vintage.
Malm, Andreas and Wim Carton. 2024. *Overshoot: How the World Surrendered to Climate Breakdown*. Verso.
Mantha, Alexis. 2020. 'Late Pre-Hispanic Communities of the Upper Maranon: Lineages, Houses, or Simply Ayllus?' *Andean Past* 13: 295–338.

Markley, Stephen. 2023. *The Deluge*. Simon & Schuster.
McCarraher, Eugene. 2019. *The Enchantments of Mammon: How Capitalism Became the Religion of Modernity*. Harvard University Press.
McGuire, Bill. 2022. *Hothouse Earth: An Inhabitant's Guide*. Icon Books.
McKay, George. 2011. *Radical Gardening: Politics, Idealism and Rebellion in the Garden*. Frances Lincoln.
Médaille, John. 2010. *Toward A Truly Free Market: A Distributist Perspective on the Role of Government, Taxes, Health Care, Deficits and More*. ISI Books.
Miller, Brian. 2023. *Kayaking With Lambs: Notes from an East Tennessee Farmer*. Front Porch Republic Books.
Milner, Murray. 1994. *Status and Sacredness: A General Theory of Status Relations and an Analysis of Indian Culture*. Oxford University Press.
Netting, Robert. 1993. *Smallholders, Householders: Farm Families and the Ecology of Intensive, Sustainable Agriculture*. Stanford University Press.
North, Claire. 2021. *Notes from the Burning Age*. Orbit.
Oldenburg, Veena Talwar. 2010. *Dowry Murder: Reinvestigating a Cultural Whodunnit*. Penguin Books.
Oosthuizen, Susan. 2019. *The Emergence of the English*. Arc Humanities Press.
Orrell, David. 2010. *Economyths: How the Science of Complex Systems is Transforming Economic Thought*. Icon.
Ortyl, Bernadetta et al. 2024. 'Trends and Drivers of Land Abandonment in Poland Under Common Agricultural Policy', *Land Use Policy* 147: 107353, https://doi.org/10.1016/j.landusepol.2024.107353.
Ostrom, Elinor. 1990. *Governing the Commons: The Evolution of Institutions for Collective Action*. Cambridge University Press.
Ott, Sandra. 1981. *The Circle of Mountains: A Basque Shepherding Community*. Clarendon Press.
Paprocki, Kasia. 2016. '"Selling our own skin:" Social Dispossession Through Microcredit in Rural Bangladesh', *Geoforum* 74: 29–38.
Paprocki, Kasia. 2021. *Threatening Dystopias: The Global Politics of Climate Change Adaptation in Bangladesh*. Cornell University Press.
Patel, Ian Sanjay. 2022. *We're Here Because You Were There: Immigration and the End of Empire*. Verso.
Patterson, Orlando. 1990. *Slavery and Social Death: A Comparative Study*. Harvard University Press.
Ploeg, Jan Douwe van der. 2008. *The New Peasantries: Struggles for Autonomy and Sustainability in an Era of Empire and Globalization*. Earthscan.
Polanyi, Karl. [1944] 2001. *The Great Transformation: The Political and Economic Origins of Our Time*. Beacon Press.
Price, Neil. 2020. *The Children of Ash and Elm: A History of the Vikings*. Penguin.

Quilley, Stephen. 2024a. 'Schumacher Against Globalism and Ecomodernism: Ecology, Subsidiarity and the Politics of Scale', *European Journal of Social Theory* 27 (3): 456–81.

Quilley, Stephen. 2024b. 'Ecology "After Virtue" and After Modernity', *New Polity* 5 (2): 63–77.

Rankin-Gee, Rosa. 2021. *Dreamland*. Scribner.

Rees, William. 2023. 'Cities, Energy and the Uncertain Future of Urban Civilization', *Oxford Development Studies* 51 (1): 11–17.

Rigg, Jonathan. 2001. *More Than the Soil: Rural Change in Southeast Asia*. Prentice Hall.

Robbins, Peter. 2003. *Stolen Fruit: The Tropical Commodities Disaster*. Zed.

Rodsky, Eve. 2019. *Fair Play*. Quercus.

Rofel, Lisa and Silvia Yanagisako. 2018. *Fabricating Transnational Capitalism: A Collaborative Ethnography of Italian-Chinese Global Fashion*. Duke University Press.

Sahlins, Marshall. 1972. *Stone Age Economics*. Tavistock.

Sahlins, Marshall. 2013. *What Kinship Is – And Is Not*. University of Chicago Press.

Sahlins, Marshall. 2022. *The New Science of the Enchanted Universe: An Anthropology of Most of Humanity*. Princeton University Press.

Sayer, Andrew. 2016. *Why We Can't Afford the Rich*. Policy.

Sayers, Paul et al. 2022. 'Responding to Climate Change Around England's Coast – The Scale of the Transformational Challenge', *Ocean and Coastal Management* 225: 106187, https://doi.org/10.1016/j.ocecoaman.2022.106187.

Schumacher, E.F. 1974. *Small Is Beautiful*. Abacus.

Scoones, Ian. 2015. *Sustainable Livelihoods and Rural Development*. Practical Action.

Scott, James. 2009. *The Art of Not Being Governed: An Anarchist History of Upland Southeast Asia*. Yale University Press.

Scott, James. 2017. *Against the Grain: A Deep History of the Earliest States*. Yale University Press.

Scott, Manda. 2024. *Any Human Power*. September.

Sen, Amartya. 1981. *Poverty and Famines: An Essay on Entitlement and Deprivation*. Oxford University Press.

Shepard, Paul. 1998. *Coming Home to the Pleistocene*. Shearwater.

Siedentop, Larry. 2014. *Inventing the Individual: The Origins of Western Liberalism*. Penguin.

da Silva, Mariana Piva et al. 2022. 'From "Prison" to 'Paradise"? Seeking Freedom at the Rainforest Frontier Through Urban–Rural Migration', *World Development* 160: 106077, https://:doi.org/10.1016/j.worlddev.2022.106077.

Smaje, Chris. 2020. *A Small Farm Future: Making the Case for a Society Built Around Local Economies, Self-Provisioning, Agricultural Diversity and a Shared Earth*. Chelsea Green.

Smaje, Chris. 2023. *Saying NO to a Farm-Free Future*. Chelsea Green.

Smaje, Chris. 2025. 'Wild Communities, Tamed Publics', *The Land* 35: 24–31.

Smil, Vaclav. 2017. *Energy and Civilization: A History*. MIT Press.
Smil, Vaclav. 2022. *How the World Really Works*. Penguin.
Soper, Kate. 2020. *Post-Growth Living: For an Alternative Hedonism*. Verso.
Stoll, Steven. 2017. *Ramp Hollow: The Ordeal of Appalachia*. Hill and Wang.
Stone, Glenn Davis. 2022. *The Agricultural Dilemma: How Not to Feed the World*. Routledge.
Strange, Marty. 1988. *Family Farming: A New Economic Vision*. University of Nebraska Press.
Streeck, Wolfgang. 2016. *How Will Capitalism End?* Verso.
Subedi, Yuba Raj et al. 2022. 'Drivers and Consequences of Agricultural Land Abandonment and Its Reutilisation Pathways: A Systematic Review', *Environmental Development* 42: 100681, https://doi.org/10.1016/j.envdev.2021.100681.
Tainter, Joseph. 2019. 'Cahokia: Urbanization, Metabolism and Collapse', *Frontiers in Sustainable Cities* 1 (6): 000006, https://doi.org/10.3389/frsc.2019.00006.
Tambiah, Stanley. 2013. 'The Galactic Polity in Southeast Asia', *Hau: Journal of Ethnographic Theory* 3 (3): 503–34.
Taylor, Temis and Joseph Tainter. 2016. 'The Nexus of Population, Energy, Innovation, and Complexity', *American Journal of Economics and Sociology* 75 (4): 12162, https://doi.org/10.1111/ajes.12162.
Thoreau, Henry David. [1851] 2019. 'Walking'. Dover.
Todd, Zoe. 2018. 'Refracting the State Through Human-Fish Relations', *Decolonization: Indigeneity, Education and Society* 7 (1): 60–75.
Tree, Isabella. 2018. *Wilding: The Return of Nature to a British Farm*. Picador.
Urbina, Ian. 2019. *The Outlaw Ocean: Crime and Survival in the Last Untamed Frontier*. Bodley Head.
Vizenor, Gerald. 2008. *Survivance: Narratives of Native Presence*. University of Nebraska Press.
Wallace-Wells, David. 2019. *The Uninhabitable Earth: A Story of the Future*. Penguin.
White, Damian et al. 2008. 'Anti-Environmentalism: Prometheans, Contrarians, and Beyond.' In *Sage Handbook in Environment and Society*, edited by Jules Pretty et al. Sage.
White, Lynn. 2018. *Rural Roots of Reform Before China's Conservative Change*. Routledge.
Whittle, Jane. 1998. 'Individualism and the Family-Land Bond: A Reassessment of Land Transfer Patterns Among the English Peasantry c.1270–1580', *Past and Present* 160: 25–63.
Williams, Raymond. 1980. 'Advertising: The Magic System.' In *Problems in Materialism and Culture*, edited by Raymond Williams. Verso.
Woodcock, George and Ivan Avakumovic. 1968. *The Doukhobors*. Oxford University Press.
Worpole, Ken. 2021. *No Matter How Many Skies Have Fallen: Back to the Land in Wartime Britain*. Little Toller.
Xu, Chi et al. 2020. 'Future of the Human Climate Niche'. *PNAS* 117 (21): 11350–55, https://doi.org/10.1073/pnas.1910114117.

Yunkaporta, Tyson. 2019. *Sand Talk: How Indigenous Thinking Can Save the World*. Text Publishing.

Yunkaporta, Tyson. 2023. *Right Story, Wrong Story: Adventures in Indigenous Thinking*. Text Publishing.

Zeihan, Peter. 2022. *The End of the World Is Just the Beginning: Mapping the Collapse of Globalization*. Harper Business.

INDEX

A

After Virtue (MacIntyre) 125–6, 161
agony columns 74
agrarian populism 25, 117
agrarianism, historical 18
agricultural extension 126
agricultural frontiers 57
agriculture, 'scientific' 126
Albert, Michael 38, 40, 63, 187, 203
Albertus, Michael 46
Alfred, King xiv, 157
Always Coming Home (Le Guin) 85
American Solidarity Party 58
Amish 89
Amsterdam 3, 6
anarchism 26, 75, 89, 175
anarcho-primitivism 14
Andean *ayllu* association 108
anthropology 73–4, 177
Appalachia, US 45
Appalachian whisky currency 134
Aquarians 194, 200, 204
Aquinas, St Thomas 162, 167
Aristotelean ethics 161–2, 164
Aristotle 161, 167
Asian financial crisis (1997) 7
atheism 184
Australian Aboriginal people 109, 151
author's farm, Somerset xiv, 34–5
    average household size 61
    campsite 35–6, 37, 51
    economic structure 145
    embracing benevolence 49
    firewood making 66–7, 69
    freezer flashpoint 98–9, 101
    gendered work roles 82–3
    market garden 33, 98–9, 102, 107, 139–40, 148
    'no blame, no shame' approach 88, 107
    rainforest 31–2
    restoring balance 32–3
    spare capacity 63
    telehandler incident 79
    willow coppice 68
    wood commons 66–7, 93–4
authoritarianism 89, 174, 175, 181, 182
Avebury 194, 196, 204

B

back-to-the-land movements 58, 87
Bakhtin, Mikhail 144, 145, 153
banditry 176
Bank of England 130
banks 131
Belloc, Hilaire 166
beloved community 90
Beowulf xii
Berry, Wendell 166
biodiversity 115
Black Panthers 57
Blue Book of Nebo, The (Ros) 119
Boaty McBoatface 179
Bookchin, Murray 57
Bouie, Jamelle 181
breadbasket regions 2, 137
    decline 2, 47
Bright Ages, The 18
Bristol 3, 5, 196–7, 198, 201, 203, 204
Britain/UK 22, 100, 124, 130, 136, 152, 155
    back-to-the-land movements 58

Britain/UK (*continued*)
   ceramic manufacture in post-Roman 127
   comedy in politics 179–80
   flying over future 5–6
   flying over present 3
   modern yearning for land 92
   pulling away of Scotland, Wales and Northern Ireland 175
   rainforests 31–2
   scapegoating of farmers 58
Brown, Azby 39
Bruderhof communities 89
building new structures 31–43
   states of refuge 35–8
   suns, supernovas and solar systems 38–43
bureaucracy 173, 174
   vs record keeping 129–30
Butler, Octavia 53

C

Cahokia 4, 8
Campbell, Rebecca 128
Canada 13, 190
capital 51
   dangers of incoming 104
   degrading 140
   fictitious 102
   imbalance with resources 22–3
   as limiting factor 55
   overproduction 152
   preventing accumulation 105
capital flows 151, 152
capitalism 15–16, 85, 97, 102, 131–2, 134, 146, 147, 171
   feudalized 203, 204
   as 'religion of modernity' 170
caring 71–90
   communities 85–90
   families 71–80
   patriarchs and matrilines 80–5
carnival/s 105, 144, 145, 153, 201
Catholic Church 145, 165–6

Catholic Social Teaching 24
Catholic Worker Movement, US 58, 89, 166
Catholicism 144, 145, 165–6, 169, 170
centre-pivot irrigation systems 2
changing times 7–10
Cheddar dairying practices (1724) 64–5, 67
Chesterton, G.K. 75, 166
Chicago 2, 4, 5
children and child-rearing 77–90
   benefits of farming backgrounds 78–80
   challenges for single mothers 76
   distributist view 77–8
China
   energy use 9
   household responsibility system 62
   Warring States period 18
Christianity xiii, 162, 166, 168
civic republicanism 158, 160
Clastres, Pierre 88
climate change xiv, 6–7, 188
   as dynamic of world system collapse 7–8
   and European migration east 132
   in fiction 11–12
   as hoax 8
   and land distribution 46
   and small-scale farming 46–7
'climax' states of biological life 32
Cold War 7
Cole, G.D.H. 146–7
colonialism 43, 46, 92, 114, 131–2, 138, 171
Colorado River 1–2, 4
comedy in politics 155, 157, 179–81
common good 97, 103, 104, 113, 133, 168, 169
   and livelihood communities 185
   in republicanism 159, 160, 161, 162, 165
   and state sovereignty 182
commons 59, 60, 64–70, 111
   and dark-age distributism 108–9
   definition 93

INDEX

vs free-for-alls 65–6
freeriding 68, 69
and guilds 146
and occupancy rights 70
ownership structures 93–4
political moralism about 68–9
communism 39–40, 134
Communist Manifesto, The (Marx and Engels) 90
communitarianism 89–90
community/ies 59, 60, 85–9
    as aggregations of promises 130–1
    conflict resolution 87–8
    and guilds 146
    money as power of 130–1, 135, 36, 137, 145
    power inequalities 89
    vs publics 8–9, 89–90, 130
    return of sovereignty to 26–7
    see also livelihood communities
community land trusts 103, 148
Community Supported Agriculture 148
conflict resolution 87–8
Conservative Party, UK 179–80
construction 127, 128
Corbyn, Jeremy 179–80
cottagecore 50
Cottam, Hilary 27, 125
Covid pandemic 126, 148
Cram, Ralph Adam 146
credit-based commercial accounting 108

D

Dark Age Ahead (Jacobs) 17
dark age ahead 17–29
    from liberalism to distributism 21–9
dark-age distributism 107–19
    accessing land 109–14
    being indigenous 114–19
Dark Ages xii–xiii, 17–19, 28, 93, 96, 156
Davis, Mike 47
Day, Dorothy 58, 166
death/estate taxes 103
decarbonization 9

Defoe, Daniel 64–5
Deluge, The (Markley) 11–12, 16, 17, 20, 21, 43, 135, 182
Democrats, US 182
Deneen, Patrick 21
Department of Government Efficiency (DOGE), US 129
derivatives 22, 132
Detroit 2, 4
'development', Promethean narratives of 23, 25
distributism 24, 26, 68, 89, 97–8
    Catholic roots 166
    and child-rearing 77–8
    'common sense' appeal 166–7
    connecting immanence and local livelihood 169
    conservative 112
    dark-age 107–19
    distributist moment 203–6
    and families 75
    and land ownership 24, 46, 47–8, 98–105
    and money/value imbalances 133–4
    US 89, 166
    and work 123
divine comedy: or, the stranger king 173–85
    taming kingship 177–85
Doggerland 3, 6
Domencic, Sean 24
Domesday Book xiii
Doukhobors, Russia 89
Drax power station 121, 123
Drowned World, The (Ballard) 6
Dutch Republic 3

E

Earth
    arc of future 3–6, 10, 18, 37, 41, 50, 112, 183
    arc of present 1–3
    green Earth rising xv, 20, 203–4, 205
    rights 105

East Anglia 3, 6, 112, 119
ecological economics 132
ecology 164
   human 79, 109, 129, 171
   local 23, 109, 116
economic depression 12, 135
economic growth 23, 38, 62, 131, 136, 147, 174, 182
   consequences 7
economic rent 101–2
economics, etymology 60
economy
   disembedded from human relationships 52
   endless reinvention 36
   see also global economy; liberal market economy; moral economy; Mordor economy; oligarchic economy
education 125–6, 129
egalitarianism 108, 164
employment patterns 123–4
energy
   as dynamic of world system collapse 9
   global consumption 1750/2000/2023 9
   transition to low-carbon 9–10, 14
energy prices
   current system 99–100, 137
   livelihood communities 138
Engels, Friedrich 90
England xii, xiii, 57, 81, 105, 121, 139
   household size (1574–1821) 62
   kin-based household residence (2021) 72–3
   prehistoric private property rights 96
   premodern open field systems 69–70
Enlightenment 18, 80
entrepreneurship 54, 55
environmentalism
   Indigenous/non-Indigenous dualism 115–16
   modernist mindset 144–5
   Promethian 11

European Union 165
   referendum 179
Extinction Rebellion 57

F
Fair Play (Rodsky) 82
Fairlie, Simon 65
family/ies 59, 60, 71–80
   abolition 74, 75–6, 85
   and anthropology 73–4
   distributist view 75
   historical size 72
   importance 72–3, 77
   liberal-modernist critique 74, 75
   present socioeconomic reality 76
   usefulness in livelihood-making 72
family businesses 74, 78, 79, 104
Farage, Nigel 180
farmers
   deskilled 126
   STEM knowledge 126
farms and farming
   apprentice/internship arrangements 139–40
   benefits for child-rearing 78–80
   dismal economics 139
   energy constraint 127
   importance in the future 124–5
   inheritance tax 104
   land value/income disparity 22–3
   as lifehouses 58
   projected future 193, 197, 200
   see also author's farm; small-scale farms
fascism 134, 181, 182
feminism 60
Fenrir xiv
Finding Our Niche (Loring) 12
Flatpack Democracy (Macfadyen) 155, 157
food, locally produced 125, 148–9
   cost 137, 138
food commodity prices 137
food prices
   current system 99–100, 111, 137

INDEX

livelihood communities 138
food security 47
foragers vs farmers 78–9
fossil fuels 9, 48, 112, 132
founding moments 83–4
Francis of Assisi 143–4
Frankenfoods 54
Frankenstein (Mary Shelley) 11, 54
free-trade ideology 151
Fressoz, Jean-Baptiste 9–10
Frome 155–6, 197, 197, 202, 203, 204
   'The People's Republic of' 157
Frome Town Council 155, 156
Front Porch Republic, US 58

G

Gandhi, Mohandas 25
gardening/livestock mix 92
Gardner, Richard 79
gender
   and devaluation of household 60
   and work roles 82–3
George, Henry 101, 102
Ghosh, Amitav 169
Gilbert, David 48
Glastonbury 194, 204
global economy 7, 110, 131, 149, 151, 195–6
   monetary and energetic imbalances 133, 134
   money-value mismatch 134–5
   political ruination of 21–3
global financial crisis (2007–9) 7
global modernization 43
Global North 15, 17, 22, 102
Global South 22, 25, 50, 57, 102, 151
global trading system, disintegration 7
globalization xiii, 128, 147
   and the slave trade 3
gods 177
golf courses 2, 4
Google Earth 1
government employment 129–30
Goulson, Dave 187

Graeber, David 19, 53, 73
grain production 41, 52
Graves, Carwyn 118, 119
Great Reshuffle 46, 62
   future 58
Greece and Rome, classical 158, 163
Greenfield, Adam 41, 57, 175
Greenland 3, 5, 190
Grillo, Beppe 180
Guild Socialism (Cole) 146–7
guilds 145–9
Guldi, Jo 45, 46, 47

H

Hagens, Nate 22, 52
Hamilton, Alexander 134
Hardin, Garret 65
Havasu, Lake 1, 4
health care 125
Heathrow airport third runway 174
hero's journey myths 11–16
heteronormativity 81
hierarchy/popular egalitarianism tension 164
high-context cultures 109, 151
High Plains, US 2, 4
Hobbes, Thomas 42, 173
Holmgren, David 50
home, present concept of 60
home economics
   caring 71–90
   modern devaluation 60
   producing 59–70
homelessness 36
Honohan, Iseult 158, 159, 161
Hoover Dam 2
horticulture 36, 96, 125, 140
   and matriliny 84–5
household/s 59, 60, 61–4
   advantages of underproduction 63–4
   consumption only 61, 64
   joint production/consumption 61, 62–4, 107–8
   kin-based 72–3

household/s (*continued*)
   productivity 62–3
   size 61–2
   structure of underproduction 62–3
housing prices
   current system 99, 137, 153
   livelihood communities 138
human services 125, 129
hunger, as modernizing phenomenon 47
hunter-gatherers 78–9, 96, 170

I
icecap depletion 5
ID cards 192
Ieyasu, Tokugawa 39
Illich, Ivan 166
immanence 168–71
immigration/migration 151–2, 191
improvement ideology 205–6
Independents for Frome 155, 165, 174
India 9, 42, 43, 46
indigenous, being 114–19
Indigenous peoples 88, 170–1
   American salmon girl story 12–13
   historic and current narratives 114–15
   ideas about the wild 167
   low-impact livelihoods 115–16
   self-determination 116–18
individual/collective dualism 74–5
individual rights 158–9, 163
individualism/individualization 21, 98, 162
inheritance, land 103–4
inheritance tax on farmland 22, 104
Ireland 3, 46

J
J.P. Morgan 6–7
Jackson, Wes 114
Jacobs, Jane 17
Japan, Edo-era 39, 40, 81
Jesus, Caesar/God assertion 183, 184
Johnson, Boris 180

Jones, Andrew Willard 77–8
Joyce, Patrick 169–70, 171
jubilees 108, 130
Just Enough (Azby) 39

K
Kansas 54, 56, 57, 112, 119, 137, 183
Kearney, Melissa 76, 81
Khmer courts, Cambodia 42
King, Martin Luther, Jr. 90
kings 177 *see also* stranger kings
Kingsnorth, Paul 22, 52
kinship *see* families
Klein, Naomi 37
Kofyar people, Nigeria 96

L
labour
   as fictitious commodity 51–2, 52–4, 60
   industrial 'servants' 134
   price of 137–8, 139
   see also wage labour; work
Labour Party, UK 179–80, 182, 192
land 91–105
   accessing 109–14
   cultural inviolability 105
   defences against speculation 103–4
   as fictitious commodity 51–2, 101
   see also landownership
land prices
   agricultural land 100
   current system 99–100, 137, 153
   livelihood communities 138
land value tax 101, 102, 104, 111
land wisdom 170, 171
landowners
   negotiating with 109–10
   perspective on co-creating communities 110–12
   overthrowing 112, 113–14
landlordism 100–2, 197–8
landownership 93–8
   distributed 24, 46, 47–8, 98–105
   at parish level 57–8

INDEX

republican ceilings on 160
Las Vegas 2, 4
laughter 144, 153
Le Guin, Ursula 85
left-wing politics
   collective labour as redemptive 69
   corporate turn 78–9
   and liberal modernism 21
   Promethian narrative 15–16
   realignment with the right 26, 58
Lenin, Vladimir 39, 160
Leo XIII, Pope 166
Leviathan (Hobbes) 173
Lewis, C.S. 163
ley lines, South West England 169
liberal market economy 53–4, 55
liberal-modernism 21, 26, 29, 115, 166, 168, 169, 204
   critique of the family 74, 75
   state-or-market thinking 123
   turning away from 28
   worship 184, 185
liberal-modernist states 25, 27, 41, 46, 56, 95, 105, 117, 124–5
liberalism 21, 82, 144
   practical 88–9, 160
   republicanism compared 159
libertarianism 57, 160
   republicanism compared 158–9
Lifehouse (Greenfield) 41–2
lifehouses 41, 56–8, 104, 193
Lincoln, Abraham 2, 183
Lindisfarne Viking raid (793) xii
livelihood communities 26, 87, 109, 153, 166
   Britain, twentieth century 92
   building 14–15, 19, 27–8, 117
   disinterring knowledge of 13
   grounding worship 185
   land/housing/food/energy costs 138
   landholder/incomer co-creation 110–12
   making small plots of land available 141

money as currency and capital 141
   vs publics 8–9, 116
livelihood republics 157–61, 165, 175, 183
   left alone by the state 178–9
local food production 125, 148–9
local markets 152–3
localism 59, 77, 80, 157, 197
   historical 18
London 3, 112, 119, 175, 183, 188–9, 192, 203
London Grows initiative 190–1, 193
Long Land War, The (Guldi) 45
Loring, Philip 12–13, 91, 167, 168, 169
Los Angeles 1, 4, 50, 54
low-context cultures 109
Luddism 105, 138, 164

M

Macfadyen, Peter 155, 156, 157, 174
Machiavelli, Niccoló 158
MacIntyre, Alasdair 17, 27–8, 125–6, 161, 162, 164, 182
Majapahit empire, Java 42
making a living 121–41
   money 130–41
   work 123–30
Malthus, Thomas Robert 15
mandala states 42
manifest destiny 11–12, 14
manufacturing 127–8
Markley, Stephen 11–12, 16, 17, 20, 21, 43, 135, 182
marriage
   as failed commons 82
   as small state 75
   socioeconomic pressures, US 76
Marx, Karl 90
matriliny 84–5
   and horticultural societies 84–5
Maurin, Peter 58, 166
McCarraher, Eugene 11, 14, 143–4
McGuire, Bill 187
Mead, Lake 2, 4

Médaille, John 130–1, 132, 134, 135, 140
medieval era 145, 146
 bad press 156
 philosophy 162
 politics 156–7
men
 hearth-fasting 81, 85
 'masterless' 81–2
 socioeconomic pressures on 76
Mennonites 89
meta-crisis xv, 19, 90, 152, 165
migration/immigration 151–2, 191
Miller, Brian 78, 80
modern monetary theory (MMT) 21–2
 and money/value imbalances 132–3
modernism 144
 bewitched by brands and advertising 170
 joyless, materialist worldview 143, 144, 146
 and patriarchy 80
Monbiot, George 48, 51
money 130–41
 as fictitious commodity 51–2, 54
 mismatch with value 132–5
 as power of oligarchic community 131, 136, 137
 as power of the whole community 130–1, 135, 136, 137, 145
 see also capital
monopoly, political and monetary 131
'moonshot', as neo-Malthusian giveaway 16
moral economy 104, 148
moral philosophy 126
Mordor economy 22, 52, 153
mosaic landscapes 32–3
MST (Movimento dos Trabalhadores Rurais Sem Terra), Brazil 83–4, 113–14
Musk, Elon 129
mutuality of being 87, 108
mysteries and passions 143, 150, 167

N
natural law 75, 161–71
nature
 cultural power over 144
 hierarchy with humanity 164
 price 138
 rights of 105, 164
Navigating the Polycrisis (Albert) 38
neighbours 86
neofeudalism 38, 187, 203
neo-Malthusianism 15–16, 45, 46, 116, 124
Netting, Robert 96, 97
Nevada 2, 4
New Deal 2
New England 3, 5, 50, 112, 183, 187–8
New Guinea animism 168
New York 112
'no blame, no shame' 88, 107
Noordzeekanaal 3
Norman conquest xiii
North, Claire 128
Northern Ireland 175
nuclear power stations 201

O
Obama, Barack 8
occupancy rights 45–6, 49–50, 51, 109, 117
 commons perspective 70
Occupy 57
Of Torture in Primitive Societies (Clastres) 88
Ogallala Aquifer 2
oligarchic economy 137–8
oligarchy 138, 160
 money as power of 131, 136, 137
Oosthuizen, Susan 18–19
open country 45–58
 fictitious commodities 51–6
 lifehouses 56–8
open field systems, premodern England 69–70
Orthodox Christian forest churches 58
Ostrom, Elinor 66, 70

INDEX

overcapitalization 102, 104, 138
Overshoot (Malm and Carton) 17

P

paddy rice cultures, Asia 79
Parable of the Sower, The (Butler) 53
Parker Dam 1
patriarchy 60–1, 75, 80–4, 87
Peasant's Republic of Wessex, The 157
peasants and peasant culture 169–70
    Indigenous people compared 170–1
    land wisdom 171
people, sovereignty of 177
periphery-to-centre pipelines 22, 50, 54
Perón, Juan 160
Perry, Matthew 39
pigs 31, 33, 34, 50, 200
Polanyi, Karl 51–2
Polish peasant culture 170
political order 51
    dark-age scrambling 56
    liberal-modern extension 56
politics
    apocalyptic spirit xiv–xv
    comedy in 155, 157, 179–81
    impact of economic growth 7
    see also left-wing politics; right-wing politics; state/s; stranger kings
politics of the people 24–5, 155–71
    livelihood republics 157–61
    natural law 161–71
Popular Party, US 25
populism 24–5, 26
    Pyrrhic victories 25
Potomac defences 190
power inequalities 89
private property 94–7
    extreme form 95–6, 96–7
    as a form of commons 94
    mitigating patriarchy 85
    in non-capitalist societies 96
    and ownership of ancestors 168
    as property of communities 110
    republican view 158–9

producing 59–70
    commons 64–70
    households 61–4
Progress and Poverty (George) 101
Prometheus 11, 12, 16
Promethian environmentalism 11
Promethian hero myth 14, 15, 25
    left- and right-wing versions 15–16
Protestantism 166, 169, 170
public property 97–8
publics vs communities 8–9, 89–90, 130

Q

Quilley, Stephen 26, 58

R

racism 114, 115, 116, 151, 166
Radical Help (Cottam) 27
Ragnarök revisited? xi–xv
record keeping vs bureaucracy 129–30
Rees, William 50
Reform Party, UK 180
religion 184–5, 200–1
religious communities 89, 90
Remembering Peasants (Joyce) 169–70
republicanism 157–62, 197, 204
    definition 158
Republicans, US 182
'Rerum Novarum' (Pope Leo XIII) 166
resource cycling, Edo-era Japan 39
resources
    consequences of economic growth 7
    imbalance with capital 22–3
    transfer from poor to rich 22
Retrosuburbia (Holmgren) 50
rewilding, Wales 118–19
right-wing politics
    and liberal-modernism 21
    realignment with the left 26
'Rights of Man, The' (Spence) 57–8
Rodsky, Eve 82
Rojava, Syria 41
Roman Empire, fall 18, 28, 163
Roman law 95

Romantic movement 11, 14
Roosevelt, Franklin D. 2, 181
Ros, Manon Steffan 119
ruralism 47–9, 50
Russia, energy use 9

S

Sahlins, Marshall 73, 168, 169
salmon girl story 12–13
salvation narratives 21, 25
'saviour' technologies 13–14
Saying NO to a Farm Free Future (Smaje) 136
scarring rituals 88
School of the Tillers, China 18
Schumacher, Fritz 25, 166
Scotland 175
Scott, James 40–1, 49, 79
Scottish Highlands 3, 5
sea-level rises 8
'Seeress's Prophecy, The' xi, xii, xv, 20, 203, 205
Seymour, John 118
sheep overproduction 118–19
sheepskins 202
Shelley, Mary 11, 16, 54
site residence fees 99, 111
slave trade 3, 149
slavery
    as a product of civilization 53
    Thai offshore fisheries 136
    wage labour as 138
Slow Cities 58
Small Farm Future, A (Smaje) 24
small-scale farming
    alleged hunger risk 47
    and economic growth 62
    and ruralization 47–9
    productivity 46–7
    projected future 195–6
    and wheat growing 136–7
social care 125
socialism
    corporate-friendly 78, 79, 104

    and money/value imbalances 133
    republicanism compared 159
solar electricity 9
solar panels 4
solar system (galactic) states 42–3, 98, 178, 183, 204
solarpunk 50
Solon 160
Somerset xiv, 34, 112, 189, 194–202
Somerset Levels xiv, 127–8, 199–200
Soper, Kate 63
Southeast Asia 42, 43
Sparta 161, 167
Spence, Thomas 57–8, 141, 192
Starmer, Keir 180, 182
state/s
    abandonment by 20
    bureaucracy 173, 174
    competitiveness 173, 174
    consolidation phase (control by markets) 22, 24, 172, 182
    decline and collapse, effects 19–20, 175–6
    detaching sovereignty 26–7
    freedom-in-principle though monopoly 23–4
    Great Reshuffle of land entitlement 46
    inattention to 143–4
    incapability of solving present crisis 8, 20
    leaving future livelihood republics alone 178–9
    in loco parentis 75
    and modern monetary theory 21–2, 133
    possible future forms 38–43
    possible responses to dark-age crisis 37
    and public property 97–8
    and socialisms 133
    see also liberal-modernist states solar system (galactic) states; sun-states; supernova states

INDEX

state sovereignty 173, 174
   and the common good 182
   divine form 177, 179
   possible responses to loss 26–7
   tensions in 174–5
state-technology-high-energy nexus 14
STEM (science, technology, engineering and mathematics) knowledge 125–6
Stoll, Stephen 45
stranger kings 177–9, 181, 204
Streeck, Wolfgang 22, 24
Street Goat project, Bristol 50
Strong Towns 58
subsidiarity 24, 43, 47, 67, 72, 77, 78, 103, 166
subtreasuries 141
sun-states 38–40, 43, 56, 58, 156
supernova states 43, 43
supply chains
   disruptions 148
   effects of crumbling 19–20

T

technological sublime 11–12, 170
technology/ies 205
   as helpmate 16
   problems and risks of 11, 16
   and Promethian myths 11
   'saviour' 13–14
   and workplace misery 136
Thai offshore fisheries 135–6
Thomism 162
Thoreau, Henry David 33, 187–8
thrutopia 43, 187
Todd, Zoe 13
totalitarianism 181
Tour Through the Whole Island of Great Britain (Defoe) 64–5
trade 129, 149–53
   overinflation 128
   three planks of sustainable 150–1
trade unionism 138
'Tragedy of the Commons, The' (Hardin) 65

Trainer, Ted 50
transcendent cultures 168
transformative culture 87–8
transport work 128
Tree, Isabella 127
Trump, Donald 2, 180, 181

U

UK *see* Britain/UK
Universal Basic Income 123
universities 125, 126
urban-rural balance 52
urban-rural population shift 57, 112
urban/suburban farming 49
urbanism 47–8, 50, 51, 58
US 24, 61, 62, 123, 124, 126, 151, 175
   distributist tradition 89, 166
   energy use 9
   flight over present 1–3, 53–4
   flight over future 4–5, 18, 47, 183
   'manifest destiny' 11
   sea-level rises 8
   socioeconomic pressures on families 76
   and the technological sublime 11–12
   Trump as stranger king 180, 181
   urban-rural shift 50, 57
utility industries 128

V

Vietnam War 62
Vikings xii–xiii, 1
virtue ethics 165
vitalist politics 169
Vizenor, Gerald 167
volcanic eruptions, sixth century xi–xii

W

wage labour 138
Wales 3, 175
   kin-based household residence (2021) 72–3
   learning to be indigenous in 118–19

Wallace, David Foster 184, 185
Walled Towns (Cram) 146
walking west 187–202
Warminster 194, 196
Washington, DC 2, 5, 183
Washington, George 2, 134, 183
'Waste Land, The' (Eliot) 5, 6
'we', meaning of 15
Wengrow, David 19, 53
Wessex xiv, 157
Western Europe 28, 127, 151, 165
Westphalia, Peace of (1648) 156, 165–6
Westphalian system 156
What Kinship Is – And Is Not (Sahlins) 73
wheat growing 136–7
wild, the 167
wildness 33–4, 187–8
William, Duke of Normandy xiii, xiv
William III of England 3, 177
William of Ockham 162
Wiltshire 193–4
women
    advantages of ruralism 49
    association with household 60
    families as trap 74
    and land inheritance 103
    and patriarchy 80
    see also gender; matrilines
Women's Island 199–200
wood fuel, good or bad? 66, 121–2
work 123–30
    distributist approach 123
    gendered work roles 82–3
    see also labour; wage labour
working for others 143–53
    guilds 145–9
    trade 149–53
world environmental problems
    framework 16, 48, 91
world systems collapse 6–7
    dynamics of 7–8
worship 90, 184–5
WWOOF (Worldwide Opportunities on Organic Farms) 139

Y

Yggdrasil xii, xiv
Yunkaporta, Tyson 109, 151

Z

Zapata, Emiliano 25
Zelensky, Volodymyr 180
Zomia 40–1, 49

ABOUT THE AUTHOR

Chris Smaje has coworked a small farm in Somerset, South West England, for the last twenty years. Previously, he was a university-based social scientist, working in the department of sociology at the University of Surrey and the department of anthropology at Goldsmiths, University of London in the UK. Since switching focus to the practice and politics of agroecology, he's written for publications such as *The Land*, *Dark Mountain*, *Permaculture* magazine and Stats & Data Science Views, as well as academic journals such as *Agroecology and Sustainable Food Systems* and the *Journal of Consumer Culture*. He has also worked with the Ecological Land Cooperative and the Landworkers' Alliance. Chris is the author of *A Small Farm Future* and *Saying No to a Farm-Free Future*, writes the Small Farm Future blog at www.chrissmaje.com and is a featured author at www.resilience.org.

the politics and practice of sustainable living
CHELSEA GREEN PUBLISHING

Chelsea Green Publishing sees books as tools for effecting cultural change and seeks to empower citizens to participate in reclaiming our global commons and become its impassioned stewards. If you enjoyed *Finding Lights in a Dark Age*, please consider these other great books related to ecological thinking and agriculture.

SAYING NO TO A FARM-FREE FUTURE
The Case for an Ecological Food System and Against Manufactured Foods
CHRIS SMAJE
9781915294166
Paperback

A SMALL FARM FUTURE
Making the Case for a Society Built Around Local Economies, Self-Provisioning, Agricultural Diversity and a Shared Earth
CHRIS SMAJE
9781603589024
Paperback

GHOSTS OF THE FARM
Two Women's Journeys Through Time, Land and Community
NICOLA CHESTER
9781915294678
Hardcover

THE NATURE OF FASHION
A Botanical Story of Our Material Lives
CARRY SOMERS
9781915294791
Hardcover

For more information, visit **www.chelseagreen.com**.

the politics and practice of sustainable living
CHELSEA GREEN PUBLISHING

RADIANCE OF THE ORDINARY
Essays on Life, Death, and the Sinews that Bind
TARA COUTURE
9781645023098
Hardcover

HOW TO FALL IN LOVE WITH THE FUTURE
*A Time Traveller's Guide
to Changing the World*
ROB HOPKINS
9781915294517
Hardcovert

THE ACCIDENTAL SEED HEROES
Growing a Delicious Food Future for All of Us
ADAM ALEXANDER
9781915294432
Hardcover

AT WORK IN THE RUINS
*Finding Our Place in the Time of
Climate Crises and Other Emergencies*
DOUGALD HINE
9781645022800 (US)
9781645022916 (UK)
Paperback

For more information,
visit **www.chelseagreen.com**.